the
Cheesecake
bible

the Cheesecake bible

Includes **200** recipes

George Geary

Robert ROSE

Design and Production: Daniella Zanchetta/PageWave Graphics Inc.
Editor: Sue Sumeraj
Recipe Tester: Jennifer MacKenzie
Proofreader: Sheila Wawanash
Indexer: Gillian Watts
Photography: Colin Erricson and Mark T. Shapiro
Food Styling: Kathryn Robertson and Kate Bush
Prop Styling: Charlene Erricson

Cover image: Blue Ribbon Cheesecake (page 26)

We acknowledge the financial support of the Government of Canada through the Book Publishing Industry Development Program (BPIDP) for our publishing activities.

Published by Robert Rose Inc.
120 Eglinton Avenue East, Suite 800, Toronto, Ontario, Canada M4P 1E2
Tel: (416) 322-6552 Fax: (416) 322-6936

Printed and bound in Canada
1 2 3 4 5 6 7 8 9 CPL 16 15 14 13 12 11 10 09 08

To my mom.
I love you more than you will ever know.

Contents

Introduction

NAME A DESSERT THAT APPEARS on both fast-food menus and the dessert menus of high-end restaurants and is the most-requested recipe at major cooking magazines. The answer? Cheesecake. Everybody loves them. Simple, yet elegant, cheesecakes are much easier to make than other traditional cakes, such as layer cakes, yet they're equally, if not more, impressive.

When I took my mom to one of my book-signing events, the host served a cheesecake from my first book. My mom kept saying she would enjoy the cake more than the other guests would, so we should take the leftovers back to the hotel. My mom is a cheesecake-oholic, if there is such a thing. You have to watch her. She could eat a whole cheesecake by herself in one day. Come to think of it, maybe she has. But then, she does walk more than six miles a day and dances many nights of the week.

I hope the 200 cheesecake recipes in this book will inspire equally excited responses from your family and friends.

Tools and Equipment for Perfect Cheesecakes

One of the keys to creating a perfect cheesecake every time is having the proper tools. The wrong-size pan or poor-quality tools will cause problems that are not easy to solve. Many of the tools you'll need will have other uses in your kitchen and will last a long time, so it's worth purchasing quality equipment the first time.

Hand Tools

Rubber spatulas

A rubber spatula is the perfect tool for scraping a bowl clean. It also allows for the most thorough mixing of ingredients, the least waste when turning ingredients into the baking pan and an easy cleanup. The new silicone spatulas, which are heatproof to 800°F (427°C), are ultra-efficient because they can go from the mixing bowl to the stovetop. Commercial-quality spatulas are more flexible and durable than grocery-store brands.

Balloon whisk

To achieve perfectly beaten egg whites or whipped cream, use a sturdy whisk. They come in many sizes for different jobs. If you buy only one whisk, select a medium-sized one.

Liquid measuring cups

The most accurate way to measure liquid ingredients is with a glass or Pyrex measuring cup with a pouring spout. They are widely available in sizes ranging from 1 cup (250 mL) to 8 cups (2 L). Place the measure on a flat surface and add the liquid until it reaches the desired level. When checking for accuracy, bend over so that your eye is level with the measure. (Angled liquid measures are now available that allow you to measure ingredients without bending — the markings are inside the cup for easy viewing.) Pyrex cups can also be used in the microwave to melt butter and heat water.

Dry measuring cups

The most accurate way to measure dry ingredients is with nesting metal measuring cups. They usually come in sets of four to six cups in sizes ranging from ¼ cup (50 mL) to 1 cup (250 mL). Spoon the dry ingredient into the appropriate cup, then level it off by sliding the flat end of a knife or spatula across the top of the cup. Brown sugar and shortening need to be packed firmly in the cup for correct measurement.

Measuring spoons

The most accurate measuring spoons are metal. You'll need a set of sturdy spoons ranging from ⅛ tsp (0.5 mL) to 1 tbsp (15 mL) to measure small amounts of both liquid and dry ingredients.

Mixing bowls

A nested set of small, medium and large mixing bowls will be used countless times. Having the right size of bowl for the job, whether it's beating an egg white or whipping a quart (1 L) of cream, helps the cooking process. Ceramic, glass and stainless steel bowls all have their merits, but I think stainless steel is the most versatile.

Microplane zester/grater

A Microplane zester/grater with a handle is the best tool for quickly removing zest from lemons and other citrus fruits. To use it, rub the Microplane over the skin so you can see the zest. Do not zest any of the white pith, as it has a bitter taste. The Microplane is also good for grating hard cheeses and chocolate.

Garlic press

A garlic press is the fastest way to turn a clove of garlic into small bits. When you use a garlic press, your crushed garlic will have a stronger flavor, because of the release of oils, than garlic minced with a knife.

Baking Pans

Invest in quality pans — they conduct heat more efficiently, so cooking is more even and the desired results are achieved on top and bottom. (See Sources, page 276, for sources of quality baking pans.)

If your storage is limited or you are frugal, you can get by with one 9-inch (23 cm) cheesecake pan with 3-inch (7.5 cm) sides and one 13- by 9-inch (3 L) metal baking pan with 2-inch (5 cm) sides, which can also serve as a water bath.

However, having an assortment of baking pans on hand will give you the most flexibility and allow you to make a variety of cheesecakes. In addition to the pans mentioned above, a good selection would include:

- a 6-inch (15 cm) cheesecake pan with 3-inch (7.5 cm) sides
- an 8-inch (20 cm) cheesecake pan with 3-inch (7.5 cm) sides
- a 10-inch (25 cm) cheesecake pan with 3-inch (7.5 cm) sides
- a jellyroll pan or half-sheet pan
- a 12-cup muffin tin
- a 9-inch (23 cm) pie plate

Pie plates come in a variety of materials, but I like metal best, simply because glass and ceramic can break when dropped.

Cheesecake pans versus springform pans

I recommend using a good-quality cheesecake pan instead of a springform pan for several reasons. A cheesecake pan has solid sides with a pop-up bottom — a flat metal disc similar to a tart pan bottom. The sides do not have a spring that can rust, and the pan does not need to be greased.

A springform pan, on the other hand, needs to be replaced after only a few uses because the sides buckle and the spring in the release stops working. The bottom must fit very tightly into the pan edge, or it leaks. As well, the pan bottom has a zigzag texture and a lip that make it hard to unmold the cheesecake. When using a springform pan, lightly grease the pan or cut a circle of bleached parchment paper for the bottom. I would also make a band of parchment for the sides of the pan. Avoid using unbleached parchment paper, as it will brown your cheesecake, making it look too dark.

Baking instructions for shallower pans

If you have shallower pans than the ones I recommend, you can still make the recipes in this book. Here's a good rule of thumb: If you are using a pan that is $2\frac{1}{2}$ inches (6 cm) deep instead of 3 inches (7.5 cm) deep, the diameter of the pan should be 1 inch (2.5 cm) larger than what is called for in the recipe. For example, in place of a 9-inch (23 cm) pan with 3-inch (7.5 cm) sides, substitute a 10-inch (25 cm) pan with $2\frac{1}{2}$-inch (6 cm) sides. Bake for 5 to 10 minutes less than the recipe specifies, because the cheesecake will not be as deep.

Decorating Tools

Pastry bag and tips

A pastry bag with a variety of tips allows you to pipe beautiful garnishes and decorations to make perfect-looking cheesecakes. They can also be used for cookies, appetizers, mashed potatoes and more. Pastry bags come in a variety of materials, so choose one that's easy to wash. I use a poly bag.

Offset spatula

This tool has a long handle and a flexible metal blade set at an angle. It's ideal for smoothing out batters in pans without dragging your knuckles through the mixture, and is great for spreading icing over cheesecakes. Offset spatulas come in a variety of lengths and thicknesses. Choose one that feels comfortable in your hand.

Electric Equipment

Stand mixer

Tough jobs such as beating cream cheese with sugar require the power of a stand mixer. Select one that's sturdy and that comes with a rounded bowl and with whip and paddle attachments. When making cheesecakes, you'll use the paddle to mix batter and the whip to whip cream. Professional quality is not essential, but a KitchenAid stand mixer is a delight to use and takes care of all your mixing needs.

Hand-held mixer

A hand-held mixer is great for small jobs. It allows easy access around the bowl when you're beating egg whites or whipping cream. It also makes it easier to mix ingredients in pots that are on the stove.

Food processor

Select a sturdy processor that is large enough to handle the volume of ingredients in the recipes you use most often. My 11-cup (2.75 L) Cuisinart has worked well for me over many years.

Common Ingredients
Cheese

Regular versus lower-fat cheese

There is a big difference between regular and lower-fat cheese. For the best results when baking cheesecakes, use regular (full-fat) cheese only. The process of removing fat from cheese reduces the flavor and texture. Lower-fat and non-fat cheeses do not melt properly — and sometimes not at all — when they are baked or heated. Substituting a lower-fat cheese in a standard cheesecake recipe will diminish the final product. Save lower-fat cheeses for use in cold dips, spreads and sandwiches.

Storing fresh and ripened cheeses

The cheeses used in this book can typically be categorized as fresh cheeses and ripened cheeses.

Fresh cheese is usually soft and needs to be wrapped tightly in plastic wrap, placed in an airtight container and stored in the coldest part of the refrigerator. If any mold develops, it's time to toss the cheese out.

Ripened cheese is typically firm or semi-firm and should be wrapped in waxed paper and stored in the warmest section of the refrigerator. Storing the cheese in its original wrapping inside a resealable bag will prevent it from assuming the odors of other items in the refrigerator. If any mold develops on the surface, there's no harm done; just slice it off before using.

Cream cheese

Cream cheese is a fresh cheese made from cow's milk. By law, it must contain 33% milk fat and no more than 55% moisture to be classified as cream cheese. When buying cream cheese, select name brands only. Some of the store brands have added sorbic gum acids and moisture, which diminish the texture of cheesecake.

Neufchâtel cheese is a reduced-fat cream cheese that contains 23% milk fat, which means a few less calories.

Light or lower-fat cream cheese has about half the calories of regular cream cheese. Whipped cream cheese, which is soft because it has air whipped into it, has slightly fewer calories. Non-fat cream cheese, of course, has no calories from fat and is best used on a bagel or sandwich, not for baking cheesecake.

Regional cheeses
(Used to add richness and body)

- *Cottage cheese* is a fresh cow's-milk cheese that comes in small, medium and large curds with various fat contents. The moisture content is high. The creamed style has extra cream added and extra calories as a result. Cottage cheese is drained to become other styles of cheese, of which the driest version is farmer's cheese.
- *Farmer's cheese* is dry enough to slice or crumble and is a good all-purpose cheese.
- *Hoop cheese* is a dry drained cottage cheese, but not as dry as farmer's. It is common in Russian cooking. If it's not available in your grocery store, you might find it in a Jewish delicatessen.
- *Quark* is a German-style soft cheese that is similar in texture and flavor to sour cream, with a hint of sweetness. It comes only in lower-fat and non-fat versions, but due to natural extra flavor and texture, it's a good substitute for lower-fat sour cream and yogurt.

- *Provolone* is a cheese of Italian origin that is aged for up to a year, or even more, to create a mild, smoky flavor. It is good for cooking. The varieties that are aged the longest are firm enough to grate.
- *Ricotta* is an Italian-style soft fresh cheese made with the by-products of provolone and mozzarella. It is a standard ingredient in lasagna, manicotti and cheesecake. Ricotta comes in whole milk, lower-fat and non-fat varieties. I use the whole milk variety. If there is a buildup of liquid on top when you open the container, I suggest draining it over a piece of cheesecloth for one hour or overnight in the refrigerator.
- *Mascarpone* is an Italian double- or triple-cream cheese. The delicate, buttery texture is delicious with fruit, but it is very versatile and is found in both savory and sweet recipes.

Flavored cheeses
(Ripened for flavor and texture)

- *Cheddar* is a firm ripened cheese that can be mild to sharp in flavor. In color, it ranges from white to orange. (Orange Cheddar get its color from annaito, a natural dye.) It is popular served plain with crackers, cooked in casseroles and sauces or shredded as a garnish.
- *Swiss*, which is ripened to a light yellow with distinctive holes, is styled after the famous cheeses made in Switzerland: Gruyère and Emmentaler. The nutty flavor makes these cheeses popular in sandwiches and in cooking.
- *Blue cheese* is aptly named, because it has blue veins running through it — a result of being treated with molds and ripened. The aging process intensifies the flavor of the cheese, which is popular in salads and salad dressings and served with fruit. It is also used in cooking. The texture is firm enough for crumbling. My favorites are Maytag Blue from Iowa and Point Reyes from Northern California. Well-known names for international blue cheeses include Gorgonzola from Italy, Stilton from England and Roquefort from France.
- *Parmesan* is ripened for two or more years to a hard, dry state, which makes it perfect for grating or shaving. The rich, sharp flavor of the premium aged versions imported from Italy is easily distinguished from that of the grocery-store pre-grated brands.

Chocolate

Whenever I'm asked what brand of chocolate I like, I always say that chocolate is like wine. Some people prefer white, some reds. Pastry chefs generally lean toward rich French chocolate, while others love the creamy Belgian and even American artisan chocolates. I say, go with a good-quality brand that has a high percentage of cocoa butter and no tropical oils, and you can't lose.

I tend to stay clear of chip varieties in my recipes, as they do not melt easily and are better used in cookies and quick desserts.

Baking, bitter or unsweetened chocolate

Use this type of chocolate when you're baking something with a lot of sugar. It is the only chocolate I melt in the microwave, because it doesn't have any sugar to cook faster than the chocolate. You can still burn it, though, so be careful.

Bittersweet, semisweet or sweet chocolate

These chocolates can be used interchangeably in most recipes without any change to the outcome other than the taste. Bittersweet must contain at least 35% chocolate liquor (a by-product of the manufacturing of the cocoa beans into chocolate). Semisweet and sweet must contain at least 15% to 35% chocolate liquor.

Milk chocolate

I use milk chocolate only when I want a sweeter taste in my pastry. It cannot be used interchangeably with other chocolates. Melt over steam from a double boiler only and not over direct heat. Milk chocolate must contain at least 12% milk solids and 10% chocolate liquor.

White chocolate

Not really a chocolate, white chocolate is a mixture of cocoa butter, milk solids, vanilla and lecithin. U.S. regulations do not allow it to be classified as chocolate, because it does not contain any chocolate liquor.

Dutch-process cocoa powder

This dark, rich cocoa powder gives a cheesecake a glorious deep color. It is processed with alkali, which neutralizes the cocoa powder's natural acidity.

Sugar

Sugar has many uses besides sweetening. As an ingredient in pastry dough, it adds tenderness. It adds body to help egg whites become meringues. It is a natural preservative that allows jelly and jam to have a long shelf life. Heat makes it turn brown, so it adds an attractive color to many baked goods and candies.

Granulated sugar

Granulated, or white, sugar is the most common form. When it is pulverized, which is easily done in a blender, it is called superfine sugar. Because superfine sugar melts so quickly, it is used to sweeten cold liquids and in delicate sweets such as meringues. When it is crushed to an even finer powder, with a bit of cornstarch added, it is called powdered sugar or confectioner's (icing) sugar, which is excellent for icings and candy or as a decoration.

Brown sugar

Light and dark brown sugars are created when white sugar is mixed with molasses. The light variety is lighter in taste, but both have nutritional value from the molasses, while white sugar has none. Brown sugar has some calcium, phosphorus, iron, potassium and sodium, making it a popular addition to cookies and cereal.

Unless a recipe specifies, you can use either light or dark brown sugar. Because it is very moist and tends to clump, brown sugar should be packed tightly in a measuring cup to get the exact amount required.

Store brown sugar in an airtight container or in the refrigerator. If the sugar becomes too hard, restore its moisture by placing an apple slice in the container or by warming the sugar in a low oven with a few drops of water for 20 minutes.

Granulated and liquid brown sugars are good for cereal or fruit but should not be substituted in baking recipes because of their different moisture contents.

Natural, or raw, sugar looks and tastes much like brown sugar, but it's not brown sugar. It is a by-product of sugarcane and is prized for having nutritional value. If it is purified, as is commonly done in the United States, the nutritional value is lost.

Liquid sugars

Liquid sugars come in a variety of flavors and can be used to add sweetness to baked goods, including cheesecake. Store in a cool, dry place for the best shelf life.

- **Honey** is made by bees from flower nectar and is therefore a natural sugar, but that doesn't mean it has fewer calories. It actually has a few more. Because it is sweeter, use less honey if substituting it for other liquid sweeteners.
- **Molasses**, made from sugarcane or sugar beet syrup, is available in three varieties: light (fancy), dark and blackstrap. Light molasses is typically used as table syrup, while dark molasses provides the distinctive sweet flavor of gingerbread and Boston baked beans. Blackstrap molasses is only slightly more nutritious than the other versions and is not commonly used in baking.
- **Corn syrup** is made from cornstarch and is available in light and dark varieties. Popular in baking, it does not crystallize, and it makes baked products brown more quickly than granulated sugar does. The dark version is best used when color doesn't matter and the caramel flavor is an asset to the recipe. Both types are used as table syrups and in frostings, candy and jam.

Eggs

The recipes in this book were tested using large eggs. Eggs are easier to separate when cold. After separating, allow eggs to come to room temperature before using. Leftover whites and yolks will keep for up to two days in a covered container in the refrigerator. Both can be frozen as well. Store eggs in the carton in which they came in the refrigerator for up to a month.

Nuts

Nuts provide nutritional value, including a generous amount of the good monounsaturated fat. But because of the fat content, they have the corresponding calories, too. They add flavor and texture to baked goods. Refrigerate or freeze shelled nuts that won't be used right away. For the best results, defrost and toast before proceeding with the recipe.

To toast nuts, preheat the oven to 350°F (180°C). Spread the nuts on a baking sheet and bake for 10 to 12 minutes, checking a few times to make sure they don't burn. Let cool before chopping. Some nuts may require longer baking; just watch to make sure they do not burn.

Cookies and Crackers for Crusts

Making crusts from cookies and crackers is easily done in a food processor or with a rolling pin. If using a food processor, place whole cookies or crackers in a work bowl fitted with a metal blade and pulse on and off until the crumbs resemble wet sand. There is no need to remove the center filling of a sandwich cookie. If using a rolling pin, put cookies or crackers in a plastic bag and grind using a rolling action. Many recipes call for $1\frac{1}{2}$ cups (375 mL) of crumbs to make a 9-inch (23 cm) cheesecake crust. Here are some measurements that make that amount:

- 20 graham cracker squares
- 45 vanilla wafers
- 15 chocolate sandwich cookies
- 30 Ritz-style crackers

Flavorings and Spices

Oils and extracts

- **Pure vanilla extract** is created by soaking vanilla beans in bourbon or vodka and then aging the liquid. The flavor and aroma are unmistakable. (See Sources, page 276, for sources of vanilla.)
- **Pure vanilla paste** is created by scraping the seeds out of a vanilla bean and mixing with oil. I tend to use vanilla paste only when I want to see specks of vanilla in my cheesecake.
- **Imitation vanilla** is created with man-made products and barely resembles what it attempts to imitate. Despite being half the cost of the real thing, it is not worth substituting for pure vanilla extract.
- **Almond oil** is made by pressing the oil from sweet almonds. The best versions are imported from France and have the aroma and flavor of toasted almonds.

- **Almond extract** is made from almond oil and alcohol and should be used carefully, as the flavor is very intense.
- **Lemon oil, tangerine oil, lime oil** and **orange oil** are made from the oils in the skins of the citrus fruits. Their base is oil rather than alcohol, which is found in extracts. A small amount delivers a lot of flavor.
- **Mint** is grown in many varieties, but the two most common flavors for extracts and oils used in baking are spearmint and peppermint.

Citrus zest and juice

Because I reside in the citrus-growing area of Southern California, I use a range of citrus fruits in my recipes. Every year, a new variety seems to spring up. Aside from the common orange, lemon and lime, the citrus fruits I've used in this book include tangerines (clementines), mandarin oranges, blood oranges, Meyer lemons and Key limes. All citrus fruits are interchangeable, so if your region does not have one of the fruits called for in a recipe, by all means substitute another.

The amount of zest and juice yielded by a citrus fruit depend on the weight and thickness of the rind. When making your selection, choose fruits that feel heavy.

Spices

Indispensable spices for savory and sweet cheesecakes are cinnamon, cloves, poppy seeds, nutmeg and allspice. Spices go stale all too quickly, especially the finely ground ones. If they are no longer fragrant, discard them. Keep spices tightly sealed and store in a cool, dry, dark place. For the best flavor, purchase whole spices and grind them as you need them.

Herbs

The herbs most frequently used in savory cheesecakes are basil, tarragon, thyme and rosemary. Dried herbs are more intensely flavored than fresh, so if you must substitute dried for fresh, use half as much as the recipe specifies. Dried herbs go stale quickly, especially the finely ground ones. When dried herbs lose their aroma, be ruthless and discard them. Keep dried herbs in tightly closed containers and store in a cool, dry, dark place.

Basic Techniques for Perfect Cheesecakes

Preparation Is Key

To make a perfect cheesecake every time, prepare like a professional. Get all the ingredients out and on the counter. Unless you live in a very hot climate, allow the cold ingredients, such as eggs and cheese, to sit out for about three hours or until they reach room temperature. This will ensure easy and thorough mixing with no lumps. Prepare all the other ingredients, measuring each one so that it's ready to use. Don't wait to toast and chop nuts until they are called for in the recipe. Preparing ahead saves many greasy hands on the refrigerator door, fumbling for a forgotten item, or discovering that you need to go to the store.

Thorough Blending Technique

Thorough mixing is the second critical step for perfect cheesecake. Use the paddle attachment, not the whip, on a stand mixer. Beat the cream cheese thoroughly. Add the sugar slowly and beat in thoroughly, making sure that there are no lumps and that the mixture looks creamy, not granular. Watch the sides of the bowl and the paddle for cheese that has adhered, and scrape down both with a rubber spatula.

Add the eggs one at a time and beat well after each addition. Stop the mixer occasionally and carefully scrape down the bowl to make sure nothing is left on the sides or bottom.

Whipping Technique

Cream

To whip cream, use chilled cream in a cold bowl and a hand-held mixer with cold beaters or a cold whisk. Whip the chilled cream on medium-high speed until it thickens, then lower the speed and continue whipping until soft peaks or firm peaks form, as specified in the recipe. Be careful after the soft-peak stage, as cream turns to butter if overbeaten, and you will have to start over. Only whipping cream, or heavy cream, has a milk fat content of 35%, which is high enough to allow it to become whipped cream. Half-and-half will not whip properly.

Egg whites

To whip egg whites to form soft peaks, begin with a spotless metal or glass bowl and whisk or hand-held mixer. Any grease in the bowl or on the whisk, and any egg yolk in the whites, will ruin your effort. Start over if you break a yolk, and wash the tools beforehand to be sure they are grease-free. Eggs separate more easily when cold, but let the whites sit on the counter after separating and don't beat them until they have reached room temperature.

Adding Flavors

Extracts and oils can be poured directly into the batter to blend. Melted chocolate must be cooled before it is added to the main mixture. First, stir a small amount of the batter into the container with the melted chocolate. This will help the ingredients combine into a finer batter.

Oven Temperature and Rack Check

When making cheesecake, always preheat the oven and place the rack in the center of the oven. Perfect cheesecake requires accurate oven temperatures. Check your oven temperature for accuracy against an oven thermometer. To do this, preheat the oven to 350°F (180°C) for 15 minutes. Place an independent oven thermometer inside for a few minutes, then take a reading. If it indicates that the oven is above or below 350°F (180°C), either recalibrate the oven or rely on the thermometer and adjust your control setting until 350°F (180°C) is attained. It is not difficult to recalibrate an oven. If your owner's manual does not have instructions, contact a repairperson.

It's Done When It Jiggles

Bake the cheesecake in the center of the oven for 45 to 55 minutes or until the top starts to brown lightly. When you pull out the oven rack to remove the cheesecake, the center of the cheesecake should have a slight jiggle to it, with the sides looking somewhat dry. Don't worry about the wobbling center — the cheesecake will continue to bake as it cools and the center will firm up.

Getting It Out of the Pan
Cheesecake pan
To unmold the cheesecake from a cheesecake pan, first run a warm wet cloth over the outside. Then run a small spatula between the cheesecake and the pan, being careful not to scrape the metal pan. Place a heavy can on the counter, with the cheesecake pan on top. Press the sides of the pan downward. The cheesecake will be left sitting on the disk. Have a serving platter close by. Insert a large offset spatula between the disk and the cheesecake crust to loosen the cake. Slide the cake onto the platter.

Springform pan
To unmold the cheesecake from a springform pan, first run a warm wet cloth over the outside. Then run a small spatula between the cheesecake and the pan, being careful not to scrape the metal pan. Carefully release the spring latch. Have a serving platter close by. Insert a large offset spatula between the metal lip and the cheesecake crust to loosen the cake. Slide the cake onto the platter.

Storing and Freezing
Proper storage for maintaining flavor
After the cheesecake has cooled on a rack for two hours, cover it tightly with plastic wrap and refrigerate for at least six hours or overnight before serving. Refrigerate leftovers after serving.

Wrapping for the freezer and getting it out in time to serve
After covering the cheesecake tightly with plastic wrap, wrap it again in foil. Cheesecake freezes well for up to three months. To serve, take it out of the freezer and let it thaw in the refrigerator for 24 hours.

Troubleshooting
To prevent cracking
Bring all ingredients to room temperature before using. Incorporate eggs one at a time. Preheat oven to 350°F (180°C). Remove the cheesecake from the oven while the center still jiggles.

To prevent a grainy texture

Bring fat, cream cheese or butter to room temperature before beating. Add sugar slowly, beating well until incorporated and dissolved. Scrape the sides of the bowl often to make sure there are no lumps.

To prevent overbaking and dryness

Remove the cheesecake from the oven while the center still jiggles. A firm center in a hot cheesecake means it is overcooked.

Solutions to underbaking

You can always put the cheesecake back in the oven for a few more minutes if the center seems more liquid than jiggling. Most underbaking errors can be remedied by refrigerating before serving.

Frequently Asked Questions from My Cheesecake Classes

Why do cheesecakes crack?

One great myth about cheesecakes is that cracks or crevices are caused by drafts inside the oven or during the cooling process. The truth is simply that eggs are proteins, which create pockets in the fat that explode when exposed to heat. Adding the eggs slowly, one at a time, and beating well after each addition will help eliminate the pockets and the resulting crevices.

It is also important to let all ingredients come to room temperature, to preheat the oven to 350°F (180°C) and to remove the cheesecake from the oven while the center still jiggles. If the center does split or crack, cover it with a decorative topping. The cheesecake will still taste wonderful.

Why do you press the crumbs only on the bottom of the cheesecake pan and not up the sides?

If you do press crumbs up the sides, you'll have a thick area of crust that you won't be able to get a fork into once it is baked. I also think the sides look better without a crust when the cheesecake is served.

Do I have to bake the crust first?

Most recipes do not require baking the crust first. The best place for the crust is in the freezer until the filling is ready to be poured into it. If the crust is properly made in a cheesecake pan, it will not stick. It is not necessary to grease the pan unless you're using a springform pan (see page 11).

How do you get the white icing out of chocolate sandwich cookies to make the crust?

It would be fun to eat it out, but that's not necessary. Put whole chocolate sandwich cookies, icing and all, in a food processor and pulse on and off until crumbs form. The icing disappears like magic.

Can I freeze a cheesecake?

Wrapped properly to be airtight, in plastic wrap and an outer covering of foil, cheesecake suffers no loss of texture for up to three months in the freezer. Let it thaw in the refrigerator for 24 hours before serving. Decorate and refrigerate two hours before serving.

How can I make perfect-looking cheesecakes?

Most perfect-looking cheesecakes are decorated with whipped cream and other items. It's called "finishing off" the cake. Throughout this book, I provide instructions on how to finish off a cake to make it look perfect!

A World of Cheesecakes

Blue Ribbon Cheesecake

SERVES 10 TO 12

I have won numerous awards with this recipe, also affectionately called "Patty's Favorite Cheesecake" after my mom, my biggest fan.

Tips

Zest lemons and limes before juicing and freeze the zest for another recipe.

This cheesecake freezes well for up to 4 months before decorating. Defrost in the refrigerator the day before use and then decorate.

Variation

If fresh berries are not available, spread 1 cup (250 mL) strawberry preserves on top.

- Preheat oven to 350°F (180°C)
- 9-inch (23 cm) cheesecake pan, ungreased, or springform pan with 3-inch (7.5 cm) sides, greased

Crust

1¼ cups	graham cracker crumbs	300 mL
¼ cup	unsalted butter, melted	50 mL

Filling

4	packages (each 8 oz/250 g) cream cheese, softened	4
1¼ cups	granulated sugar	300 mL
4	eggs	4
3 tbsp	freshly squeezed lemon juice	45 mL
1 tsp	vanilla extract	5 mL

Topping

½ cup	sour cream	125 mL
¼ cup	granulated sugar	50 mL
1 tbsp	freshly squeezed lemon juice	15 mL
½ tsp	vanilla extract	2 mL

Decoration

2 cups	fresh strawberries, sliced	500 mL

1. *Crust:* In a bowl, combine graham cracker crumbs and butter. Press into bottom of cheesecake pan and freeze.
2. *Filling:* In a mixer bowl fitted with paddle attachment, beat cream cheese and sugar on medium-high speed until very smooth, for 3 minutes. Add eggs, one at a time, beating after each addition. Mix in lemon juice and vanilla.
3. Pour over frozen crust, smoothing out to sides of pan. Bake in preheated oven until top is light brown and center has a slight jiggle to it, 45 to 55 minutes. Let cool on the counter for 10 minutes (do not turn the oven off). The cake will sink slightly.
4. *Topping:* In a small bowl, combine sour cream, sugar, lemon juice and vanilla. Pour into center of cooled cake and spread out to edges. Bake for 5 minutes more. Let cool in pan on a wire rack for 2 hours. Cover with plastic wrap and refrigerate for at least 6 hours before decorating or serving.
5. *Decoration:* Top with sliced strawberries when completely chilled.

New York–Style Cheesecake

SERVES 10 TO 12

In my first pastry job, I made a New York–style cheesecake. I never knew what it meant until I stepped into a deli in Manhattan, a Mecca for cheesecake fans.

Tip

Save leftover egg whites or egg yolks by freezing them for up to 6 months. Freeze them in an ice cube tray. When frozen, pop them out and place cubes in plastic freezer bags.

Variation

For a different taste, you can replace the lemon and orange zest with 1 tsp (5 mL) rum extract.

- Preheat oven to 500°F (260°C)
- 9-inch (23 cm) cheesecake pan, ungreased, or springform pan with 3-inch (7.5 cm) sides, greased

Crust

1½ cups	graham cracker crumbs	375 mL
¼ cup	unsalted butter, melted	50 mL

Filling

5	packages (each 8 oz/250 g) cream cheese, softened	5
1¼ cups	granulated sugar	300 mL
3 tbsp	all-purpose flour	45 mL
1½ tsp	grated lemon zest	7 mL
1½ tsp	grated orange zest	7 mL
5	eggs	5
2	egg yolks	2
1 tsp	vanilla extract	5 mL
¼ cup	whipping (35%) cream	50 mL

1. *Crust:* In a bowl, combine graham cracker crumbs and butter. Press into bottom of cheesecake pan and freeze.

2. *Filling:* In a mixer bowl fitted with paddle attachment, beat cream cheese and sugar on medium-high speed until very smooth, for 3 minutes. Mix in flour, lemon zest and orange zest. Add whole eggs and egg yolks, one at a time, beating after each addition. Mix in vanilla and cream.

3. Pour over frozen crust, smoothing out to sides of pan. Bake for 10 minutes at 500°F (260°C). Reduce heat to 200°F (100°C) and bake until top is light golden and puffy like a soufflé, about 60 minutes. Let cool in pan on a wire rack for 2 hours. Cover with plastic wrap and refrigerate for at least 6 hours before serving.

Brooklyn Cheesecake

SERVES 14 TO 16

New Yorkers love cheesecake of many varieties. I just had to recreate this crustless one after tasting it in a Brooklyn deli.

Tip

To drain ricotta, place a fine-mesh strainer over a bowl, place the cheese in the strainer and let stand in the refrigerator for at least 1 hour or overnight.

Variation

Substitute plain yogurt for the sour cream.

- Preheat oven to 350°F (180°C)
- 10-inch (25 cm) cheesecake pan, ungreased, or springform pan with 3-inch (7.5 cm) sides, greased

2	packages (each 8 oz/250 g) cream cheese, softened	2
1 lb	ricotta cheese, drained (see tip, at left)	500 g
1½ cups	sour cream	375 mL
1½ cups	granulated sugar	375 mL
4	eggs	4
3 tbsp	cornstarch	45 mL
3 tbsp	all-purpose flour	45 mL
¼ cup	unsalted butter, melted	50 mL
1 tbsp	freshly squeezed lemon juice	15 mL
1½ tsp	vanilla extract	7 mL

1. In a mixer bowl fitted with paddle attachment, beat cream cheese, ricotta cheese, sour cream and sugar on medium-high speed until very smooth, for 3 minutes. Add eggs, one at a time, beating after each addition. Stir in cornstarch, flour, butter, lemon juice and vanilla.

2. Pour into cheesecake pan, smoothing out to sides of pan. Bake in preheated oven until top is light brown and center has a slight jiggle to it, 55 to 65 minutes. Let cool in pan on a wire rack for 2 hours. Cover with plastic wrap and refrigerate for at least 6 hours before serving.

Farmer's Cheesecake

SERVES 10 TO 12

Farmer's cheese is made from cottage cheese but is dry enough to slice or crumble. It's a good all-purpose cooking cheese.

Tip

To preserve a big harvest of lemons, I zest all of my lemons on one day to break down the walls of the lemon; the next day I juice them. Store the zest in plastic bags in the freezer. Freeze the juice in ice cube trays. When frozen, pop them out and store the cubes in plastic freezer bags.

Variation

If your supermarket doesn't stock farmer's cheese, try a specialty store or substitute small-curd cottage cheese, drained.

- Preheat oven to 325°F (160°C)
- 9-inch (23 cm) cheesecake pan, ungreased, or springform pan with 3-inch (7.5 cm) sides, greased

Crust

2 cups	butter cookie crumbs	500 mL
1 cup	granulated sugar	250 mL
¼ cup	walnuts, chopped	50 mL
1 tsp	ground cinnamon	5 mL
½ cup	unsalted butter, melted	125 mL

Filling

½ cup	unsalted butter, softened	125 mL
4	egg yolks	4
1 cup	granulated sugar	250 mL
2 lbs	farmer's cheese	1 kg
1 tbsp	grated lemon zest	15 mL
¼ cup	freshly squeezed lemon juice	50 mL
¼ cup	all-purpose flour	50 mL
1 tsp	vanilla extract	5 mL
1 tsp	baking powder	5 mL
4	egg whites	4
2 tbsp	granulated sugar	25 mL

Decoration

¼ cup	walnuts, chopped	50 mL

1. *Crust:* In a bowl, combine cookie crumbs and sugar. Add walnuts and cinnamon. Add butter and stir. Press about half the crust mixture into bottom of cheesecake pan and freeze.
2. *Filling:* In a mixer bowl fitted with paddle attachment, beat butter, egg yolks and the 1 cup (250 mL) sugar on medium-high speed until very smooth, for 3 minutes. Stir in cheese, lemon zest, lemon juice, flour, vanilla and baking powder. Set aside.
3. In a clean mixer bowl fitted with whip attachment, whip egg whites on medium speed until frothy. Gradually sprinkle in the 2 tbsp (25 mL) sugar and whip until stiff peaks form. Fold into batter by hand.
4. Pour over frozen crust, smoothing out to sides of pan. Crumble remainder of the crust mixture over filling. Bake in preheated oven until top is light brown and center has a slight jiggle to it, 60 to 75 minutes. Let cool in pan on a wire rack for 2 hours. Cover with plastic wrap and refrigerate for at least 6 hours before decorating or serving.
5. *Decoration:* Sprinkle with chopped walnuts.

Austrian Cheesecake

SERVES 10 TO 12

Cottage cheese keeps this cake light. It's great served with berries or fresh fruits of the season.

Tips

To check that your baking powder is still effective, do not rely on the expiration date only. Place 2 tsp (10 mL) into a glass with a little warm water. The baking powder should start bubbling.

If the cottage cheese has a wet look to it, drain it through a fine-mesh sieve. Too much moisture will change the texture of the cheesecake.

If small-curd cottage cheese is not available, purée cottage cheese in a food processor before adding to the cream cheese.

- Preheat oven to 350°F (180°C)
- 9-inch (23 cm) cheesecake pan, ungreased, or springform pan with 3-inch (7.5 cm) sides, greased

Crust

1 cup	all-purpose flour	250 mL
½ tsp	salt	2 mL
2 tsp	packed light brown sugar	10 mL
2 tsp	baking powder	10 mL
¼ cup	unsalted butter, cut into cubes	50 mL
¼ cup	milk	50 mL
1	egg	1

Filling

2 cups	small-curd cottage cheese, drained (see tips, at left)	500 mL
½ cup	granulated sugar	125 mL
¾ cup	all-purpose flour	175 mL
5	egg yolks	5
½ cup	milk	125 mL
½ tsp	grated lemon zest	2 mL
1 tsp	vanilla extract	5 mL
5	egg whites	5
¼ cup	confectioner's (icing) sugar	50 mL
¼ cup	golden raisins, chopped	50 mL

Decoration

Classic Whipped Cream Topping (see recipe, page 262)

1. *Crust:* In a bowl, combine flour, salt, brown sugar and baking powder. Using a pastry fork or two knives, cut butter into dry mixture until it resembles cornmeal. Add milk and egg, blending into a ball. Press into bottom of cheesecake pan. Bake in preheated oven for 10 minutes or until golden brown. Set aside.

2. *Filling:* In a mixer bowl fitted with paddle attachment, beat cottage cheese and sugar on medium-high speed until very smooth, for 3 minutes. Mix in flour. Add egg yolks, one at a time, beating after each addition. Stir in milk, lemon zest and vanilla. Set aside.

Variation

You can substitute dried cranberries for the raisins in the filling and add some on top for decoration.

3. In a clean mixer bowl fitted with whip attachment, whip egg whites on medium speed until frothy. Gradually sprinkle in confectioner's sugar and whip until stiff peaks form. Fold into batter by hand. Fold in raisins.

4. Pour over baked crust, smoothing out to sides of pan. Bake in preheated oven until top is light brown and center has a slight jiggle to it, 55 to 65 minutes. Let cool in pan on a wire rack for 2 hours. Cover with plastic wrap and refrigerate for at least 6 hours before decorating or serving.

5. *Decoration:* Ice top of cake with Classic Whipped Cream Topping or pipe rosettes around top of cake, if desired.

German Quark Cheesecake

SERVES 10 TO 12

German quark cheese is a flavorful soft cheese found in German delis and cheese shops. It's worth the search. You will be delighted with this soft-textured cheesecake.

Tip

If you use homemade cookies in the crust, you may not need to use any butter, because fresh cookies have more moisture. The crust should feel like wet sand.

Variation

If quark cheese is difficult to locate, substitute mascarpone cheese. It's a bit sweeter.

- Preheat oven to 325°F (160°C)
- 9-inch (23 cm) cheesecake pan, ungreased, or springform pan with 3-inch (7.5 cm) sides, greased

Crust

1½ cups	butter cookie crumbs	375 mL
1 tsp	ground cinnamon	5 mL
¼ cup	unsalted butter, melted	50 mL

Filling

1 lb	quark cheese	500 g
2 cups	sour cream	500 mL
1 cup	granulated sugar	250 mL
4	egg yolks	4
⅔ cup	all-purpose flour	150 mL
1 tbsp	grated orange zest	15 mL
¼ cup	freshly squeezed orange juice	50 mL
1 tbsp	vanilla extract	15 mL

Decoration

	Classic Whipped Cream Topping (see recipe, page 262)	
1 tbsp	grated orange zest	15 mL

1. *Crust:* In a bowl, combine cookie crumbs, cinnamon and butter. Press into bottom of cheesecake pan and freeze.
2. *Filling:* In a mixer bowl fitted with paddle attachment, beat quark, sour cream and sugar on medium-high speed until very smooth, for 3 minutes. Add egg yolks, one at a time, beating after each addition. Stir in flour, orange zest, orange juice and vanilla.
3. Pour over frozen crust, smoothing out to sides of pan. Bake in preheated oven until top is light brown and center has a slight jiggle to it, 65 to 75 minutes. Let cool in pan on a wire rack for 2 hours. Cover with plastic wrap and refrigerate for at least 6 hours before decorating or serving.
4. *Decoration:* Ice top of cake with Classic Whipped Cream Topping or pipe a ribbon around border, if desired. Top with a sprinkling of orange zest.

Blue Ribbon Cheesecake (page 26)
Overleaf: Café au Lait Cheesecake (page 34)

Italian Ricotta Cheesecake

SERVES 10 TO 12

Using a chopped pecan crust makes this cheesecake pure Italian!

Tips

Fresh ricotta cheese creates a huge difference in taste and texture. Find an Italian deli that makes its own ricotta.

A sugar dredger or shaker is a container with a mesh lid used to lightly dust icing sugar, flour or cocoa as decoration.

Variation

Substitute 1 tsp (15 mL) almond-flavored liqueur or vanilla extract for the almond extract.

- Preheat the oven to 325°F (160°C)
- 9-inch (23 cm) cheesecake pan, ungreased, or springform pan with 3-inch (7.5 cm) sides, greased

Crust

1½ cups	pecans, toasted (see tip, page 34) and ground	375 mL

Filling

1½ lbs	ricotta cheese, drained (see tip, page 28)	750 g
1 cup	granulated sugar	250 mL
¼ cup	all-purpose flour	50 mL
4	eggs	4
1 tsp	almond extract	5 mL

Decoration

¼ cup	confectioner's (icing) sugar	50 mL

1. *Crust:* Sprinkle bottom of cheesecake pan evenly with ground pecans. Set aside.

2. *Filling:* In a mixer bowl fitted with paddle attachment, beat ricotta cheese and sugar on medium-high speed until very smooth, for 3 minutes. Add flour and mix for about 3 minutes. Add eggs, one at a time, beating after each addition. Mix in almond extract.

3. Pour over crust, smoothing out to sides of pan. Bake in preheated oven until top is light brown and center has a slight jiggle to it, 55 to 65 minutes. Let cool in pan on a wire rack for 2 hours. Cover with plastic wrap and refrigerate for at least 6 hours before decorating or serving.

4. *Decoration:* After cake has chilled, dust top with a sprinkling of confectioner's sugar, using a sugar dredger or flour sifter.

Overleaf: English Trifle Cheesecake (page 40)

Carrot Cake Cheesecake (page 54)

Café au Lait Cheesecake

. . . .

SERVES 10 TO 12

The richness of coffee, chocolate and hazelnuts make this cheesecake a winner for the fall season.

Tips

Toasting brings out the natural oils and flavor of nuts. Place nuts in a single layer on a baking sheet and bake at 350°F (180°C) until fragrant, 10 to 12 minutes.

Neufchâtel cheese is a reduced-fat cream cheese that contains 23% milk fat, which means a few less calories. You could also use a light cream cheese.

- Preheat oven to 350°F (180°C)
- 9-inch (23 cm) cheesecake pan, ungreased, or springform pan with 3-inch (7.5 cm) sides, greased

Crust

1½ cups	chocolate sandwich cookie crumbs	375 mL
¼ cup	packed light brown sugar	50 mL
1 tsp	instant espresso powder	5 mL
½ tsp	ground cinnamon	2 mL
⅓ cup	unsalted butter, melted	75 mL

Filling

2 tbsp	milk	25 mL
1½ tsp	instant espresso powder	7 mL
2 tbsp	unsalted butter	25 mL
2	packages (each 8 oz/250 g) Neufchâtel cheese (see tip, at left)	2
1	package (8 oz/250 g) cream cheese, softened	1
⅔ cup	granulated sugar	150 mL
4	eggs	4
¼ cup	milk	50 mL
⅓ cup	hazelnuts, toasted (see tip, at left) and chopped	75 mL
2 tbsp	coffee-flavored liqueur	25 mL

Decoration

	Coffee-Flavored Syrup (see recipe, page 267)	
⅓ cup	hazelnuts, toasted and chopped	75 mL

1. *Crust:* In a bowl, combine crumbs, brown sugar, espresso powder, cinnamon and butter. Press into bottom of cheesecake pan and freeze.

2. *Filling:* In a saucepan, heat 2 tbsp (25 mL) milk, espresso powder and butter until butter melts. Set aside.

3. In a mixer bowl fitted with paddle attachment, beat Neufchâtel cheese, cream cheese and sugar on medium-high speed until very smooth, for 3 minutes. Add eggs, one at a time, beating after each addition. Reduce to low speed and mix in milk, hazelnuts, liqueur and espresso mixture.

4. Pour over frozen crust, smoothing out to sides of pan. Bake in preheated oven until top is light brown and center has a slight jiggle to it, 45 to 55 minutes. Let cool in pan on a wire rack for 2 hours. Cover with plastic wrap and refrigerate for at least 6 hours before decorating or serving.

5. *Decoration:* Place a slice on a plate. Pour 2 tbsp (25 mL) Coffee-Flavored Syrup on top and sprinkle with hazelnuts.

Coffee Liqueur Cheesecake

A coffee-flavored liqueur enhances the taste of this rich cake.

Tip

You may have to add additional butter to the crust, depending on the brand of cookies you use. Just make sure the crust is like wet sand.

Variation

For an even richer, creamier cake, substitute mascarpone cheese for the sour cream.

- Preheat oven to 325°F (160°C)
- 9-inch (23 cm) cheesecake pan, ungreased, or springform pan with 3-inch (7.5 cm) sides, greased

Crust

1⅓ cups	chocolate sandwich cookie crumbs	325 mL
¼ cup	unsalted butter, melted	50 mL

Filling

2	packages (each 8 oz/250 g) cream cheese, softened	2
⅓ cup	granulated sugar	75 mL
¼ tsp	salt	1 mL
1 cup	sour cream	250 mL
3	eggs	3
¼ cup	coffee-flavored liqueur	50 mL
2 tbsp	unsalted butter, melted	25 mL

Decoration

Coffee-Flavored Syrup (see recipe, page 267)

1. *Crust:* In a bowl, combine cookie crumbs and butter. Press into bottom of cheesecake pan and freeze.
2. *Filling:* In a mixer bowl fitted with paddle attachment, beat cream cheese and sugar on medium-high speed until very smooth, for 3 minutes. Mix in salt and sour cream. Add eggs, one at a time, beating after each addition. Mix in liqueur and melted butter.
3. Pour over frozen crust, smoothing out to sides of pan. Bake in preheated oven until top is light brown and center has a slight jiggle to it, 40 to 50 minutes. Let cool in pan on a wire rack for 2 hours. Cover with plastic wrap and refrigerate for at least 6 hours before decorating or serving.
4. *Decoration:* When ready to serve, pour about 2 tbsp (25 mL) Coffee-Flavored Syrup on individual plates and position a piece of cake on top.

Espresso Cheesecake

SERVES 10 TO 12

Café society thrills to the rich flavor created by combining espresso, coffee liqueur and candied coffee beans.

Tips

Toasting brings out the natural oils and flavor of nuts. Place nuts in a single layer on a baking sheet and bake at 350°F (180°C) until fragrant, 10 to 12 minutes.

Shaved chocolate looks great on this cheesecake. Create chocolate shavings by moving a spatula in an up-and-down motion along the side of a bar of chocolate (or use a potato peeler on a cold bar of chocolate).

- Preheat oven to 325°F (160°C)
- 9-inch (23 cm) cheesecake pan, ungreased, or springform pan with 3-inch (7.5 cm) sides, greased

Crust

1½ cups	hazelnuts, toasted (see tip, at left) and ground	375 mL
⅓ cup	granulated sugar	75 mL
1 tbsp	unsweetened cocoa powder	15 mL
3 tbsp	unsalted butter, melted	45 mL

Filling

1 cup	brewed espresso	250 mL
3	packages (each 8 oz/250 g) cream cheese, softened	3
1⅓ cups	granulated sugar	325 mL
3	eggs	3
3	egg yolks	3
1½ tbsp	cornstarch	22 mL
¼ tsp	salt	1 mL
⅓ cup	whipping (35%) cream	75 mL
2 tsp	grated lemon zest	10 mL
1 tbsp	freshly squeezed lemon juice	15 mL
1 tbsp	coffee-flavored liqueur	15 mL
1 tsp	vanilla extract	5 mL

Decoration

Classic Whipped Cream Topping (see recipe, page 262)

1. *Crust:* In a bowl, combine hazelnuts, sugar, cocoa and butter. Press into bottom of cheesecake pan. Bake in preheated oven for 10 minutes. Set aside. Increase oven temperature to 350°F (180°C).
2. *Filling:* In a small saucepan, boil espresso until it reduces to ¼ cup (50 mL). Let cool completely.

Variation

Substitute pecans if
hazelnuts are difficult
to find.

3. In a mixer bowl fitted with paddle attachment, beat cream cheese and sugar on medium-high speed until very smooth, for 3 minutes. Add whole eggs and egg yolks, one at a time, beating after each addition. Mix in cornstarch and salt. Reduce to low speed and mix in reduced espresso, cream, lemon zest, lemon juice, liqueur and vanilla.

4. Pour over baked crust, smoothing out to sides of pan. Bake in preheated oven until top is light brown and center has a slight jiggle to it, 60 to 75 minutes. Let cool in pan on a wire rack for 2 hours. Cover with plastic wrap and refrigerate for at least 6 hours before decorating or serving.

5. *Decoration:* Ice top of cake with Classic Whipped Cream Topping or pipe rosettes around top of cake, if desired.

Mocha Cheesecake

SERVES 10 TO 12

Double the pleasure of a coffee break with a slice of mocha cheesecake.

Tips

If the cottage cheese has a wet look to it, drain it through a fine-mesh sieve. Too much moisture will change the texture of the cheesecake.

If small-curd cottage cheese is not available, purée cottage cheese in a food processor before adding to the cream cheese.

- Preheat oven to 350°F (180°C)
- 9-inch (23 cm) cheesecake pan, ungreased, or springform pan with 3-inch (7.5 cm) sides, greased

Crust

1½ cups	chocolate sandwich cookie crumbs	375 mL
¼ cup	unsalted butter, melted	50 mL

Filling

2 tbsp	instant coffee powder or granules	25 mL
1 tbsp	hot water	15 mL
3	packages (each 8 oz/250 g) cream cheese, softened	3
1 cup	small-curd cottage cheese (see tips, at left)	250 mL
1½ cups	granulated sugar	375 mL
4	eggs	4
1 tsp	vanilla extract	5 mL

Topping

1 tsp	instant coffee powder or granules	5 mL
½ tsp	hot water	2 mL
½ cup	sour cream	125 mL
¼ cup	granulated sugar	50 mL
1 tbsp	freshly squeezed lemon juice	15 mL
½ tsp	vanilla extract	2 mL

Decoration

Classic Whipped Cream Topping (see recipe, page 262)

1. *Crust:* In a bowl, combine cookie crumbs and butter. Press into bottom of cheesecake pan and freeze.
2. *Filling:* In a small bowl, dissolve coffee powder in hot water. Set aside.
3. In a mixer bowl fitted with paddle attachment, beat cream cheese, cottage cheese and sugar on medium-high speed until very smooth, for 3 minutes. Add eggs, one at a time, beating after each addition. With the mixer running, pour in coffee in a steady stream. Mix in vanilla.

Variation

Add 2 tbsp (25 mL) rum with the vanilla in the filling for a little kick in flavor.

4. Pour over frozen crust, smoothing out to sides of pan. Bake in preheated oven until top is light brown and center has a slight jiggle to it, 45 to 55 minutes. Let cool on the counter for 10 minutes (do not turn the oven off). The cake will sink slightly.

5. *Topping:* In a small bowl, dissolve coffee powder in hot water. Stir in sour cream, sugar, lemon juice and vanilla. Pour into center of cooled cake and spread out to edges. Bake for 5 minutes more. Let cool in pan on a wire rack for 2 hours. Cover with plastic wrap and refrigerate for at least 6 hours before decorating or serving.

6. *Decoration:* Ice top of cake with Classic Whipped Cream Topping or pipe rosettes around top of cake, if desired.

English Trifle Cheesecake

SERVES 10 TO 12

This delicious dessert tastes just like an old-fashioned English trifle, but with the texture of cheesecake.

Tips

It's much easier to slice a cake horizontally when it is frozen than when it's at room temperature. Some bakeries will sell you un-iced layers if you are in a hurry.

Be sure your cake layers are no more than $1/2$ inch (1 cm) thick to make sure the filling doesn't overflow the pan.

Variation

Substitute strawberries and strawberry preserves for the raspberries and raspberry preserves.

- Preheat oven to 325°F (160°C)
- 9-inch (23 cm) cheesecake pan, ungreased, or springform pan with 3-inch (7.5 cm) sides, greased

Crust

1	9-inch (23 cm) yellow cake, sliced horizontally in half	1
$1/4$ cup	cream sherry, divided	50 mL
$1/2$ cup	raspberry preserves, divided	125 mL

Filling

4	packages (each 8 oz/250 g) cream cheese, softened	4
1 cup	granulated sugar	250 mL
5	eggs	5
1 tbsp	vanilla extract	15 mL

Decoration

	Classic Whipped Cream Topping (see recipe, page 262)	
1 cup	fresh raspberries	250 mL

1. *Crust:* Press half of cake into bottom of cheesecake pan. Brush with half the sherry. Spread half the raspberry preserves on top. Set aside.
2. *Filling:* In a mixer bowl fitted with paddle attachment, beat cream cheese and sugar on medium-high speed until very smooth, for 3 minutes. Add eggs one at a time, beating after each addition. Mix in vanilla.
3. Pour half the batter over cake layer in pan, smoothing out to sides of pan. Place second cake layer on top, brush with the remaining sherry and spread the remaining raspberry preserves on top. Pour the remaining batter on top of cake layer, smoothing out to sides of pan (the pan will be filled to the top edge). Bake in preheated oven until top is very light brown and center has a slight jiggle to it, 50 to 55 minutes. Let cool in pan on a wire rack for 2 hours. Cover with plastic wrap and refrigerate for at least 6 hours before decorating or serving.
4. *Decoration:* Ice top of cake with Classic Whipped Cream Topping or pipe rosettes around top of cake, if desired. Top with fresh raspberries.

Dulce de Leche Cheesecake

SERVES 10 TO 12

Put a Latin American spin on the menu with the popular caramel flavor produced by cooking condensed milk until it caramelizes.

Tip

You can prepare the sweetened condensed milk a few days ahead. Just reheat in a double boiler until fluid but not hot before adding to filling.

- Preheat oven to 350°F (180°C)
- 9-inch (23 cm) cheesecake pan, ungreased, or springform pan with 3-inch (7.5 cm) sides, greased

Crust

1¼ cups	graham cracker crumbs	300 mL
¼ cup	unsalted butter, melted	50 mL

Filling

1	can (14 oz/396 g or 300 mL) sweetened condensed milk	1
4	packages (each 8 oz/250 g) cream cheese, softened	4
1 cup	packed brown sugar	250 mL
4	eggs	4
1 tsp	vanilla extract	5 mL

Decoration

Classic Whipped Cream Topping (see recipe, page 262)

1. *Crust:* In a bowl, combine graham cracker crumbs and butter. Press into bottom of cheesecake pan and freeze.

2. *Filling:* In a heatproof bowl set over a saucepan of lightly simmering water, heat condensed milk, stirring occasionally, until light caramel in color and thick, about 60 to 70 minutes. Check water periodically and add more if necessary to keep the level of water just below the bottom of the bowl. Set aside, reserving 2 tbsp (25 mL) for decorating.

3. In a mixer bowl fitted with paddle attachment, beat cream cheese and brown sugar on medium-high speed until very smooth, for 3 minutes. Add eggs, one at a time, beating after each addition. Mix in vanilla and cooked condensed milk.

4. Pour over frozen crust, smoothing out to sides of pan. Bake in preheated oven until top is light brown and center has a slight jiggle to it, 45 to 55 minutes. Let cool in pan on a wire rack for 2 hours. Cover with plastic wrap and refrigerate for at least 6 hours before decorating or serving.

5. *Decoration:* Ice top of cake with Classic Whipped Cream Topping or pipe rosettes around top of cake, if desired. Drizzle reserved cooked condensed milk on top.

White Chocolate Crème Brûlée Cheesecake

SERVES 10 TO 12

The Spanish, English and French all take credit for creating "burnt cream," an egg custard with a sugar glaze on top. I am adding to the history of the dish by expanding its influence to American cheesecake.

Tips

Completely cold cheesecake is essential to creating the sugar glaze; otherwise, the sugar will just melt into the cheesecake.

Don't skip the pan of boiling water on the lower oven rack, as the extra moisture helps.

- Preheat oven to 400°F (200°F)
- 9-inch (23 cm) cheesecake pan, ungreased, or springform pan with 3-inch (7.5 cm) sides, greased
- 13- by 9-inch (3 L) baking pan, filled with 2 inches (5 cm) boiling water
- Blowtorch or broiler

Filling

3	packages (each 8 oz/250 g) cream cheese, softened	3
1½ cups	sour cream	375 mL
½ cup	granulated sugar	125 mL
4	eggs	4
12 oz	white chocolate, chopped, melted (see page 63) and cooled	375 g
1 tbsp	vanilla extract	15 mL
1 tsp	freshly squeezed lemon juice	5 mL
½ tsp	salt	2 mL

Topping

¼ cup	packed light brown sugar	50 mL

1. *Filling:* In a mixer bowl fitted with paddle attachment, beat cream cheese, sour cream and sugar on medium-high speed until very smooth, for 3 minutes. Add eggs, one at a time, beating after each addition. With the mixer running, pour in melted chocolate in a steady stream. Mix in vanilla, lemon juice and salt.

2. Pour into cheesecake pan, smoothing out to sides of pan. Center cheesecake pan on the middle rack in the oven with a baking pan of boiling water on the lower rack. Bake at 400°F (200°C) for 10 minutes. Reduce oven temperature to 350°F (180°C) and bake until top is light brown and center has a slight jiggle to it, 45 to 55 minutes. Let cool in pan on a wire rack for 2 hours. Cover with plastic wrap and refrigerate for at least 6 hours before topping or serving.

3. *Topping:* Sprinkle brown sugar evenly on top of chilled cheesecake. Using a blowtorch or broiler, heat sugar just until bubbling, about 3 minutes. Let cool until sugar has hardened. Serve immediately.

English Toffee Cheesecake

SERVES 10 TO 12

I like to use English toffee from Littlejohn's candy company in Los Angeles, a family-run, artisan candy company open since 1924. If you're not in Los Angeles, you can use any English toffee in this cheesecake.

Tip

If you can't find vanilla bean paste, split 1 whole vanilla bean lengthwise and scrape the seeds into the batter.

- Preheat oven to 350°F (180°C)
- 9-inch (23 cm) cheesecake pan, ungreased, or springform pan with 3-inch (7.5 cm) sides, greased

Crust

1¼ cups	graham cracker crumbs	300 mL
¼ cup	unsalted butter, melted	50 mL

Filling

4	packages (each 8 oz/250 g) cream cheese, softened	4
1¼ cups	granulated sugar	300 mL
4	eggs	4
6 oz	English toffee, broken into small pieces	175 g
1 tbsp	pure vanilla bean paste (see tip, at left)	15 mL
1 tsp	freshly squeezed lemon juice	5 mL

Decoration

	Classic Whipped Cream Topping (see recipe, page 262)

1. *Crust:* In a bowl, combine graham cracker crumbs and butter. Press into bottom of cheesecake pan and freeze.
2. *Filling:* In a mixer bowl fitted with paddle attachment, beat cream cheese and sugar on medium-high speed until very smooth, for 3 minutes. Add eggs, one at a time, beating after each addition. Fold in toffee, vanilla bean paste and lemon juice by hand.
3. Pour over frozen crust, smoothing out to sides of pan. Bake in preheated oven until top is light brown and center has a slight jiggle to it, 45 to 55 minutes. Let cool in pan on a wire rack for 2 hours. Cover with plastic wrap and refrigerate for at least 6 hours before decorating or serving.
4. *Decoration:* Ice top of cake with Classic Whipped Cream Topping or pipe rosettes around top of cake, if desired.

Toffee Cheesecake with Caramel Sauce

SERVES 10 TO 12

A rich caramel center makes this cheesecake a perfect birthday cake.

Tips

Place pieces of the toffee candy bar in a sealable plastic bag and roll a rolling pin over them a few times until crushed to desired coarseness.

When making the Caramel Sauce, use a heavy-bottomed saucepan to avoid hot spots and burning caramel. Store extra Caramel Sauce at room temperature until serving time.

- Preheat the oven to 350°F (180°C)
- 9-inch (23 cm) cheesecake pan, ungreased, or springform pan with 3-inch (7.5 cm) sides, greased

Crust

1½ cups	graham cracker crumbs	375 mL
¼ cup	packed light brown sugar	50 mL
¼ cup	unsalted butter, melted	50 mL

Filling

4	packages (each 8 oz/250 g) cream cheese, softened	4
1 cup	sour cream	250 mL
1¼ cups	granulated sugar	300 mL
5	eggs	5
1 tbsp	vanilla extract	15 mL
2 tsp	freshly squeezed lemon juice	10 mL
5 oz	toffee candy bar, crushed (see tip, at left)	150 g

Caramel Sauce

1¼ cups	granulated sugar	300 mL
⅓ cup	water	75 mL
1 cup	whipping (35%) cream, at room temperature	250 mL
½ cup	unsalted butter, softened	125 mL
1 tsp	vanilla extract	5 mL

Decoration

Classic Whipped Cream Topping (see recipe, page 262)

1. *Crust:* In a bowl, combine graham cracker crumbs, brown sugar and butter. Press into bottom of cheesecake pan and freeze.

2. *Filling:* In a mixer bowl fitted with paddle attachment, beat cream cheese, sour cream and sugar on medium-high speed until very smooth, for 3 minutes. Add eggs, one at a time, beating after each addition. Mix in vanilla and lemon juice. Fold in crushed candy bar pieces by hand.

Variation
You can omit the Caramel
Sauce and call it a Toffee
Candy Cheesecake.

3. Pour over frozen crust, smoothing out to sides of pan. Bake in preheated oven until top is light brown and center has a slight jiggle to it, 45 to 55 minutes. Let cool in pan on a wire rack for 2 hours. Cover with plastic wrap and refrigerate for at least 6 hours before topping.

4. *Caramel Sauce:* In a small saucepan over low heat, heat sugar and water until sugar melts. Increase heat and boil without stirring until mixture is a rich caramel color, about 8 minutes. Reduce heat to low and add cream, stirring constantly to smooth the bubbles. Stir in butter until melted. Add vanilla. Let cool slightly. Pour about two-thirds of mixture into center of cake and spread out to edges. Chill cake until caramel is set, about 2 hours.

5. *Decoration:* Ice top of cake with Classic Whipped Cream Topping or pipe rosettes around top of cake, if desired. Use remaining caramel sauce to garnish each slice of the cheesecake.

Sticky Toffee Pudding Cheesecake

SERVES 10 TO 12

One of my favorite desserts when traveling in the U.K. is sticky toffee pudding, an intense cake with toffee sauce. My version doubles the flavor by using toffee candy in the cake instead of the traditional dates.

Tip

If caramel sauce is too thick to drizzle, warm it in the microwave for 30 seconds.

Variation

Stir 1 to 2 tbsp (15 to 25 mL) brandy into the whipped cream to cut the sweetness.

- Preheat oven to 350°F (180°C)
- 9-inch (23 cm) cheesecake pan, ungreased, or springform pan with 3-inch (7.5 cm) sides, greased

Crust

1¼ cups	graham cracker crumbs	300 mL
¼ cup	unsalted butter, melted	50 mL

Filling

4	packages (each 8 oz/250 g) cream cheese, softened	4
½ cup	sour cream	125 mL
1 cup	packed brown sugar	250 mL
5	eggs	5
¾ cup	caramel sauce (store-bought or see recipe, page 44)	175 mL
1 tsp	vanilla extract	5 mL
1 cup	toffee bits	250 mL

Decoration

	Classic Whipped Cream Topping (see recipe, page 262)	
2 tbsp	caramel sauce	25 mL

1. *Crust:* In a bowl, combine graham cracker crumbs and butter. Press into bottom of cheesecake pan and freeze.

2. *Filling:* In a mixer bowl fitted with paddle attachment, beat cream cheese, sour cream and brown sugar on medium-high speed until very smooth, for 3 minutes. Add eggs, one at a time, beating after each addition. Mix in caramel sauce and vanilla. Fold in toffee bits by hand.

3. Pour over frozen crust, smoothing out to sides of pan. Bake in preheated oven until top is light brown and center has a slight jiggle to it, 45 to 55 minutes. Let cool in pan on a wire rack for 2 hours. Cover with plastic wrap and refrigerate for at least 6 hours before decorating or serving.

4. *Decoration:* Ice top of cake with Classic Whipped Cream Topping or pipe rosettes around top of cake, if desired. Drizzle caramel sauce on top.

Tiramisu Cheesecake

SERVES 10 TO 12

Half cheesecake, half layer cake, absolutely decadent. Prepare this dessert a few days before serving to allow the flavor and texture to fully develop.

Tips

It's much easier to slice a cake horizontally when it is frozen than when it's at room temperature. Some bakeries will sell you un-iced layers if you are in a hurry.

Be sure your cake layers are no more than ½ inch (1 cm) thick to make sure the filling doesn't overflow the pan.

Variation

Stir in 6 oz (175 g) semisweet chocolate chunks with the vanilla in the filling.

- Preheat oven to 325°F (160°C)
- 9-inch (23 cm) cheesecake pan, ungreased, or springform pan with 3-inch (7.5 cm) sides, greased

Crust

1	9-inch (23 cm) yellow cake, sliced horizontally in half	1
½ cup	coffee-flavored liqueur	125 mL
2 tbsp	instant espresso powder	25 mL

Filling

1 lb	mascarpone cheese	500 g
2	packages (each 8 oz/250 g) cream cheese, softened	2
1 cup	granulated sugar	250 mL
5	eggs	5
1 tbsp	vanilla extract	15 mL

Decoration

	Classic Whipped Cream Topping (see recipe, page 262)	
1 tsp	sweetened cocoa powder	5 mL

1. *Crust:* Place half the cake in bottom of cheesecake pan. In a bowl, combine liqueur and espresso power. Brush about one-quarter of the mixture on cake layer in pan. Brush the other cake layer with one-quarter of the mixture. Set the cake layers and remaining mixture aside.

2. *Filling:* In a mixer bowl fitted with paddle attachment, beat mascarpone, cream cheese and sugar on medium-high speed until very smooth, for 3 minutes. Add eggs one at a time, beating after each addition. Mix in vanilla and remaining liqueur mixture.

3. Pour half the batter over cake layer in pan, smoothing out to sides of pan. Place second cake layer on top and pour in the remaining batter, smoothing out to sides of pan (the pan will be filled to the top edge). Bake in preheated oven until top is very light brown and center has a slight jiggle to it, 50 to 55 minutes. Let cool in pan on a wire rack for 2 hours. Cover with plastic wrap and refrigerate for at least 6 hours before decorating or serving.

4. *Decoration:* Ice top of cake with Classic Whipped Cream Topping or pipe rosettes around top of cake, if desired. Sprinkle with cocoa powder.

Zabaglione Cheesecake

SERVES 10 TO 12

Serve this decadent treat after an Italian feast!

Tips

To quickly prepare cookie crumbs, place whole cookies in a food processor fitted with a metal blade and pulse a few times. You can add the butter to the food processor and pulse until blended. When mixed with the butter, the crumbs should feel like wet sand.

Use the remaining wine to make Chicken Marsala.

Variation

Substitute graham cracker crumbs and ½ tsp (2 mL) almond extract for the almond cookie crumbs.

- Preheat oven to 350°F (180°C)
- 9-inch (23 cm) cheesecake pan, ungreased, or springform pan with 3-inch (7.5 cm) sides, greased

Crust

1½ cups	almond cookie crumbs	375 mL
3 tbsp	unsalted butter, melted	45 mL

Filling

2	packages (each 8 oz/250 g) cream cheese, softened	2
1 lb	mascarpone cheese	500 g
1 cup	granulated sugar	250 mL
5	egg yolks	5
¼ cup	Marsala wine	50 mL
2 tsp	vanilla extract	10 mL

1. *Crust:* In a bowl, combine cookie crumbs and butter. Press into bottom of cheesecake pan and freeze.

2. *Filling:* In a mixer bowl fitted with paddle attachment, beat cream cheese, mascarpone and sugar on medium-high speed until very smooth, for 3 minutes. Add egg yolks, one at a time, beating after each addition. Mix in wine and vanilla.

3. Pour over frozen crust, smoothing out to sides of pan. Bake in preheated oven until top is light brown and center has a slight jiggle to it, 45 to 55 minutes. Let cool in pan on a wire rack for 2 hours. Cover with plastic wrap and refrigerate for at least 6 hours before serving.

Creamy Amaretto Cheesecake

SERVES 10 TO 12

When touring the Banff Springs area in the 1980s, I came across a light almond cheesecake. This is just like the one served to me on that cold fall evening.

Tips

To avoid making almond butter when grinding the almonds, process with the graham crackers in a food processor fitted with a metal blade. If you're preparing a recipe that doesn't call for crumbs, mix in 2 tbsp (25 mL) all-purpose flour with the nuts.

For a smoother texture, purée the cottage cheese in a food processor before adding to filling.

Variation

Substitute 1 tsp (5 mL) almond extract for the liqueur.

- Preheat oven to 350°F (180°C)
- 9-inch (23 cm) cheesecake pan, ungreased, or springform pan with 3-inch (7.5 cm) sides, greased

Crust

1¼ cups	graham cracker crumbs	300 mL
¼ cup	almonds, toasted (see tip, page 50) and ground	50 mL
¼ cup	unsalted butter, melted	50 mL

Filling

3	packages (each 8 oz/250 g) cream cheese, softened	3
1 cup	small-curd cottage cheese (see tip, at left)	250 mL
1½ cups	granulated sugar	375 mL
½ tsp	salt	2 mL
4	eggs	4
1 tsp	grated orange zest	5 mL
½ cup	almond-flavored liqueur	125 mL

Decoration

	Classic Whipped Cream Topping (see recipe, page 262)	
⅓ cup	slivered almonds, toasted	75 mL

1. *Crust:* In a bowl, mix graham cracker crumbs, ground almonds and butter. Press into bottom of cheesecake pan and freeze.
2. *Filling:* In a mixer bowl fitted with paddle attachment, beat cream cheese, cottage cheese, sugar and salt on medium-high speed until very smooth, for 3 minutes. Add eggs, one at a time, beating after each addition. Stir in orange zest and liqueur.
3. Pour over frozen crust, smoothing out to sides of pan. Bake in preheated oven until top is light brown and center has a slight jiggle to it, 45 to 55 minutes. Let cool in pan on a wire rack for 2 hours. Cover with plastic wrap and refrigerate for at least 6 hours before decorating or serving.
4. *Decoration:* Ice top of cake with Classic Whipped Cream Topping or pipe rosettes around top of cake, if desired. Sprinkle with toasted almonds.

Rum Raisin Cheesecake

When it's cold outside, this hearty cheesecake will warm you up.

Tips

Toasting brings out the natural oils and flavor of nuts. Place nuts in a single layer on a baking sheet and bake at 350°F (180°C) until fragrant, 10 to 12 minutes.

Infuse the raisins with extra flavor by soaking them in the rum for about 10 minutes before adding both to the recipe.

Variation

Substituting dried cranberries for the raisins adds a tart element that highlights the sweetness of the cheesecake.

- Preheat oven to 350°F (180°C)
- 9-inch (23 cm) cheesecake pan, ungreased, or springform pan with 3-inch (7.5 cm) sides, greased

Crust

1 cup	graham cracker crumbs	250 mL
¼ cup	pecans, toasted (see tip, at left) and ground	50 mL
¼ cup	packed brown sugar	50 mL
¼ cup	unsalted butter, melted	50 mL

Filling

2	packages (each 8 oz/250 g) cream cheese, softened	2
1 cup	small-curd cottage cheese (see tips, page 51), drained if necessary	250 mL
1 cup	sour cream	250 mL
1¼ cups	packed brown sugar	300 mL
4	eggs	4
1 cup	golden raisins	250 mL
3 tbsp	dark rum	45 mL
1 tbsp	freshly squeezed lemon juice	15 mL
1 tbsp	vanilla extract	15 mL
½ tsp	freshly grated nutmeg	2 mL

1. *Crust:* In a bowl, combine graham cracker crumbs, pecans, brown sugar and butter. Press into bottom of cheesecake pan and freeze.
2. *Filling:* In a mixer bowl fitted with paddle attachment, beat cream cheese, cottage cheese, sour cream and brown sugar on medium-high speed until very smooth, for 3 minutes. Add eggs, one at a time, beating after each addition. Fold in raisins, rum, lemon juice, vanilla and nutmeg by hand.
3. Pour over frozen crust, smoothing out to sides of pan. Bake in preheated oven until top is light brown and center has a slight jiggle to it, 45 to 55 minutes. Let cool in pan on a wire rack for 2 hours. Cover with plastic wrap and refrigerate for at least 6 hours before serving.

Three-Cinnamon Cheesecake

SERVES 10 TO 12

Yes, three types of cinnamon in one amazing cheesecake. The real deal from Ceylon is much lighter in color and more delicate in flavor than the pungent spice most commonly sold here.

Tips

Treat yourself to a sensory experience by trying imported brands of cinnamon. I use Penzeys Spices from Wisconsin. Check my listing of suppliers on page 277 to contact them directly.

If the cottage cheese has a wet look to it, drain it through a fine-mesh sieve. Too much moisture will change the texture of the cheesecake.

If small-curd cottage cheese is not available, purée cottage cheese in a food processor before adding to the cream cheese.

- Preheat oven to 325°F (160°C)
- 9-inch (23 cm) cheesecake pan, ungreased, or springform pan with 3-inch (7.5 cm) sides, greased

Crust

1½ cups	butter cookie crumbs	375 mL
¼ cup	unsalted butter, melted	50 mL
1 tsp	Ceylon ground cinnamon	5 mL

Filling

3	packages (each 8 oz/250 g) cream cheese, softened	3
1 cup	small-curd cottage cheese (see tips, at left)	250 mL
1 cup	sour cream	250 mL
1½ cups	granulated sugar	375 mL
4	eggs	4
1	egg yolk	1
1 tsp	Vietnamese ground cinnamon	5 mL
½ tsp	Ceylon ground cinnamon	2 mL
½ tsp	Korintje cassia ground cinnamon	2 mL

Decoration

Classic Whipped Cream Topping
(see recipe, page 262)

1. *Crust:* In a bowl, combine cookie crumbs, butter and Ceylon cinnamon. Press into bottom of cheesecake pan and freeze.

2. *Filling:* In a mixer bowl fitted with paddle attachment, beat cream cheese, cottage cheese, sour cream and sugar on medium-high speed until very smooth, for 3 minutes. Add whole eggs and egg yolk, one at a time, beating after each addition. Stir in the three cinnamons.

3. Pour over frozen crust, smoothing out to sides of pan. Bake in preheated oven until top is light brown and center has a slight jiggle to it, 45 to 55 minutes. Let cool in pan on a wire rack for 2 hours. Cover with plastic wrap and refrigerate for at least 6 hours before decorating or serving.

4. *Decoration:* Ice top of cake with Classic Whipped Cream Topping or pipe rosettes around top of cake, if desired.

Lavender Honey Cheesecake

SERVES 10 TO 12

Look for lavender honey in health food stores or farmers' markets. Purchase culinary lavender at health food stores or spice stores, as some lavender is best used for aroma only.

Tip

Extra lavender buds can be used in salads or breads, or to perfume a bowl of sugar.

- Preheat oven to 350°F (180°C)
- 9-inch (23 cm) cheesecake pan, ungreased, or springform pan with 3-inch (7.5 cm) sides, greased

Crust

1¼ cups	graham cracker crumbs	300 mL
¼ cup	unsalted butter, melted	50 mL

Filling

2	packages (each 8 oz/250 g) cream cheese, softened	2
1 lb	ricotta cheese, drained	500 g
½ cup	liquid lavender honey	125 mL
3	eggs	3
1 tbsp	all-purpose flour	15 mL
2 tsp	grated lemon zest	10 mL
1 tsp	vanilla extract	5 mL
½ tsp	salt	2 mL

Decoration

	Classic Whipped Cream Topping (see recipe, page 262)	
½ tsp	fresh or dried lavender buds	2 mL

1. *Crust:* In a bowl, combine graham cracker crumbs and butter. Press into bottom of cheesecake pan and freeze.

2. *Filling:* In a mixer bowl fitted with paddle attachment, beat cream cheese, ricotta cheese and honey until very smooth, for 3 minutes. Add eggs, one at a time, beating after each addition. Stir in flour, lemon zest, vanilla and salt.

3. Pour over frozen crust, smoothing out to sides of pan. Bake in preheated oven until top is light brown and center has a slight jiggle to it, 45 to 55 minutes. Let cool in pan on a wire rack for 2 hours. Cover with plastic wrap and refrigerate for at least 6 hours before decorating or serving.

4. *Decoration:* Ice top of cake with Classic Whipped Cream Topping or pipe rosettes around top of cake, if desired. Sprinkle with lavender buds.

Ginger and Honey Cheesecake

SERVES 10 TO 12

A perfect cheesecake to finish off the flavors of an Asian-style meal. The candied and dry ginger in this cheesecake will give your taste buds a tingle.

Tip

Use fresh candied ginger. It should feel soft. If ginger is hard, soften it in hot water for about 15 minutes and drain well before mincing it.

- Preheat oven to 350°F (180°C)
- 9-inch (23 cm) cheesecake pan, ungreased, or springform pan with 3-inch (7.5 cm) sides, greased

Crust

1½ cups	gingersnap cookie crumbs	375 mL
¼ cup	unsalted butter, melted	50 mL

Filling

2	packages (each 8 oz/250 g) cream cheese, softened	2
1 cup	sour cream	250 mL
⅓ cup	all-purpose flour	75 mL
⅔ cup	packed light brown sugar	150 mL
¼ cup	liquid honey	50 mL
2	eggs	2
2 tsp	minced candied ginger	10 mL
½ tsp	ground ginger	2 mL
¼ tsp	ground cinnamon	1 mL

Decoration

	Classic Whipped Cream Topping (see recipe, page 262)	
¼ tsp	ground ginger	1 mL
⅛ tsp	ground cinnamon	0.5 mL

1. *Crust:* In a bowl, combine cookie crumbs and butter. Press into bottom of cheesecake pan and freeze.

2. *Filling:* In mixer bowl fitted with paddle attachment, beat cream cheese and sour cream on medium-high speed until very smooth, for 3 minutes. Mix in flour, brown sugar and honey until well blended, about 2 minutes. Add eggs, one at a time, beating after each addition. Add candied ginger, ground ginger and cinnamon.

3. Pour over frozen crust, smoothing out to sides of pan. Bake in preheated oven until top is light brown and center has a slight jiggle to it, 55 to 65 minutes. Let cool in pan on a wire rack for 2 hours. Cover with plastic wrap and refrigerate for at least 6 hours before decorating or serving.

4. *Decoration:* Ice top of cake with Classic Whipped Cream Topping or pipe a ribbon around border, if desired. Sprinkle with ground ginger and cinnamon.

Carrot Cake Cheesecake

Your guests will ask if it's a cheesecake or a carrot cake. It's the best of both worlds.

Tips

Toasting brings out the natural oils and flavor of nuts. Place nuts in a single layer on a baking sheet and bake at 350°F (180°C) until fragrant, 10 to 12 minutes.

You can use the same mixer bowl for the cheesecake batter and the carrot cake batter; there's no need to wash it in between.

- Preheat oven to 350°F (180°C)
- 9-inch (23 cm) cheesecake pan or springform pan with 3-inch (7.5 cm) sides, sprayed with nonstick spray, outside of pan wrapped with foil

Cheesecake Batter

2	packages (each 8 oz/250 g) cream cheese, softened	2
¾ cup	granulated sugar	175 mL
1 tbsp	all-purpose flour	15 mL
2	eggs	2
1 tsp	vanilla extract	5 mL
1 tsp	ground cinnamon	5 mL

Carrot Cake Batter

1¼ cups	all-purpose flour	300 mL
1¼ tsp	baking soda	6 mL
¼ tsp	ground cinnamon	1 mL
¼ tsp	salt	1 mL
⅛ tsp	freshly grated nutmeg	0.5 mL
1¼ cups	granulated sugar	300 mL
2	eggs	2
⅓ cup	vegetable oil	75 mL
1 tsp	vanilla extract	5 mL
½ cup	well-drained crushed pineapple (about one 8-oz/227 mL can)	125 mL
½ cup	flaked sweetened coconut	125 mL
½ cup	pecans, toasted (see tip, at left) and chopped	125 mL
1 cup	shredded carrots	250 mL

Icing

2 oz	cream cheese, softened	60 g
1 tbsp	unsalted butter, softened	15 mL
1¾ cups	confectioner's (icing) sugar	425 mL
½ tsp	vanilla extract	2 mL

1. *Cheesecake batter:* In a mixer bowl fitted with paddle attachment, beat cream cheese, sugar and flour on medium-high speed until very smooth, for 3 minutes. Add eggs one at a time, beating after each addition. Stir in vanilla and cinnamon. Transfer to a bowl and set aside.

Remove the foil from
the pan as soon as it
comes out of the oven;
otherwise, it will stick.

2. *Carrot cake batter:* In a bowl, whisk together flour, baking soda, cinnamon, salt, and nutmeg. In a mixer bowl fitted with paddle attachment, combine sugar, eggs, oil and vanilla until well blended, for 2 minutes. Add pineapple, coconut and pecans; mix for 1 minute. Gradually stir in flour mixture. Stir in carrots.

3. Divide carrot cake batter in half and smooth half the batter over bottom of prepared pan. Bake in preheated oven just until cake is light brown and just set, 18 to 22 minutes (it will not be fully cooked).

4. Gently drop cheesecake batter by large spoonfuls over carrot cake. Top with large spoonfuls of remaining carrot cake batter, allowing some of the cheesecake batter to show through. Bake in preheated oven until a tester inserted in the top layer of carrot cake comes out clean, 55 to 60 minutes. Let cool in pan on a wire rack for 2 hours. Cover with plastic wrap and refrigerate for at least 6 hours before icing or serving.

5. *Icing:* In a mixer bowl fitted with paddle attachment, beat cream cheese and butter on medium speed until fluffy, about 4 minutes. Add sugar and vanilla; beat until creamy and light, about 3 minutes. Pipe large rosettes around top of cake.

Lemongrass Cheesecake

SERVES 10 TO 12

Combining lemongrass and coconut milk with cheesecake creates a fusion that would be fun to serve after a Pacific Rim meal.

Tips

Lemongrass can be found in Asian markets and some supermarkets, often where the fresh herbs are displayed.

Coconut is often burned by pastry chefs. To avoid crying over burnt coconut, follow this technique. Spread coconut in a single layer on a baking sheet. Bake in a 350°F (180°C) oven for 3 minutes. Check the coconut and stir. Set the timer for another 3 minutes. Repeat until coconut is lightly browned.

Variation

Substitute whipping (35%) cream for the coconut milk.

- Preheat oven to 350°F (180°C)
- 9-inch (23 cm) cheesecake pan, ungreased, or springform pan with 3-inch (7.5 cm) sides, greased

Crust

1¼ cups	butter cookie crumbs	300 mL
¼ cup	pecans, toasted (see tip, page 54) and ground	50 mL
3 tbsp	unsalted butter, melted	45 mL

Filling

1	stalk fresh lemongrass, coarsely chopped	1
½ cup	coconut milk	125 mL
4	packages (each 8 oz/250 g) cream cheese, softened	4
1½ cups	granulated sugar	375 mL
3	eggs	3
2	egg yolks	2
2 tsp	vanilla extract	10 mL

Decoration

	Classic Whipped Cream Topping (see recipe, page 262)	
¼ cup	shredded sweetened coconut, toasted (see tip, at left)	50 mL

1. *Crust:* In a bowl, combine cookie crumbs, pecans and butter. Press into bottom of cheesecake pan and freeze.
2. *Filling:* In a saucepan, cook lemongrass and coconut milk over medium heat until milk starts to bubble. Strain milk and discard lemongrass. Set aside.
3. In a mixer bowl fitted with paddle attachment, beat cream cheese and sugar on medium-high speed until very smooth, for 3 minutes. Add whole eggs and egg yolks, one at a time, beating after each addition. Mix in coconut milk and vanilla.
4. Pour over frozen crust, smoothing out to sides of pan. Bake in preheated oven until top is light brown and center has a slight jiggle to it, 45 to 55 minutes. Let cool in pan on a wire rack for 2 hours. Cover with plastic wrap and refrigerate for at least 6 hours before decorating or serving.
5. *Decoration:* Ice top of cake with Classic Whipped Cream Topping or pipe rosettes around top of cake, if desired. Sprinkle with toasted coconut.

Vanilla Bean Cheesecake

SERVES 10 TO 12

For rich vanilla flavor, it is worth the extra expense and effort to use real vanilla beans in this recipe. Specialty food stores and online vendors stock vanilla beans and paste.

Tip

If you can't find vanilla bean paste, use an equal amount of vanilla extract or split 2 whole vanilla beans lengthwise and scrape the seeds into the batter.

- Preheat oven to 350°F (180°C)
- 9-inch (23 cm) cheesecake pan, ungreased, or springform pan with 3-inch (7.5 cm) sides, greased

Crust

1¼ cups	graham cracker crumbs	300 mL
¼ cup	unsalted butter, melted	50 mL

Filling

4	packages (each 8 oz/250 g) cream cheese, softened	4
1¼ cups	granulated sugar	300 mL
4	eggs	4
2 tbsp	pure vanilla bean paste (see tip, at left)	25 mL
1 tsp	freshly squeezed lemon juice	5 mL

Decoration

Classic Whipped Cream Topping
(see recipe, page 262)

1. *Crust:* In a bowl, combine graham cracker crumbs and butter. Press into bottom of cheesecake pan and freeze.

2. *Filling:* In a mixer bowl fitted with paddle attachment, beat cream cheese and sugar on medium-high speed until very smooth, for 3 minutes. Add eggs, one at a time, beating after each addition. Mix in vanilla bean paste and lemon juice.

3. Pour over frozen crust, smoothing out to sides of pan. Bake in preheated oven until top is light brown and center has a slight jiggle to it, 45 to 55 minutes. Let cool in pan on a wire rack for 2 hours. Cover with plastic wrap and refrigerate for at least 6 hours before decorating or serving.

4. *Decoration:* Ice top of cake with Classic Whipped Cream Topping or pipe rosettes around top of cake, if desired.

Vanilla Sour Cream Cheesecake

SERVES 10 TO 12

When purchasing vanilla bean paste, you should see specks of the vanilla bean, which says authentic vanilla was used.

Tip

If you can't find vanilla bean paste, split 1 whole vanilla bean lengthwise and scrape the seeds into the batter. The seeds of 1 bean are equivalent to 1 tbsp (15 mL) paste.

- Preheat oven to 325°F (160°C)
- 9-inch (23 cm) cheesecake pan, ungreased, or springform pan with 3-inch (7.5 cm) sides, greased

Crust

1½ cups	vanilla cookie crumbs	375 mL
¼ cup	unsalted butter, melted	50 mL

Filling

3	packages (each 8 oz/250 g) cream cheese, softened	3
1 cup	small-curd cottage cheese (see tips, page 51)	250 mL
1 cup	sour cream	250 mL
1½ cups	granulated sugar	375 mL
5	eggs	5
1 tbsp	pure vanilla bean paste (see tip, at left)	15 mL
1 tsp	grated lemon zest	5 mL

Decoration

Classic Whipped Cream Topping (see recipe, page 262)

1. *Crust:* In a bowl, combine cookie crumbs and butter. Press into bottom of cheesecake pan and freeze.
2. *Filling:* In a mixer bowl fitted with paddle attachment, beat cream cheese, cottage cheese, sour cream and sugar on medium-high speed until very smooth, for 3 minutes. Add eggs, one at a time, beating after each addition. Mix in vanilla bean paste and lemon zest.
3. Pour over frozen crust, smoothing out to sides of pan. Bake in preheated oven until top is light brown and center has a slight jiggle to it, 45 to 55 minutes. Let cool in pan on a wire rack for 2 hours. Cover with plastic wrap and refrigerate for at least 6 hours before decorating or serving.
4. *Decoration:* Ice top of cake with Classic Whipped Cream Topping or pipe rosettes around top of cake, if desired.

Chocolate
Cheesecakes

Aztec Cheesecake

SERVES 10 TO 12

The Aztec civilization of south-central Mexico introduced Europeans to chocolate about 500 years ago with a hot drink made from cocoa beans. The rest, as they say, is history.

Tips

Using Dutch-process cocoa powder creates a richer cheesecake.

A small whisk is perfect for the small, but important, job of dissolving cocoa powder in hot water.

If you can't find vanilla bean paste, split 1 whole vanilla bean lengthwise and scrape the seeds into the batter. The seeds of 1 bean are equivalent to 1 tbsp (15 mL) paste.

Variation

Add 2 tbsp (25 mL) of coffee-flavored liqueur to the batter with the dissolved cocoa for an added punch.

- Preheat oven to 350°F (180°C)
- 9-inch (23 cm) cheesecake pan, ungreased, or springform pan with 3-inch (7.5 cm) sides, greased

Crust

1¼ cups	chocolate sandwich cookie crumbs	300 mL
¼ cup	unsalted butter, melted	50 mL

Filling

¼ cup	unsweetened Dutch-process cocoa powder	50 mL
3 tbsp	hot water	45 mL
4	packages (each 8 oz/250 g) cream cheese, softened	4
1½ cups	granulated sugar	375 mL
5	eggs	5
1 tbsp	pure vanilla bean paste (see tip, at left)	15 mL
1 tsp	ground cinnamon	5 mL

Decoration

Truffle Fudge Topping (see recipe, page 263)

1. *Crust:* In a bowl, combine cookie crumbs and butter. Press into bottom of cheesecake pan and freeze.
2. *Filling:* In a small bowl, dissolve cocoa powder in hot water. Set aside.
3. In a mixer bowl fitted with paddle attachment, beat cream cheese and sugar on medium-high speed until very smooth, for 3 minutes. Add eggs, one at a time, beating after each addition. Stir in vanilla bean paste, cinnamon and dissolved cocoa.
4. Pour over frozen crust, smoothing out to sides of pan. Bake in preheated oven until top is light brown and center has a slight jiggle to it, 45 to 55 minutes. Let cool in pan on a wire rack for 2 hours. Cover with plastic wrap and refrigerate for at least 6 hours before decorating or serving.
5. *Decoration:* Top each slice with a spoonful of Truffle Fudge Topping.

Milk Chocolate Cheesecake

A sweet milk chocolate layer is paired with a rich vanilla layer.

Tip

Be careful not to blend the two cheesecake batters. If you do, swirl the chocolate into the vanilla and call it a Milk Chocolate Swirl Cheesecake.

Variation

Dust cocoa powder on top instead of shaved chocolate.

- Preheat oven to 350°F (180°C)
- 9-inch (23 cm) cheesecake pan, ungreased, or springform pan with 3-inch (7.5 cm) sides, greased

Crust

1½ cups	chocolate sandwich cookie crumbs	375 mL
¼ cup	unsalted butter, melted	50 mL

Filling

4	packages (each 8 oz/250 g) cream cheese, softened	4
1¼ cups	granulated sugar	300 mL
4	eggs	4
1 cup	sour cream	250 mL
1 tbsp	vanilla extract	15 mL
4 oz	milk chocolate, melted (see page 63) and cooled	125 g

Decoration

	Classic Whipped Cream Topping (see recipe, page 262)	
¼ cup	shaved chocolate	50 mL

1. **Crust:** In a bowl, combine cookie crumbs and butter. Press into bottom of cheesecake pan and freeze.

2. **Filling:** In a mixer bowl fitted with paddle attachment, beat cream cheese and sugar on medium-high speed until very smooth, for 3 minutes. Add eggs, one at a time, beating after each addition. Mix in sour cream and vanilla.

3. Divide batter in half. Stir milk chocolate into one portion and pour over frozen crust, smoothing out to sides of pan. Pour remaining batter over chocolate portion, smoothing out to sides of pan. Bake in preheated oven until top is light brown and center has a slight jiggle to it, 55 to 65 minutes. Let cool in pan on a wire rack for 2 hours. Cover with plastic wrap and refrigerate for at least 6 hours before decorating or serving.

4. **Decoration:** Ice top of cake with Classic Whipped Cream Topping or pipe rosettes around top of cake, if desired. Top with chocolate shavings.

German Chocolate Cheesecake

• •

SERVES 10 TO 12

A rich German chocolate filling is at the heart of this decadent cheesecake.

Tips

Toasting brings out the natural oils and flavor of nuts. Place nuts in a single layer on a baking sheet and bake at 350°F (180°C) until fragrant, 10 to 12 minutes.

To melt bittersweet chocolate in the microwave, break into squares and place in a microwave-safe dish. Microwave on High for 1 to 2 minutes, stirring after 30 seconds.

You can prepare the coconut mixture up to 3 days ahead. Cover and store in the refrigerator. Bring to room temperature and stir well before using.

- Preheat oven to 350°F (180°C)
- 9-inch (23 cm) cheesecake pan, ungreased, or springform pan with 3-inch (7.5 cm) sides, greased

Crust

1¼ cups	chocolate sandwich cookie crumbs	300 mL
¼ cup	pecans, toasted (see tip, at left) and ground	50 mL
3 tbsp	unsalted butter, melted	45 mL

Filling

1 cup	packed brown sugar	250 mL
2 tbsp	unsalted butter, softened	25 mL
2	egg yolks, stirred	2
1½ cups	flaked sweetened coconut	375 mL
¾ cup	pecan halves	175 mL
3	packages (each 8 oz/250 g) cream cheese, softened	3
1 cup	granulated sugar	250 mL
3	eggs	3
6 oz	bittersweet chocolate, melted (see box, opposite, and tip, at left) and cooled	175 g
1 tsp	vanilla extract	5 mL

1. *Crust:* In a bowl, combine cookie crumbs, ground pecans and butter. Press into bottom of cheesecake pan and freeze.

2. *Filling:* In a saucepan over medium-high heat, melt brown sugar and butter for 3 minutes. Remove from heat. Slowly drizzle stirred egg yolks into mixture. Return to medium heat and cook, stirring, for about 3 minutes. Add coconut and pecan halves. Let cool in the refrigerator for 20 minutes.

Variation

Toasted almonds are a tasty substitute for pecans.

3. In a mixer bowl fitted with paddle attachment, beat cream cheese and sugar on medium-high speed until very smooth, for 3 minutes. Add whole eggs, one at a time, beating after each addition. With the mixer running, pour in melted chocolate in a steady stream. Mix in vanilla. Fold half of the coconut mixture into batter by hand. Set the remainder aside for decorating.

4. Pour over frozen crust, smoothing out to sides of pan. Bake in preheated oven until top is light brown and center has a slight jiggle to it, 45 to 55 minutes. Let cool in pan on a wire rack for 2 hours. Cover with plastic wrap and refrigerate for at least 6 hours before decorating or serving.

5. *Decoration:* Spread remaining coconut mixture on top of cake.

Melting Chocolate

Milk and White Chocolate: Finely chop chocolate and place in a heatproof stainless steel bowl that fits snugly on top of a saucepan. In saucepan, bring water to a boil. Remove from heat and place bowl of chopped chocolate on top, making sure the bottom of the bowl doesn't touch the water. Let stand, allowing the steam to melt the chocolate. When it is almost melted, stir until smooth. The more finely you chop the chocolate, the faster it will melt.

Dark Chocolate (Semisweet and Bittersweet): Finely chop chocolate and place in a heatproof stainless steel bowl that fits snugly on top of a saucepan. In saucepan, bring water to a boil. Reduce heat to the lowest setting, so that the water just ripples. Place bowl of chopped chocolate on top, making sure the bottom of the bowl doesn't touch the water. When it is almost melted, stir until smooth. The more finely you chop the chocolate, the faster it will melt.

Triple-Chocolate Cheesecake

SERVES 10 TO 12

Not two, but three chocolates make this a chocoholic's dream!

Tip

A small whisk is perfect for the small, but important, job of dissolving cocoa powder in hot water.

Variation

Dust additional cocoa powder on top and around the edge of the individual serving plates.

- Preheat oven to 350°F (180°C)
- 9-inch (23 cm) cheesecake pan, ungreased, or springform pan with 3-inch (7.5 cm) sides, greased

Crust

1¼ cups	pecans, toasted (see tip, page 62) and ground	300 mL
3 tbsp	all-purpose flour	45 mL
3 tbsp	unsalted butter, melted	45 mL

Filling

¼ cup	unsweetened Dutch-process cocoa powder	50 mL
3 tbsp	hot water	45 mL
4	packages (each 8 oz/250 g) cream cheese, softened	4
1½ cups	granulated sugar	375 mL
5	eggs	5
2 tbsp	freshly squeezed lemon juice	25 mL
1 tsp	vanilla extract	5 mL
8 oz	bittersweet chocolate chunks	250 g
6 oz	white chocolate chunks	175 g

Decoration

Fresh Raspberry Sauce (see recipe, page 271)

1. *Crust:* In a bowl, combine pecans, flour and butter. Press into bottom of cheesecake pan and bake in preheated oven for 12 minutes. Let cool on the counter until filling is ready (do not turn the oven off).

2. *Filling:* In a small bowl, dissolve cocoa powder in hot water. Set aside.

3. In a mixer bowl fitted with paddle attachment, beat cream cheese and sugar on medium-high speed until very smooth, for 3 minutes. Add eggs, one at a time, beating after each addition. Mix in lemon juice and vanilla. Fold in dissolved cocoa and chocolate chunks by hand.

4. Pour over baked crust, smoothing out to sides of pan. Bake in preheated oven until top is light brown and center has a slight jiggle to it, 45 to 55 minutes. Let cool in pan on a wire rack for 2 hours. Cover with plastic wrap and refrigerate for at least 6 hours before decorating or serving.

5. *Decoration:* Top each slice with a spoonful of Fresh Raspberry Sauce.

German Chocolate Cheesecake (page 62)
Overleaf: Neapolitan Cheesecake (page 69)

Chocolate Cookie Cheesecake

SERVES 10 TO 12

In the 1980s the rage was chocolate cookie ice cream; now try chocolate sandwich cookies in a rich cheesecake.

Tips

This recipe takes less than 1 lb (500 g) of cookies. You can eat the rest! Cookies with double filling made into crumbs have enough moisture in them that you can omit the butter in the crust.

If the wall of cookies starts to fall, don't worry; you can prop them up when you pour the filling into the pan.

Variation

During Halloween you can find chocolate sandwich cookies with orange centers. These would make a great spooky dessert.

- Preheat oven to 350°F (180°C)
- 9-inch (23 cm) cheesecake pan, ungreased, or springform pan with 3-inch (7.5 cm) sides, greased

Crust

1¼ cups	chocolate sandwich cookie crumbs	300 mL
¼ cup	unsalted butter, melted	50 mL
10	chocolate sandwich cookies	10

Filling

3	packages (each 8 oz/250 g) cream cheese, softened	3
1 cup	sour cream	250 mL
¾ cup	granulated sugar	175 mL
4	eggs	4
2 tsp	vanilla extract	10 mL
4	chocolate sandwich cookies, quartered	4

Decoration

Classic Whipped Cream Topping
(see recipe, page 262)

1. *Crust:* In a bowl, combine cookie crumbs and butter. Press into cheesecake pan. Cut sandwich cookies in half at the cream filling. Place each half, cookie side out, against side of pan, one after another, creating a wall of chocolate sandwich cookies. Set aside in the freezer to firm.

2. *Filling:* In a mixer bowl fitted with paddle attachment, beat cream cheese, sour cream and sugar on medium-high speed until very smooth, for 3 minutes. Add eggs, one at a time, beating after each addition. Mix in vanilla. Fold in quartered cookies by hand.

3. Pour over frozen crust, smoothing out to sides of pan. Bake in preheated oven until top is light brown and center has a slight jiggle to it, 45 to 55 minutes. Let cool in pan on a wire rack for 2 hours. Cover with plastic wrap and refrigerate for at least 6 hours before decorating or serving.

4. *Decoration:* Ice top of cake with Classic Whipped Cream Topping or pipe rosettes around top of cake, if desired.

Overleaf: Minty Chocolate Cheesecake (page 70)

Chocolate Espresso Swirl Cheesecake (page 72)

Chocolate Truffle Cheesecake

SERVES 10 TO 12

Chocolate truffles are made with chocolate and cream, flavored with liqueurs and spices. The candy gets its name because it looks like the rare savory fungus, the black truffle.

Tip

You can prepare the chocolate cream mixture up to 3 days ahead.

Variation

Fold in 2 tbsp (25 mL) Chambord (or other raspberry-flavored liqueur) and ¼ cup (50 mL) fresh raspberries with the chocolate mixture to make Raspberry Chocolate Truffle Cheesecake.

- Preheat oven to 350°F (180°C)
- 9-inch (23 cm) cheesecake pan, ungreased, or springform pan with 3-inch (7.5 cm) sides, greased

Crust

1½ cups	chocolate sandwich cookie crumbs	375 mL
¼ cup	unsalted butter, melted	50 mL

Filling

½ cup	whipping (35%) cream	125 mL
8 oz	bittersweet chocolate, finely chopped	250 g
3	packages (each 8 oz/250 g) cream cheese, softened	3
1 cup	granulated sugar	250 mL
2	eggs	2
¼ cup	unsweetened Dutch-process cocoa powder	50 mL
1 tbsp	all-purpose flour	15 mL
½ cup	sour cream	125 mL
1 tsp	vanilla extract	5 mL

Decoration

	Classic Whipped Cream Topping (see recipe, page 262)	
½ cup	chocolate shavings	125 mL

1. *Crust:* In a bowl, combine cookie crumbs and butter. Press into bottom of cheesecake pan and freeze.
2. *Filling:* In a small saucepan over high heat, bring cream to a boil. Pour over chocolate in a bowl and stir until blended. Set aside in the freezer until very firm.
3. In a mixer bowl fitted with paddle attachment, beat cream cheese and sugar on medium-high speed until very smooth, for 3 minutes. Add eggs, one at a time, beating after each addition. Stir in cocoa powder, flour, sour cream and vanilla. Using a spoon, scrape firm chocolate mixture into small pieces and fold into batter by hand.
4. Pour over frozen crust, smoothing out to sides of pan. Bake in preheated oven until top is light brown and center has a slight jiggle to it, 45 to 55 minutes. Let cool in pan on a wire rack for 2 hours. Cover with plastic wrap and refrigerate for at least 6 hours before decorating or serving.
5. *Decoration:* Ice top of cake with Classic Whipped Cream Topping or pipe rosettes around top of cake, if desired. Top with chocolate shavings.

Red Velvet Cheesecake

SERVES 10 TO 12

Southerners are famous for appreciating the most decadent desserts, and red velvet cake is every bit as intense in cheesecake form.

Tip

A small whisk is perfect for the small, but important, job of dissolving cocoa powder in hot water.

Variation

To make a chunky cheesecake, add 6 oz (175 g) semisweet chocolate chunks to the batter.

- Preheat oven to 350°F (180°C)
- 9-inch (23 cm) cheesecake pan, ungreased, or springform pan with 3-inch (7.5 cm) sides, greased

Crust

1¼ cups	chocolate sandwich cookie crumbs	300 mL
¼ cup	unsalted butter, melted	50 mL

Filling

¼ cup	unsweetened Dutch-process cocoa powder	50 mL
3 tbsp	hot water	45 mL
4	packages (each 8 oz/250 g) cream cheese, softened	4
1 cup	sour cream	250 mL
1½ cups	granulated sugar	375 mL
3	eggs	3
2	egg yolks	2
1 oz	liquid red food coloring	30 mL
1 tbsp	vanilla extract	15 mL

Decoration

Truffle Fudge Topping (see recipe, page 263)

1. *Crust:* In a bowl, combine cookie crumbs and butter. Press into bottom of cheesecake pan and freeze.
2. *Filling:* In a small bowl, dissolve cocoa powder in hot water. Set aside.
3. In a mixer bowl fitted with paddle attachment, beat cream cheese, sour cream and sugar on medium-high speed until very smooth, for 3 minutes. Add whole eggs and egg yolks, one at a time, beating after each addition. Mix in food coloring, vanilla and dissolved cocoa.
4. Pour over frozen crust, smoothing out to sides of pan. Bake in preheated oven until top is light brown and center has a slight jiggle to it, 45 to 55 minutes. Let cool in pan on a wire rack for 2 hours. Cover with plastic wrap and refrigerate for at least 6 hours before decorating or serving.
5. *Decoration:* Top each slice with a spoonful of Truffle Fudge Topping.

White Chocolate Velvet Cheesecake

SERVES 10 TO 12

As smooth as velvet, this is an elegant cheesecake fit for a special event.

Tip

This cheesecake has no crust to interrupt the velvety texture. If you prefer to have a crust, use the one for Passion Fruit Cheesecake (page 114).

- Preheat oven to 400°F (200°F)
- 9-inch (23 cm) cheesecake pan, ungreased, or springform pan with 3-inch (7.5 cm) sides, greased
- 13- by 9-inch (3 L) baking pan, filled with 2 inches (5 cm) boiling water

Filling

3	packages (each 8 oz/250 g) cream cheese, softened	3
1 cup	sour cream	250 mL
½ cup	vanilla-flavored yogurt	125 mL
½ cup	granulated sugar	125 mL
4	eggs	4
12 oz	white chocolate, chopped, melted (see page 63) and cooled	375 g
1 tbsp	vanilla extract	15 mL
½ tsp	rum extract	2 mL

Decoration

Port Wine Berry Compote (see recipe, page 266)

1. *Filling:* In a mixer bowl fitted with paddle attachment, beat cream cheese, sour cream, yogurt and sugar on medium-high speed until very smooth, for 3 minutes. Add eggs, one at a time, beating after each addition. With the mixer running, pour in melted chocolate in a steady stream. Mix in vanilla and rum extract.

2. Pour into cheesecake pan, smoothing out to sides of pan. Center cheesecake pan on the middle rack in the oven with a baking pan of boiling water on the lower rack. Bake at 400°F (200°C) for 10 minutes. Reduce oven temperature to 350°F (180°C) and bake until top is light brown and center has a slight jiggle to it, 45 to 55 minutes. Let cool in pan on a wire rack for 2 hours. Cover with plastic wrap and refrigerate for at least 6 hours before decorating or serving.

3. *Decoration:* Top each slice with a spoonful of Port Wine Berry Compote.

Neapolitan Cheesecake

SERVES 10 TO 12

When I was a child, Neapolitan ice cream satisfied my love of chocolate and my sister's strawberry craving. But there was always that lonely center of vanilla left untouched in the carton. That won't happen with this wonderful spin on the ice cream flavor.

Tips

When shopping for white chocolate, make sure cocoa butter is listed as the oil. Try to avoid tropical oils, such as palm kernel, cottonseed or coconut oil.

Purchase white chocolate in bars rather than in chip form for this recipe.

Variation

Replace strawberries with fresh raspberries when they are in season.

- Preheat oven to 350°F (180°C)
- 9-inch (23 cm) cheesecake pan, ungreased, or springform pan with 3-inch (7.5 cm) sides, greased

Crust

1¼ cups	chocolate sandwich cookie crumbs	300 mL
¼ cup	unsalted butter, melted	50 mL

Filling

3	packages (each 8 oz/250 g) cream cheese, softened	3
¾ cup	granulated sugar	175 mL
3	eggs	3
2 tsp	vanilla extract	10 mL
2 oz	semisweet chocolate, melted (see page 63) and cooled	60 g
2 oz	white chocolate, melted and cooled	60 g
½ cup	fresh strawberries, mashed	125 mL

Decoration

3 oz	semisweet chocolate, chopped	90 g
2 tbsp	unsalted butter	25 mL

1. *Crust:* In a bowl, combine cookie crumbs and butter. Press into bottom of cheesecake pan and freeze.

2. *Filling:* In a mixer bowl fitted with paddle attachment, beat cream cheese and sugar on medium-high speed until very smooth, for 3 minutes. Add eggs, one at a time, beating after each addition. Mix in vanilla.

3. Divide batter into three equal portions. Mix semisweet chocolate into one-third of the batter. Mix white chocolate into one-third of the batter. Stir strawberries into remaining third.

4. Spread dark chocolate batter over frozen crust, smoothing out to sides of pan. Refrigerate for about 5 minutes to firm. Spread white chocolate batter carefully over dark chocolate layer, covering it completely. Refrigerate for 5 minutes to firm. Spread strawberry batter over white chocolate layer. Bake in preheated oven until top is light brown and center has a slight jiggle to it, 45 to 55 minutes. Let cool in pan on a wire rack for 2 hours. Cover with plastic wrap and refrigerate for at least 6 hours before decorating or serving.

5. *Decoration:* In top of double boiler over medium heat with water simmering, whisk chocolate and butter until fully melted. Pour over chilled cake and let drip down the sides. Serve cold.

Minty Chocolate Cheesecake

SERVES 10 TO 12

This cheesecake reminds me of Christmas — chocolate and mint! Two great flavors to savor next to a warm fire.

Tips

Purchase chocolate in bar form rather than as chips for the melted semisweet chocolate in this recipe.

When making cookie crumbs, you do not have to scrape the cream filling out of the cookies; just place them whole into the food processor and pulse.

Variation

Substitute mint chips for the semisweet chips and delete the peppermint extract.

- Preheat oven to 350°F (180°C)
- 9-inch (23 cm) cheesecake pan, ungreased, or springform pan with 3-inch (7.5 cm) sides, greased

Crust

1½ cups	chocolate sandwich cookie crumbs	375 mL
¼ cup	unsalted butter, melted	50 mL

Filling

3	packages (each 8 oz/250 g) cream cheese, softened	3
¾ cup	granulated sugar	175 mL
3	eggs	3
¼ cup	all-purpose flour	50 mL
½ cup	sour cream	125 mL
1 tsp	vanilla extract	5 mL
¼ tsp	peppermint extract	1 mL
3 oz	semisweet chocolate, melted (see page 63) and cooled	90 g
1 cup	semisweet chocolate chips	250 mL
2 tsp	all-purpose flour	10 mL

1. *Crust:* In a bowl, combine cookie crumbs and butter. Press into bottom of cheesecake pan and freeze.

2. *Filling:* In a mixer bowl fitted with paddle attachment, beat cream cheese and sugar on medium-high speed until very smooth, for 3 minutes. Add eggs, one at a time, beating after each addition. Mix in the ¼ cup (50 mL) flour. Mix in sour cream, vanilla and peppermint extract. With the mixer running, pour in melted chocolate in a steady stream. In a small bowl, combine chocolate chips and the 2 tsp (10 mL) flour. Fold into batter by hand.

3. Pour over frozen crust, smoothing out to sides of pan. Bake in preheated oven until top is light brown and center has a slight jiggle to it, 45 to 55 minutes. Let cool in pan on a wire rack for 2 hours. Cover with plastic wrap and refrigerate for at least 6 hours before serving.

Coffee-Flavored Brownie Cheesecake

SERVES 10 TO 12

Satisfy your brownie and cheesecake cravings in one dessert. A rich coffee-flavored brownie is topped with a layer of sweet cheesecake.

Tip

A second mixer bowl saves washing dishes mid-recipe.

Variation

Ice the cheesecake with cherry pie filling or Fresh Raspberry Sauce (see recipe, page 271).

- Preheat oven to 350°F (180°C)
- 9-inch (23 cm) cheesecake or springform pan with 3-inch (7.5 cm) sides, lined with parchment paper

Base

1 cup	unsalted butter, softened	250 mL
1 cup	granulated sugar	250 mL
4	eggs	4
1 lb	semisweet chocolate, melted (see page 63) and cooled	500 g
2 tbsp	coffee-flavored liqueur	25 mL
2 tsp	vanilla extract	10 mL
½ tsp	salt	2 mL
1 cup	all-purpose flour	250 mL

Filling

2	packages (each 8 oz/250 g) cream cheese, softened	2
¾ cup	granulated sugar	175 mL
4	eggs	4
2 tbsp	all-purpose flour	25 mL
¼ cup	sour cream	50 mL
2 tsp	vanilla extract	10 mL

1. *Base:* In a mixer bowl fitted with paddle attachment, beat butter and sugar on medium-high speed until light and fluffy, for 3 minutes. Add eggs, one at a time, beating after each addition. With the mixer running, pour in melted chocolate in a steady stream. Mix in liqueur, vanilla and salt. Quickly beat in flour. Smooth into prepared cheesecake pan and refrigerate for 3 minutes.

2. *Filling:* In a clean mixer bowl fitted with paddle attachment, beat cream cheese and sugar on medium-high speed until very smooth, for 3 minutes. Add eggs, one at a time, beating after each addition. Stir in flour, sour cream and vanilla.

3. Spread batter over brownie layer, smoothing out to sides of pan. Bake in preheated oven until top is light brown and center has a slight jiggle to it, 40 to 50 minutes. Let cool in pan on a wire rack for 2 hours. Cover with plastic wrap and refrigerate for at least 6 hours before serving.

Chocolate Espresso Swirl Cheesecake

SERVES 10 TO 12

Chocolate with a light espresso swirled in the cake has just a hint of coffee flavor.

Tips

To melt bittersweet chocolate in the microwave, break into squares and place in a microwave-safe dish. Microwave on High for 1 to 2 minutes, stirring after 30 seconds.

Cool melted chocolate to room temperature before adding the cheesecake batter or the chocolate will stiffen up and you will have to start all over.

- Preheat oven to 350°F (180°C)
- 9-inch (23 cm) cheesecake pan, ungreased, or springform pan with 3-inch (7.5 cm) sides, greased

Crust

1½ cups	chocolate sandwich cookie crumbs	375 mL
¼ cup	unsalted butter, melted	50 mL

Filling

4	packages (each 8 oz/250 g) cream cheese, softened	4
1½ cups	granulated sugar	375 mL
½ cup	sour cream	125 mL
4	eggs	4
1 tbsp	instant espresso powder	15 mL
1 tbsp	hot water	15 mL
1 tsp	vanilla extract	5 mL
3 oz	bittersweet chocolate, melted (see page 63 and tip, at left) and cooled	90 g

Decoration

Classic Whipped Cream Topping
(see recipe, page 262)

1. *Crust:* In a bowl, combine cookie crumbs and butter. Press into bottom of cheesecake pan and freeze.
2. *Filling:* In a small bowl, dissolve espresso powder in hot water. Set aside.
3. In a mixer bowl fitted with paddle attachment, beat cream cheese and sugar on medium-high speed until very smooth, for 3 minutes. Mix in sour cream. Add eggs, one at a time, beating after each addition. With the mixer running, pour in espresso in a steady stream. Mix in vanilla.

4. Stir 1 cup (250 mL) of the batter into melted chocolate and set aside. Pour remaining batter over frozen crust, smoothing out to sides of pan. Using a spoon, drop six large puddles of melted chocolate mixture on top of batter. Using a small knife, drag through the puddles in spiral motions to create a marbling effect. Bake in preheated oven until top is light brown and center has a slight jiggle to it, 45 to 55 minutes. Let cool in pan on a wire rack for 2 hours. Cover with plastic wrap and refrigerate for at least 6 hours before decorating or serving.

5. *Decoration:* Ice top of cake with Classic Whipped Cream Topping or pipe rosettes around top of cake, if desired.

White Chocolate Raspberry Cheesecake

SERVES 10 TO 12

This cheesecake reminds me of the pure white mountain caps of British Columbia. It will leave you with a cool feeling, too.

Tip

To melt white chocolate, bring water to a boil in the bottom of a double boiler and turn the heat off. Place chopped white chocolate in the top portion of the double boiler and stir until melted. The steam is hot enough to melt white chocolate. Do not use the microwave to melt white chocolate, as it has a lower melting point than other chocolates. If you don't have a double boiler, a saucepan with a metal bowl loosely fitted on top will also work. After the chocolate has melted, remove it from the bottom boiler and let cool until tepid.

- Preheat oven to 400°F (200°C)
- 9-inch (23 cm) cheesecake pan or springform pan with 3-inch (7.5 cm) sides, sprayed with nonstick spray and bottom lined with parchment paper
- 13- by 9-inch (3 L) baking pan, filled with 2 inches (5 cm) boiling water

Filling

3	packages (each 8 oz/250 g) cream cheese, softened	3
1/2 cup	granulated sugar	125 mL
1 tsp	freshly squeezed lemon juice	5 mL
1/2 tsp	salt	2 mL
12 oz	white chocolate, melted (see tip, at left) and cooled	375 g
1 1/2 cups	sour cream	375 mL
4	eggs	4
1 tbsp	vanilla extract	15 mL
2 1/2 cups	fresh raspberries	625 mL
1 tbsp	all-purpose flour	15 mL

Topping

1 3/4 cups	sour cream	425 mL
2 tbsp	granulated sugar	25 mL
1/2 tsp	vanilla extract	2 mL

Decoration

Fresh Raspberry Sauce (see recipe, page 271)

1. *Filling:* In a food processor fitted with a metal blade, in two batches, if necessary, combine cream cheese, sugar, lemon juice and salt for 30 seconds, scraping down sides of bowl. Add white chocolate, sour cream, eggs and vanilla; process for 30 seconds, scraping down sides of bowl. Process for 1 minute. In a bowl, toss raspberries with flour. Fold into chocolate mixture by hand.

Tip

I like to have the baking pan with water already in the oven before mixing my cheesecake batter.

2. Pour into prepared cheesecake pan, smoothing out to sides of pan. Center cheesecake pan on the middle rack in the oven with a baking pan of boiling water on the lower rack. Bake at 400°F (200°C) for 10 minutes. Reduce oven temperature to 350°F (180°C) and bake until top is light brown and center has a slight jiggle to it, 45 to 55 minutes. Let cool on the counter for 10 minutes (do not turn the oven off). The cake will sink slightly.

3. *Topping:* In a small bowl, combine sour cream, sugar and vanilla. Pour into center of cooled cake and spread out to edges. Bake for 5 minutes more. Let cool in pan on a wire rack for 2 hours. Cover with plastic wrap and refrigerate for at least 6 hours before decorating or serving.

4. *Decoration:* Top each slice with a spoonful of Fresh Raspberry Sauce.

Chocolate Cherry Cheesecake

Chocolate chunk cheesecake topped with cherries is a showstopper of a dessert!

Tip

To make chocolate chunks, cut a good-quality chocolate bar into big chunks with a knife.

Variation

Use white chocolate chunks instead of semisweet chocolate.

- Preheat oven to 350°F (180°C)
- 9-inch (23 cm) cheesecake pan, ungreased, or springform pan with 3-inch (7.5 cm) sides, greased

Crust

1¼ cups	chocolate sandwich cookie crumbs	300 mL
3 tbsp	unsalted butter, melted	45 mL

Filling

3	packages (each 8 oz/250 g) cream cheese, softened	3
1 cup	granulated sugar	250 mL
3	eggs	3
1	egg yolk	1
2 tsp	vanilla extract	10 mL
6 oz	semisweet chocolate chunks	175 g

Decoration

	Classic Whipped Cream Topping (see recipe, page 262)	
1	can (21 oz/645 mL) cherry pie filling	1

1. *Crust:* In a bowl, combine cookie crumbs and butter. Press into bottom of cheesecake pan and freeze.
2. *Filling:* In a mixer bowl fitted with paddle attachment, beat cream cheese and sugar on medium-high speed until very smooth, for 3 minutes. Add whole eggs and egg yolk, one at a time, beating after each addition. Fold in vanilla and chocolate chunks by hand.
3. Pour over frozen crust, smoothing out to sides of pan. Bake in preheated oven until top is light brown and center has a slight jiggle to it, 45 to 55 minutes. Let cool in pan on a wire rack for 2 hours. Cover with plastic wrap and refrigerate for at least 6 hours before decorating or serving.
4. *Decoration:* Pipe rosettes around top of cake with Classic Whipped Cream Topping. Fill center with cherry pie filling.

Black Forest Cheesecake

SERVES 10 TO 12

Black Forest cake has been around for years, but it may be even better as a cheesecake, rich with chocolate and topped with cherries.

Tip

Make sure the melted chocolate has cooled slightly before adding it to the batter; otherwise, the cake will have chocolate chunks.

Variation

For a stunning visual and taste sensation, cut fresh cherries in half and place them cut side down on top of the cheesecake in place of the pie filling.

- Preheat oven to 350°F (180°C)
- 9-inch (23 cm) cheesecake pan, ungreased, or springform pan with 3-inch (7.5 cm) sides, greased

Crust

1¼ cups	chocolate sandwich cookie crumbs	300 mL
3 tbsp	unsalted butter, melted	45 mL

Filling

2	packages (each 8 oz/250 g) cream cheese, softened	2
⅔ cup	granulated sugar	150 mL
2	eggs	2
6 oz	semisweet chocolate, melted (see page 63) and cooled	175 g
1 tsp	vanilla extract	5 mL

Decoration

	Classic Whipped Cream Topping (see recipe, page 262)	
1	can (21 oz/645 mL) cherry pie filling	1

1. *Crust:* In a bowl, combine cookie crumbs and butter. Press into bottom of cheesecake pan and freeze.

2. *Filling:* In a mixer bowl fitted with paddle attachment, beat cream cheese and sugar on medium-high speed until very smooth, for 3 minutes. Add eggs, one at a time, beating after each addition. With the mixer running, pour in melted chocolate in a steady stream. Mix in vanilla.

3. Pour over frozen crust, smoothing out to sides of pan. Bake in preheated oven until top is light brown and center has a slight jiggle to it, 35 to 45 minutes. Let cool in pan on a wire rack for 2 hours. Cover with plastic wrap and refrigerate for at least 6 hours before decorating or serving.

4. *Decoration:* Pipe rosettes around top of cake with Classic Whipped Cream Topping. Fill center with cherry pie filling.

Toffee Bar Cheesecake

SERVES 8 TO 10

Adding a crushed candy bar to cheesecake batter is easy and heavenly.

Tip

Place pieces of the toffee candy bar in a sealable plastic bag and roll a rolling pin over them a few times until crushed to desired coarseness.

Variation

Substitute your favorite candy bar for the toffee bar.

- Preheat oven to 325°F (160°C)
- 8-inch (20 cm) cheesecake pan, ungreased, or springform pan with 3-inch (7.5 cm) sides, greased

Crust

1 cup	chocolate sandwich cookie crumbs	250 mL
2 tbsp	unsalted butter, melted	25 mL

Filling

3	packages (each 8 oz/250 g) cream cheese, softened	3
¾ cup	packed brown sugar	175 mL
3	eggs	3
5 oz	toffee candy bar, coarsely crushed (see tip, at left)	150 g
1 tsp	vanilla extract	5 mL
½ tsp	maple extract	2 mL

Decoration

	Classic Whipped Cream Topping (see recipe, page 262)	
2 tbsp	coarsely crushed toffee candy bar	25 mL

1. *Crust:* In a bowl, combine cookie crumbs and butter. Press into bottom of cheesecake pan and freeze.

2. *Filling:* In a mixer bowl fitted with paddle attachment, beat cream cheese and brown sugar on medium-high speed until very smooth, for 3 minutes. Add eggs, one at a time, beating after each addition. Fold in crushed candy bar pieces, vanilla and maple extract by hand.

3. Pour over frozen crust, smoothing out to sides of pan. Bake in preheated oven until top is firm to the touch and center has a slight jiggle to it, 35 to 45 minutes. Let cool in pan on a wire rack for 2 hours. Cover with plastic wrap and refrigerate for at least 6 hours before decorating or serving.

4. *Decoration:* Ice top of cake with Classic Whipped Cream Topping or pipe rosettes around top of cake, if desired. Sprinkle top with crushed candy bar pieces.

Chocolate Chunk Peanut Butter Cheesecake

SERVES 10 TO 12

With its chocolate and peanut butter combination, this cheesecake is just like a candy bar.

Tip

Natural peanut butters have too much oil for this recipe.

Variation

If you think you can handle more chocolate, replace the peanut butter cookie crumbs with chocolate sandwich cookie crumbs and omit the flour.

- Preheat oven to 350°F (180°C)
- 9-inch (23 cm) cheesecake pan, ungreased, or springform pan with 3-inch (7.5 cm) sides, greased

Crust

1¼ cups	peanut butter sandwich cookie crumbs	300 mL
¼ cup	all-purpose flour	50 mL
¼ cup	unsalted butter, melted	50 mL

Filling

4	packages (each 8 oz/250 g) cream cheese, softened	4
1¼ cups	granulated sugar	300 mL
4	eggs	4
1 cup	creamy peanut butter	250 mL
3 tbsp	freshly squeezed lemon juice	45 mL
1 tsp	vanilla extract	5 mL
2 cups	semisweet chocolate chunks	500 mL

Topping

½ cup	sour cream	125 mL
¼ cup	granulated sugar	50 mL
¼ cup	creamy peanut butter	50 mL
1 tbsp	freshly squeezed lemon juice	15 mL
½ tsp	vanilla extract	2 mL
½ cup	semisweet chocolate chunks	125 mL

1. *Crust:* In a bowl, combine cookie crumbs, flour and butter. Press into bottom of cheesecake pan and freeze.

2. *Filling:* In a mixer bowl fitted with paddle attachment, beat cream cheese and sugar on medium-high speed until very smooth, for 3 minutes. Add eggs, one at a time, beating after each addition. Mix in peanut butter. Mix in lemon juice and vanilla. Fold in chocolate chunks by hand.

3. Pour over frozen crust, smoothing out to sides of pan. Bake in preheated oven until top is light brown and center has a slight jiggle to it, 45 to 55 minutes. Let cool on the counter for 10 minutes (do not turn the oven off). The cake will sink slightly.

4. *Topping:* In a bowl, combine sour cream, sugar, peanut butter, lemon juice and vanilla. Pour into center of cake and spread to edges. Sprinkle with chocolate chunks. Bake for 5 minutes more. Let cool in pan on a wire rack for 2 hours. Cover with plastic wrap and refrigerate for at least 6 hours before serving.

Chocolate Macadamia Cheesecake

SERVES 10 TO 12

Rich chocolate and rich Hawaiian macadamia nuts are a perfect marriage.

Tips

Let the melted chocolate cool to room temperature before adding it to the batter; otherwise, you'll end up with chocolate chunks in your cheesecake.

Toasting brings out the natural oils and flavor of nuts. Place nuts in a single layer on a baking sheet and bake at 350°F (180°C) until fragrant, 10 to 12 minutes.

Variation

Pecans are a less expensive alternative to macadamia nuts.

- Preheat oven to 350°F (180°C)
- 9-inch (23 cm) cheesecake pan, ungreased, or springform pan with 3-inch (7.5 cm) sides, greased

Crust
1¼ cups	chocolate sandwich cookie crumbs	300 mL
3 tbsp	unsalted butter, melted	45 mL

Filling
3	packages (each 8 oz/250 g) cream cheese, softened	3
1 cup	granulated sugar	250 mL
3	eggs	3
2	egg yolks	2
6 oz	bittersweet chocolate, melted (see page 63) and cooled	175 g
1 tsp	vanilla extract	5 mL
1 cup	macadamia nuts, toasted (see tip, at left) and chopped	250 mL

Decoration
	Classic Whipped Cream Topping (see recipe, page 262)	
¼ cup	macadamia nuts, toasted and chopped	50 mL

1. *Crust:* In a bowl, combine cookie crumbs and butter. Press into bottom of cheesecake pan and freeze.
2. *Filling:* In a mixer bowl fitted with paddle attachment, beat cream cheese and sugar on medium-high speed until very smooth, for 3 minutes. Add whole eggs and egg yolks, one at a time, beating after each addition. With the mixer running, pour in melted chocolate in a steady stream. Mix in vanilla. Fold in macadamia nuts by hand.
3. Pour over frozen crust, smoothing out to sides of pan. Bake in preheated oven until top is light brown and center has a slight jiggle to it, 45 to 55 minutes. Let cool in pan on a wire rack for 2 hours. Cover with plastic wrap and refrigerate for at least 6 hours before decorating or serving.
4. *Decoration:* Ice top of cake with Classic Whipped Cream Topping or pipe rosettes around top of cake, if desired. Sprinkle with toasted macadamia nuts.

Rocky Road Cheesecake

SERVES 10 TO 12

My grandmother always had Rocky Road ice cream on hand for us because it was everybody's favorite. Here I've recreated that memorable taste in a cheesecake.

Tip

To melt bittersweet chocolate in the microwave, break into squares and place in a microwave-safe dish. Microwave on High for 1 to 2 minutes, stirring after 30 seconds.

- Preheat oven to 350°F (180°C)
- 9-inch (23 cm) cheesecake pan, ungreased, or springform pan with 3-inch (7.5 cm) sides, greased

Crust

1½ cups	chocolate sandwich cookie crumbs	375 mL
¼ cup	unsalted butter, melted	50 mL

Filling

4	packages (each 8 oz/250 g) cream cheese, softened	4
1 cup	sour cream	250 mL
1¼ cups	granulated sugar	300 mL
4	eggs	4
4 oz	bittersweet chocolate, melted (see page 63 and tip, at left) and cooled	125 g
1 cup	walnuts, toasted (see tip, page 80) and chopped	250 mL
1 cup	quartered large marshmallows	250 mL
1 tbsp	vanilla extract	15 mL

Decoration

Classic Whipped Cream Topping (see recipe, page 262)

1. *Crust:* In a bowl, combine cookie crumbs and butter. Press into bottom of cheesecake pan and freeze.
2. *Filling:* In a mixer bowl fitted with paddle attachment, beat cream cheese, sour cream and sugar on medium-high speed until very smooth, for 3 minutes. Add eggs, one at a time, beating after each addition. With the mixer running, pour in melted chocolate in a steady stream. Fold in walnuts, marshmallows and vanilla by hand.
3. Pour over frozen crust, smoothing out to sides of pan. Bake in preheated oven until top is light brown and center has a slight jiggle to it, 55 to 65 minutes. Let cool in pan on a wire rack for 2 hours. Cover with plastic wrap and refrigerate for at least 6 hours before decorating or serving.
4. *Decoration:* Ice top of cake with Classic Whipped Cream Topping or pipe rosettes around top of cake, if desired.

Chocolate Caramel Pecan Cheesecake

SERVES 14 TO 16

Serve very thin slices of this dark, rich cheesecake — the intensity of the chocolate, caramel and pecans is almost intoxicating.

Tips

Coarsely chop a chocolate bar into chunks instead of using chocolate chips.

It's best not to spread the melted caramel mixture right to the edge of the pan. If you do, it might stick and make it difficult to remove the cake from the pan.

Variation

Dust unsweetened cocoa powder on top of the cake and around the edge of the serving plate.

- Preheat oven to 350°F (180°C)
- 9-inch (23 cm) cheesecake pan, ungreased, or springform pan with 3-inch (7.5 cm) sides, greased

Crust

1¼ cups	chocolate sandwich cookie crumbs	300 mL
¼ cup	unsalted butter, melted	50 mL

Filling

1 cup	soft caramels	250 mL
2 tbsp	evaporated milk or whipping (35%) cream	25 mL
6 oz	bittersweet chocolate chunks	175 g
2	packages (each 8 oz/250 g) cream cheese, softened	2
1 cup	sour cream	250 mL
½ cup	granulated sugar	125 mL
¼ cup	unsweetened Dutch-process cocoa powder, sifted	50 mL
3	eggs	3
1 tsp	vanilla extract	5 mL
1 cup	pecans, toasted (see tip, page 80) and chopped	250 mL

1. *Crust:* In a bowl, combine cookie crumbs and butter. Press into bottom of cheesecake pan and freeze.

2. *Filling:* In a small saucepan over low heat, melt caramels in evaporated milk, stirring often, until smooth. Reserve 3 tbsp (45 mL) for decorating; cover and refrigerate. Pour remaining caramel mixture over frozen crust, spreading evenly and leaving a ½-inch (1 cm) border uncovered. Sprinkle chocolate chunks over caramel. Set aside.

3. In a mixer bowl fitted with paddle attachment, beat cream cheese, sour cream, sugar and cocoa powder on medium-high speed until very smooth, for 3 minutes. Add eggs, one at a time, beating after each addition. Mix in vanilla. Fold in pecans by hand.

4. Pour over chocolate and caramel, smoothing out to sides of pan. Bake in preheated oven until top is light brown and center has a slight jiggle to it, 40 to 50 minutes. Let cool in pan on a wire rack for 2 hours. Cover with plastic wrap and refrigerate for at least 6 hours before decorating or serving.

5. *Decoration:* Reheat reserved caramel mixture in the microwave (or in a small saucepan over low heat) until melted. Drizzle over cake.

Fresh Fruit
Cheesecakes

Crisp Apple Cheesecake

SERVES 10 TO 12

Using the best baking apples that the fall season has to offer, such as Granny Smith or Pippin, produces the most intense apple flavors.

Tip

To prevent apples from discoloring, mix 1 tbsp (15 mL) vinegar or lemon juice in cold water and store the prepared apple slices in this mixture until ready to toss with spices.

Variation

Pecan shortbread cookie crumbs are a delicious crust alternative to graham cracker crumbs. They also combine well with crisp apple flavors.

- Preheat oven to 350°F (180°C)
- 9-inch (23 cm) cheesecake pan, ungreased, or springform pan with 3-inch (7.5 cm) sides, greased

Crust

1¼ cups	graham cracker crumbs	300 mL
3 tbsp	unsalted butter, melted	45 mL

Filling

4	packages (each 8 oz/250 g) cream cheese, softened	4
1¼ cups	packed light brown sugar	300 mL
4	eggs	4
1 tbsp	vanilla extract	15 mL
1 tsp	freshly squeezed lemon juice	5 mL

Topping

¼ cup	all-purpose flour	50 mL
¼ cup	granulated sugar	50 mL
2 tbsp	packed light brown sugar	25 mL
½ tsp	ground cinnamon	2 mL
¼ tsp	ground cloves	1 mL
1 cup	thinly sliced peeled apples	250 mL

1. *Crust:* In a bowl, combine graham cracker crumbs and butter. Press into bottom of cheesecake pan and freeze.
2. *Filling:* In a mixer bowl fitted with paddle attachment, beat cream cheese and brown sugar on medium-high speed until very smooth, for 3 minutes. Add eggs, one at a time, beating after each addition. Mix in vanilla and lemon juice. Pour over frozen crust, smoothing out to sides of pan.
3. *Topping:* In a bowl, combine flour, sugar, brown sugar, cinnamon and cloves. Add apple slices and toss to coat. Arrange slices decoratively on top of batter.
4. Bake in preheated oven until apples are light brown and slightly firm in the center, 45 to 55 minutes. Let cool in pan on a wire rack for 2 hours. Cover with plastic wrap and refrigerate for at least 6 hours before serving.

Caramel Apple Cheesecake

SERVES 10 TO 12

Caramel apples always remind me of autumn, but this flavor combination is perfect any time of year.

Tips

When cutting apples, use a porcelain knife. You won't have to coat them in lemon juice to preserve their color.

Buy pecans in bulk when they're in season and freeze to have handy whenever you need them. Not only will you save money, but the nuts will be fresher than those in the small convenience packages in the baking aisle of the grocery store.

Variation

Pears, when in season, would be a nice substitute for apples.

- Preheat oven to 350°F (180°C)
- 9-inch (23 cm) cheesecake pan, ungreased, or springform pan with 3-inch (7.5 cm) sides, greased

Crust

1¼ cups	graham cracker crumbs	300 mL
3 tbsp	unsalted butter, melted	45 mL
1	large baking apple (such as Granny Smith or Pippin), peeled and sliced into 12 slices	1
6 oz	soft caramels, cut into quarters	175 g
1 cup	pecans, chopped	250 mL

Filling

2	packages (each 8 oz/250 g) cream cheese, softened	2
1 cup	sour cream	250 mL
1 cup	granulated sugar	250 mL
3	eggs	3
1 tbsp	ground cinnamon	15 mL
1 tsp	freshly grated nutmeg	5 mL
1 tsp	vanilla extract	5 mL
½ tsp	grated lemon zest	2 mL
1 tbsp	freshly squeezed lemon juice	15 mL
1	large baking apple (such as Granny Smith or Pippin), peeled and sliced into 12 slices	1
¼ cup	pecans, chopped	50 mL

1. *Crust:* In a bowl, combine graham cracker crumbs and butter. Press into bottom of cheesecake pan. Arrange apple slices in a spiral on top of crust. Sprinkle with caramels and pecans. Bake in preheated oven for 10 minutes. Set on a wire rack to cool.

2. *Filling:* In a mixer bowl fitted with paddle attachment, beat cream cheese, sour cream and sugar on medium-high speed until very smooth, for 3 minutes. Add eggs, one at a time, beating after each addition. Stir in cinnamon, nutmeg, vanilla, lemon zest and lemon juice.

3. Pour over baked crust, smoothing out to sides of pan. Arrange apple slices and pecans decoratively on top of batter. Bake in preheated oven until apples are light brown and slightly firm in the center, 45 to 55 minutes. Let cool in pan on a wire rack for 2 hours. Cover with plastic wrap and refrigerate for at least 6 hours before serving.

French Apple Cheesecake

SERVES 10 TO 12

This cheesecake is rich with fresh apples and a topping just like a French apple pie.

Tips

You can prepare this cheesecake and freeze it, including the topping, for up to 3 weeks. To freeze, I keep my cheesecakes in the pan and cover with plastic wrap, then foil. Thaw the wrapped cheesecake in the refrigerator for 1 day before serving.

When measuring honey, lightly spray the measuring cup with a nonstick spray so the honey will release easily.

- Preheat oven to 350°F (180°C)
- 9-inch (23 cm) cheesecake pan, ungreased, or springform pan with 3-inch (7.5 cm) sides, greased

Crust

1¼ cups	graham cracker crumbs	300 mL
3 tbsp	unsalted butter, melted	45 mL

Filling

3	packages (each 8 oz/250 g) cream cheese, softened	3
1 cup	sour cream	250 mL
1 cup	packed light brown sugar	250 mL
¼ cup	liquid honey	50 mL
4	eggs	4
1 tbsp	vanilla extract	15 mL
1 tsp	freshly squeezed lemon juice	5 mL
1 tsp	ground cinnamon	5 mL
½ tsp	freshly grated nutmeg	2 mL
¼ tsp	ground cloves	1 mL

Topping

3 tbsp	cold unsalted butter, cut into cubes	45 mL
¼ cup	all-purpose flour	50 mL
¼ cup	packed light brown sugar	50 mL
½ tsp	ground cinnamon	2 mL
¼ tsp	ground cloves	1 mL
1	baking apple (such as Granny Smith or Pippin), peeled and sliced into 12 thin slices	1

Decoration

½ cup	confectioner's (icing) sugar	125 mL
2 tbsp	unsalted butter, melted	25 mL
2 tbsp	hot water	25 mL

1. *Crust:* In a bowl, combine graham cracker crumbs and butter. Press into bottom of cheesecake pan and freeze.

2. *Filling:* In a mixer bowl fitted with paddle attachment, beat cream cheese, sour cream, brown sugar and honey on medium-high speed until very smooth, for 3 minutes. Add eggs, one at a time, beating after each addition. Mix in vanilla and lemon juice. Stir in cinnamon, nutmeg and cloves. Pour over frozen crust, smoothing out to sides of pan.

Variation

Use the topping in the filling of the cheesecake instead of arranging it on top. Just blend it into the batter and bake as directed.

3. *Topping:* In a bowl, using a pastry fork or two knives, cut butter into flour as if making a pie crust. Add brown sugar, cinnamon and cloves. Add apple slices and toss to coat. Arrange slices in a spiral over batter.

4. Bake in preheated oven until apples are light brown and slightly firm in the center, 60 to 75 minutes. Let cool in pan on a wire rack for 2 hours. Cover with plastic wrap and refrigerate for at least 6 hours before decorating or serving.

5. *Decoration:* In a small bowl, whisk confectioner's sugar with butter and hot water. Drizzle over chilled cake.

Poached Pear Cheesecake

SERVES 10 TO 12

Pears poached in white Zinfandel wine create a complex sweet flavor in this elegant cheesecake.

Tips

Toasting brings out the natural oils and flavor of nuts. Place nuts in a single layer on a baking sheet and bake at 350°F (180°C) until fragrant, 10 to 12 minutes.

A Dutch oven is a large pot that can go from stovetop to oven.

You can poach the pears up to 3 days ahead. Drain, cool, cover and store in the refrigerator. Bring to room temperature before assembling cake.

- Preheat oven to 350°F (180°C)
- 9-inch (23 cm) cheesecake pan, ungreased, or springform pan with 3-inch (7.5 cm) sides, greased
- 4-quart (4 L) Dutch oven

Crust

1¼ cups	graham cracker crumbs	300 mL
¼ cup	pecans, toasted (see tip, at left) and ground	50 mL
3 tbsp	unsalted butter, melted	45 mL

Filling

2½ cups	white Zinfandel wine	625 mL
2 tbsp	granulated sugar	25 mL
½ tsp	ground cinnamon	2 mL
¼ tsp	ground cloves	1 mL
6	ripe pears, peeled, halved and cored (about 1½ lbs/750 g)	6
3	packages (each 8 oz/250 g) cream cheese, softened	3
1 cup	granulated sugar	250 mL
¼ cup	liquid honey	50 mL
4	eggs	4
1 tbsp	vanilla extract	15 mL
1 tsp	ground cinnamon	5 mL
½ tsp	ground cloves	2 mL
½ cup	pecans, toasted and chopped	125 mL

Decoration

Classic Whipped Cream Topping (see recipe, page 262)

1. *Crust:* In a bowl, combine graham cracker crumbs, ground pecans and butter. Press into bottom of cheesecake pan and freeze.

2. *Filling:* In Dutch oven, combine wine, the 2 tbsp (25 mL) sugar, cinnamon and cloves. Cover and bring to a boil over medium heat, about 4 minutes. Add pears and simmer, uncovered, until pears are fork-tender but not too soft, 3 to 6 minutes. Drain pears and let cool slightly. Thinly slice pears lengthwise and set aside.

3. In a mixer bowl fitted with paddle attachment, beat cream cheese and the 1 cup (250 mL) sugar on medium-high speed until very smooth, for 3 minutes. Mix in honey. Add eggs, one at a time, beating after each addition. Stir in vanilla, cinnamon and cloves.

4. Pour half the batter over frozen crust, smoothing out to sides of pan. Arrange half the pears on top of batter, reserving other half for decoration. Sprinkle chopped pecans over pears. Pour remaining batter over pears, smoothing out to sides of pan. Bake in preheated oven until top is light brown and center has a slight jiggle to it, 45 to 55 minutes. Let cool in pan on a wire rack for 2 hours. Cover with plastic wrap and refrigerate for at least 6 hours before decorating or serving.

5. *Decoration:* Ice top of cake with Classic Whipped Cream Topping or pipe rosettes around top of cake, if desired. Arrange the reserved pear slices in a spiral around top of cake.

Peach Melba Cheesecake

SERVES 10 TO 12

The cheesecake version of the famous dessert of peaches and raspberries, created by Escoffier for a popular opera singer, is a natural choice for a summer party with fruit at the peak of its season.

Tips

To quickly remove the peel from peaches, cut an X in the bottom with a small knife, piercing only the skin. Place fruit in rapidly boiling water for about 30 seconds. Cool in cold water. The peel should come off easily.

To avoid browning, slice peaches right before using or sprinkle with lemon juice.

Be sure your cake layers are no more than ½ inch (1 cm) thick to make sure the filling doesn't overflow the pan.

Variation

Substitute crème de cassis for the raspberry-flavored liqueur. For a non-alcoholic alternative, substitute 1 tsp (5 mL) raspberry extract for each 2 tbsp (25 mL) liqueur.

- Preheat oven to 325°F (160°C)
- 9-inch (23 cm) cheesecake pan, ungreased, or springform pan with 3-inch (7.5 cm) sides, greased.

Crust

1	9-inch (23 cm) yellow cake, sliced horizontally in half	1
¼ cup	raspberry-flavored liqueur, divided	50 mL
½ cup	raspberry preserves, divided	125 mL
2	peaches, peeled (see tip, at left) and sliced, divided	2

Filling

4	packages (each 8 oz/250 g) cream cheese, softened	4
1 cup	granulated sugar	250 mL
5	eggs	5
1 tbsp	freshly squeezed lemon juice	15 mL
1 tsp	vanilla extract	5 mL

Decoration

	Classic Whipped Cream Topping (see recipe, page 262)	
1 cup	fresh raspberries	250 mL

1. *Crust:* Press half of cake into bottom of cheesecake pan. Brush with half the liqueur. Spread with half the preserves and arrange half the peach slices in a single layer on top.

2. *Filling:* In a mixer bowl fitted with paddle attachment, beat cream cheese and sugar on medium-high speed until very smooth, for 3 minutes. Add eggs one at a time, beating after each addition. Stir in lemon juice and vanilla.

3. Pour half the batter over peaches in pan, smoothing out to sides of pan. Place second cake layer on top and brush with the remaining liqueur. Spread with the remaining raspberry preserves and top with the remaining peach slices. Pour the remaining batter on top of peaches, smoothing out to sides of pan (the pan will be filled to the top edge). Bake in preheated oven until top is light brown and center has a slight jiggle to it, 50 to 55 minutes. Let cool in pan on a wire rack for 2 hours. Cover with plastic wrap and refrigerate for at least 6 hours before decorating or serving.

4. *Decoration:* Ice top of cake with Classic Whipped Cream Topping or pipe rosettes around top of cake, if desired. Top with raspberries.

Peaches and Cream Cheesecake

SERVES 10 TO 12

This cheesecake, with its fresh peaches and creamy base, is perfect for the summer holidays.

Tip

Use ripe peaches in season. To ripen any stone fruit, such as peaches or nectarines, place in a brown paper bag for a few days until soft when lightly touched.

Variation

Try almonds or walnuts in place of pecans.

- Preheat oven to 350°F (180°C)
- 9-inch (23 cm) cheesecake pan, ungreased, or springform pan with 3-inch (7.5 cm) sides, greased

Crust

1¼ cups	graham cracker crumbs	300 mL
¼ cup	pecans, toasted (see tip, page 88) and ground	50 mL
3 tbsp	unsalted butter, melted	45 mL

Filling

4	packages (each 8 oz/250 g) cream cheese, softened	4
1 cup	whipping (35%) cream	250 mL
1 cup	granulated sugar	250 mL
4	eggs	4
¼ cup	all-purpose flour	50 mL
2 tsp	vanilla extract	10 mL
2	peaches, peeled (see tip, page 90) and sliced	2
¼ cup	pecans, chopped	50 mL

Decoration

	Classic Whipped Cream Topping (see recipe, page 262)	
1	peach, peeled and sliced	1

1. *Crust:* In a bowl, combine graham cracker crumbs, ground pecans and butter. Press into bottom of cheesecake pan and freeze.

2. *Filling:* In a mixer bowl fitted with paddle attachment, beat cream cheese, whipping cream and sugar on medium-high speed until very smooth, for 3 minutes. Add eggs, one at a time, beating after each addition. Stir in flour and vanilla.

3. Pour half the batter over frozen crust, smoothing out to sides of pan. Arrange peach slices on top of batter, then sprinkle with chopped pecans. Pour remaining batter over peaches, smoothing out to sides of pan. Bake in preheated oven until top is light brown and center has a slight jiggle to it, 45 to 55 minutes. Let cool in pan on a wire rack for 2 hours. Cover with plastic wrap and refrigerate for at least 6 hours before decorating or serving.

4. *Decoration:* Ice top of cake with Classic Whipped Cream Topping or pipe rosettes around top of cake, if desired. Top with peach slices.

Pêches Louis Cheesecake

SERVES 10 TO 12

*In my young days
working in a hotel, I
learned to infuse fresh
peaches with many
things, and that whiskey
is a great foil to rich
foods.*

Tip
Marinate the peaches
in whiskey overnight
for maximum punch.

Variation
Orange-flavored liqueur
is also delicious with
peaches or other stone
fruits. For a non-alcoholic
version, use undiluted
orange juice concentrate
in place of the whiskey.

- Preheat oven to 350°F (180°C)
- 9-inch (23 cm) cheesecake pan, ungreased, or springform pan with 3-inch (7.5 cm) sides, greased

Crust

1¼ cup	graham cracker crumbs	300 mL
¼ cup	unsalted butter, melted	50 mL

Filling

1 cup	diced peeled peaches (about 2 medium)	250 mL
2 tbsp	whiskey	25 mL
3	packages (each 8 oz/250 g) cream cheese, softened	3
1 cup	plain yogurt	250 mL
1 cup	packed brown sugar	250 mL
3	eggs	3
1 tsp	vanilla extract	5 mL

1. *Crust:* In a bowl, combine graham cracker crumbs and butter. Press into bottom of cheesecake pan and freeze.
2. *Filling:* In a small bowl, combine peaches and whiskey. Set aside.
3. In a mixer bowl fitted with paddle attachment, beat cream cheese, yogurt and brown sugar on medium-high speed until very smooth, for 3 minutes. Add eggs, one at a time, beating after each addition. Fold in soaked peaches, with juices, and vanilla by hand.
4. Pour over frozen crust, smoothing out to sides of pan. Bake in preheated oven until top is light brown and center has a slight jiggle to it, 45 to 55 minutes. Let cool in pan on a wire rack for 2 hours. Cover with plastic wrap and refrigerate for at least 6 hours before serving.

Butterscotch Peach Cheesecake

SERVES 10 TO 12

A roadside diner on the west coast of Florida inspired this peachy cheesecake.

Tips

If you use frozen peaches, dice while frozen and measure 1½ cups (375 mL). Let thaw, drain well and pat dry with paper towels before adding to cake.

A thick caramel sauce for ice cream is the easiest to work with. It should mound on a spoon when you scoop it out of the jar. The thin, squeezable type will make the cake too loose. To drizzle for decorating, you can warm the sauce slightly.

- Preheat oven to 350°F (180°C)
- 9-inch (23 cm) cheesecake pan, ungreased, or springform pan with 3-inch (7.5 cm) sides, greased

Crust

1¼ cups	graham cracker crumbs	300 mL
¼ cup	unsalted butter, melted	50 mL

Filling

3	packages (each 8 oz/250 g) cream cheese, softened	3
1 cup	sour cream	250 mL
1 cup	packed brown sugar	250 mL
5	eggs	5
¼ cup	all-purpose flour	50 mL
2	peaches, peeled (see tip, page 95) and diced	2
½ cup	thick caramel sauce (see tip, at left)	125 mL
1 tsp	vanilla extract	5 mL
Decorating		
	Classic Whipped Cream Topping (see recipe, page 262)	
¼ cup	thick caramel sauce	50 mL

1. *Crust:* In a bowl, combine graham cracker crumbs and butter. Press into bottom of cheesecake pan and freeze.
2. *Filling:* In a mixer bowl fitted with paddle attachment, beat cream cheese, sour cream and brown sugar on medium-high speed until very smooth, for 3 minutes. Add eggs, one at a time, beating after each addition. Stir in flour until blended. Fold in peaches, caramel sauce and vanilla by hand.
3. Pour over frozen crust, smoothing out to sides of pan. Bake in preheated oven until top is light brown and center has a slight jiggle to it, 45 to 55 minutes. Let cool in pan on a wire rack for 2 hours. Cover with plastic wrap and refrigerate for at least 6 hours before decorating or serving.
4. *Decoration:* Ice top of cake with Classic Whipped Cream Topping or pipe rosettes around top of cake, if desired. Drizzle caramel sauce in a bull's-eye pattern on top.

Apricot Brandy Cheesecake

SERVES 10 TO 12

While dining one summer in a teahouse in Atlanta that served a wonderful peach brandy cheesecake, I immediately thought of that other golden orange summer fruit, the apricot.

Tip

For maximum flavor and economy with an expensive ingredient, nuts should be toasted whole before they are ground. Always use unsalted nuts in baking, as salt changes the flavor drastically.

Variation

You can substitute peaches or nectarines for the apricots.

- Preheat oven to 350°F (180°C)
- 9-inch (23 cm) cheesecake pan, ungreased, or springform pan with 3-inch (7.5 cm) sides, greased

Crust

¾ cup	graham cracker crumbs	175 mL
¾ cup	pecans, toasted (see tips, at left and page 88) and ground	175 mL
¼ cup	unsalted butter, melted	50 mL

Filling

3	packages (each 8 oz/250 g) cream cheese, softened	3
½ cup	sour cream	125 mL
1 cup	granulated sugar	250 mL
4	eggs	4
4	apricots, peeled (see tip, page 95) and sliced (about 1 lb/500 g)	4
2 tbsp	brandy	25 mL
1 tsp	vanilla extract	5 mL

Decoration

	Classic Whipped Cream Topping (see recipe, page 262)	
2	apricots, peeled and sliced	2

1. *Crust:* In a bowl, combine graham cracker crumbs, ground pecans and butter. Press into bottom of cheesecake pan and freeze.

2. *Filling:* In a mixer bowl fitted with paddle attachment, beat cream cheese, sour cream and sugar on medium-high speed until very smooth, for 3 minutes. Add eggs, one at a time, beating after each addition. Fold in apricots, brandy and vanilla by hand.

3. Pour over frozen crust, smoothing out to sides of pan. Bake in preheated oven until top is light brown and center has a slight jiggle to it, 45 to 55 minutes. Let cool in pan on a wire rack for 2 hours. Cover with plastic wrap and refrigerate for at least 6 hours before decorating or serving.

4. *Decoration:* Ice top of cake with Classic Whipped Cream Topping or pipe rosettes around top of cake, if desired. Top with apricot slices.

Apricot Hazelnut Cheesecake

SERVES 10 TO 12

Legend has it that hazelnut liqueur is a 300-year-old secret recipe from a northern Italian monk. Luckily, someone has managed to recreate its unique flavor.

Tips

To avoid making hazelnut butter when grinding the hazelnuts, process with the flour in a food processor fitted with a metal blade.

To quickly remove the peel from apricots, peaches and nectarines, cut an X in the bottom with a small knife, piercing only the skin. Place fruit in rapidly boiling water for about 30 seconds. Cool in cold water. The peel should come off easily.

- Preheat oven to 350°F (180°C)
- 9-inch (23 cm) cheesecake pan, ungreased, or springform pan with 3-inch (7.5 cm) sides, greased

Crust

1¼ cups	hazelnuts, ground (see tip, at left)	300 mL
¼ cup	all-purpose flour	50 mL
3 tbsp	unsalted butter, melted	45 mL

Filling

4	packages (each 8 oz/250 g) cream cheese, softened	4
1 cup	whipping (35%) cream	250 mL
1 cup	granulated sugar	250 mL
¼ cup	all-purpose flour	50 mL
4	eggs	4
3 tbsp	hazelnut-flavored liqueur	45 mL
2 tsp	vanilla extract	10 mL
4	apricots, peeled (see tip, at left) and sliced (about 1 lb/500 g)	4
¼ cup	hazelnuts, chopped	50 mL

Decoration

	Classic Whipped Cream Topping (see recipe, page 262)	
2	apricots, peeled and sliced	2

1. *Crust:* In a bowl, combine ground hazelnuts, flour and butter. Press into bottom of cheesecake pan and freeze.

2. *Filling:* In a mixer bowl fitted with paddle attachment, beat cream cheese, whipping cream, sugar and flour on medium-high speed until very smooth, for 3 minutes. Add eggs, one at a time, beating after each addition. Mix in liqueur and vanilla.

3. Pour half the batter over frozen crust, smoothing out to sides of pan. Arrange apricot slices on top of batter and sprinkle with chopped hazelnuts. Pour remaining batter over apricots, smoothing out to sides of pan. Bake in preheated oven until top is light brown and center has a slight jiggle to it, 45 to 55 minutes. Let cool in pan on a wire rack for 2 hours. Cover with plastic wrap and refrigerate for at least 6 hours before decorating or serving.

4. *Decoration:* Ice top of cake with Classic Whipped Cream Topping or pipe rosettes around top of cake, if desired. Top with apricot slices.

Fresh Cherry Cheesecake

SERVES 10 TO 12

Fresh cherries seem to be in season for only a few weeks. I pit and freeze them during this short time span so I can bake this cake year-round.

Tips

If the cottage cheese has a wet look to it, drain it through a fine-mesh sieve. Too much moisture will change the texture of the cheesecake.

If small-curd cottage cheese is not available, purée cottage cheese in a food processor before adding to the cream cheese.

To freeze cherries in their prime, wash and pit them. Spread out on a cookie sheet and freeze until hard, then store in plastic freezer bags. Now you can pull them out one at a time, rather than in a large mass. Thaw and drain before use.

- Preheat oven to 350°F (180°C)
- 9-inch (23 cm) cheesecake pan, ungreased, or springform pan with 3-inch (7.5 cm) sides, greased

Crust

1¼ cups	butter cookie crumbs	300 mL
3 tbsp	unsalted butter, melted	45 mL

Filling

2	packages (each 8 oz/250 g) cream cheese, softened	2
1 cup	small-curd cottage cheese, drained, if necessary (see tips, at left)	250 mL
1 cup	sour cream	250 mL
½ cup	all-purpose flour	125 mL
1	can (14 oz/396 g or 300 mL) sweetened condensed milk	1
3	eggs	3
2 tbsp	freshly squeezed lemon juice	25 mL
1 tbsp	vanilla extract	15 mL
1 tsp	almond extract	5 mL
1 cup	cherries, pitted	250 mL

Decoration

¼ tsp	almond extract	1 mL
	Classic Whipped Cream Topping (see recipe, page 262)	
10 to 12	cherries	10 to 12

1. *Crust:* In a bowl, combine cookie crumbs and butter. Press into bottom of cheesecake pan and freeze.

2. *Filling:* In a mixer bowl fitted with paddle attachment, beat cream cheese, cottage cheese, sour cream and flour on medium-high speed until very smooth, for 3 minutes. Mix in condensed milk. Add eggs, one at a time, beating after each addition. Mix in lemon juice, vanilla and almond extract. Fold in cherries by hand.

3. Pour over frozen crust, smoothing out to sides of pan. Bake in preheated oven until top is light brown and center has a slight jiggle to it, 45 to 55 minutes. Let cool in pan on a wire rack for 2 hours. Cover with plastic wrap and refrigerate for at least 6 hours before decorating or serving.

4. *Decoration:* Add almond extract to Classic Whipped Cream Topping. Ice top of cake or pipe rosettes around top of cake, if desired. Top with cherries.

French Apple Cheesecake (page 86)
Overleaf: Butterscotch Peach Cheesecake (page 93)

Cherries Jubilee Cheesecake

SERVES 18 TO 20

Escoffier gets the credit for knowing that cherries were Queen Victoria's favorite fruit and preparing a flambé cherry dessert for one of her Jubilee celebrations in the late 1800s. Here's a festive cheesecake suitable for any event worth celebrating with a crowd.

Tips

You can use frozen cherries; just thaw and drain before use.

If you cannot find Kirsch, substitute port wine or cherry syrup.

- Preheat oven to 350°F (180°C)
- 10-inch (25 cm) cheesecake pan, ungreased, or springform pan with 3-inch (7.5 cm) sides, greased

Crust

2½ cups	butter cookie crumbs	625 mL
½ cup	unsalted butter, melted	125 mL

Filling

4	packages (each 8 oz/250 g) cream cheese, softened	4
1 cup	sour cream	250 mL
½ cup	all-purpose flour	125 mL
1	can (14 oz/396 g or 300 mL) sweetened condensed milk	1
4	eggs	4
1 cup	cherries, pitted	250 mL
2 tbsp	Kirsch (clear cherry-flavored liqueur)	25 mL

Decoration

	Classic Whipped Cream Topping (see recipe, page 262)	
18 to 20	cherries	18 to 20

1. *Crust:* In a bowl, combine cookie crumbs and butter. Press into bottom of cheesecake pan and freeze.
2. *Filling:* In a mixer bowl fitted with paddle attachment, beat cream cheese, sour cream and flour until very smooth, for 3 minutes. Mix in condensed milk. Add eggs, one at a time, beating after each addition. Fold in cherries and Kirsch by hand.
3. Pour over frozen crust, smoothing out to sides of pan. Bake in preheated oven until top is light brown and center has a slight jiggle to it, 55 to 65 minutes. Let cool in pan on a wire rack for 2 hours. Cover with plastic wrap and refrigerate for at least 6 hours before decorating or serving.
4. *Decoration:* Ice top of cake with Classic Whipped Cream Topping or pipe rosettes around top of cake, if desired. Top with cherries.

Overleaf: Banana Split Cheesecake (page 104)
Maui Tropical Cheesecake (page 109)

Almond Blueberry Cheesecake

Wait until you try blueberries in a chocolate almond cheesecake! A new flavor combination to love.

Tips

You can use frozen blueberries in the batter; don't thaw, just toss berries with about 1 tbsp (15 mL) flour before folding them in. Of course, you'll need thawed berries for the decoration.

Purchase the milk chocolate in bar form rather than as chips.

Variation

Substitute raspberries for the blueberries.

- Preheat oven to 350°F (180°C)
- 9-inch (23 cm) cheesecake pan, ungreased, or springform pan with 3-inch (7.5 cm) sides, greased

Crust

1¼ cups	ground almonds	300 mL
1½ tbsp	unsalted butter, melted	22 mL

Filling

4	packages (each 8 oz/250 g) cream cheese, softened	4
½ cup	unsalted butter, softened	125 mL
⅓ cup	milk	75 mL
3 tbsp	almond-flavored liqueur	45 mL
4	eggs	4
1	egg yolk	1
1 lb	milk chocolate, melted (see page 63) and cooled	500 g
1 cup	blueberries	250 mL

Decoration

2 cups	blueberries	500 mL
3 tbsp	confectioner's (icing) sugar	45 mL

1. *Crust:* In a bowl, combine almonds and butter. Press into bottom of cheesecake pan and freeze.

2. *Filling:* In a mixer bowl fitted with paddle attachment, beat cream cheese and butter on medium-high speed until very smooth, for 3 minutes. Mix in milk and liqueur. Add whole eggs and egg yolk, one at a time, beating after each addition. Remove 1 cup (250 mL) batter and stir into melted chocolate. Fold melted chocolate mixture into remaining batter by hand. Fold in blueberries.

3. Pour over frozen crust, smoothing out to sides of pan. Bake in preheated oven until top is light brown and center has a slight jiggle to it, 45 to 55 minutes. Let cool in pan on a wire rack for 2 hours. Cover with plastic wrap and refrigerate for at least 6 hours before decorating or serving.

4. *Decoration:* Top cake with blueberries and dust with confectioner's sugar.

Blueberries and Crème Cheesecake

SERVES 10 TO 12

Fresh blueberries from the northwest make this cheesecake a show-stopper at any event.

Tip

If using frozen blueberries, keep them in the freezer until ready to use.

- Preheat oven to 350°F (180°C)
- 9-inch (23 cm) cheesecake pan, ungreased, or springform pan with 3-inch (7.5 cm) sides, greased

Crust

1½ cups	butter cookie crumbs	375 mL
¼ cup	unsalted butter, melted	50 mL

Filling

4	packages (each 8 oz/250 g) cream cheese, softened	4
1 cup	granulated sugar	250 mL
4	eggs	4
1	egg yolk	1
½ cup	whipping (35%) cream	125 mL
2 tsp	vanilla extract	10 mL
1 cup	blueberries	250 mL

1. *Crust:* In a bowl, combine cookie crumbs and butter. Press into bottom of cheesecake pan and freeze.

2. *Filling:* In a mixer bowl fitted with paddle attachment, beat cream cheese and sugar on medium-high speed until very smooth, for 3 minutes. Add whole eggs and egg yolk, one at a time, beating after each addition. Mix in cream and vanilla. Fold in blueberries by hand.

3. Pour over frozen crust, smoothing out to sides of pan. Bake in preheated oven until top is light brown and center has a slight jiggle to it, 45 to 55 minutes. Let cool in pan on a wire rack for 2 hours. Cover with plastic wrap and refrigerate for at least 6 hours before serving.

Fresh Strawberry Chocolate Chunk Cheesecake

SERVES 10 TO 12

My sister Patti is a berry lover. Her favorite cheesecake is this strawberry chocolate one. It may become yours, too.

Tips

If the strawberries are not slightly crushed for the batter, you will get large pockets of liquid from the berries in the cheesecake.

Instead of using chocolate chips, I cut bar chocolate into chunks. The chunks melt and make pockets of chocolate in the cake.

Variation

Raspberries or blackberries are a delicious alternative to strawberries.

- Preheat oven to 350°F (180°C)
- 9-inch (23 cm) cheesecake pan, ungreased, or springform pan with 3-inch (7.5 cm) sides, greased
- 13- by 9-inch (3 L) baking pan, lined with parchment paper

Crust

1¼ cups	chocolate sandwich cookie crumbs	300 mL
3 tbsp	unsalted butter, melted	45 mL

Filling

4	packages (each 8 oz/250 g) cream cheese, softened	4
8 oz	ricotta cheese, drained (see tip, page 116)	250 g
¾ cup	sour cream	175 mL
1¼ cups	granulated sugar	300 mL
4	eggs	4
2 tbsp	all-purpose flour	25 mL
2 tbsp	freshly squeezed lemon juice	25 mL
1 tbsp	vanilla extract	15 mL
1 cup	strawberries, slightly crushed	250 mL
3 oz	semisweet chocolate chunks	90 g

Decoration

2 cups	whole strawberries	500 mL
3 oz	semisweet chocolate, melted (see page 63) and cooled	90 g

1. *Crust:* In a bowl, combine cookie crumbs and butter. Press into bottom of cheesecake pan and freeze.

2. *Filling:* In a mixer bowl fitted with paddle attachment, beat cream cheese, ricotta, sour cream and sugar on medium-high speed until very smooth, for 3 minutes. Add eggs, one at a time, beating after each addition. Stir in flour, lemon juice and vanilla. Fold in strawberries and chocolate chunks by hand.

3. Pour over frozen crust, smoothing out to sides of pan. Bake in preheated oven until top is light brown and center has a slight jiggle to it, 45 to 55 minutes. Let cool in pan on a wire rack for 2 hours. Cover with plastic wrap and refrigerate for at least 6 hours before decorating or serving.

4. *Decoration:* Slice stems from strawberries to create a flat bottom. Dip only the tips of berries in melted chocolate and place flat, with tips up, on lined baking pan to dry. When dried, arrange strawberries, tips up, on top of cake.

Spumoni Cheesecake

SERVES 10 TO 12

I created this cheesecake years ago for an Italian restaurant that wanted to update classic spumoni ice cream.

Tips

Toasting brings out the natural oils and flavor of nuts. Place nuts in a single layer on a baking sheet and bake at 350°F (180°C) until fragrant, 10 to 12 minutes.

Green cherries from a jar have a minty flavor rather than the almond flavor of the bright red cherries so often used as a garnish in cocktails or desserts.

- Preheat oven to 350°F (180°C)
- 9-inch (23 cm) cheesecake pan, ungreased, or springform pan with 3-inch (7.5 cm) sides, greased

Crust

1½ cups	butter cookie crumbs	375 mL
¼ cup	unsalted butter, melted	50 mL

Filling

4	packages (each 8 oz/250 g) cream cheese, softened	4
1¼ cups	granulated sugar	300 mL
4	eggs	4
2 tsp	vanilla extract	10 mL
½ cup	strawberries, mashed	125 mL
¼ cup	pistachios, toasted (see tip, at left) and chopped	50 mL
1	jar (8 oz/250 mL) green maraschino cherries, drained and finely chopped	1
½ cup	pecans, toasted and chopped	125 mL

Decoration

Classic Whipped Cream Topping (see recipe, page 262)

1. *Crust:* In a bowl, combine cookie crumbs and butter. Press into bottom of cheesecake pan and freeze.

2. *Filling:* In a mixer bowl fitted with paddle attachment, beat cream cheese and sugar on medium-high speed until very smooth, for 3 minutes. Add eggs, one at a time, beating after each addition. Mix in vanilla.

3. Divide batter into three equal portions. Fold strawberries into one-third of the batter. Fold pistachios into one-third of the batter. Fold green cherries into remaining third.

4. Spread strawberry batter over frozen crust, smoothing out to sides of pan. Refrigerate for about 5 minutes to firm. Spread pistachio batter carefully over strawberry layer, covering it completely. Refrigerate for 5 minutes to firm. Spread cherry batter over pistachio layer. Sprinkle with chopped pecans. Bake in preheated oven until top is light brown and center has a slight jiggle to it, 45 to 55 minutes. Let cool in pan on a wire rack for 2 hours. Cover with plastic wrap and refrigerate for at least 6 hours before decorating or serving.

5. *Decoration:* Pipe rosettes around top of cake with Classic Whipped Cream Topping.

Tri-Berry Cheesecake

SERVES 10 TO 12

I love berries! If there is a fresh berry on a dessert menu, I'll choose it over anything but chocolate. Berries are nature's candies — packed with flavor and beauty.

Variations

If all three berry varieties aren't available, use one or two varieties — just make sure to keep the total amount the same.

Spread 1 cup (250 mL) berry preserves on top.

- Preheat oven to 350°F (180°C)
- 9-inch (23 cm) cheesecake pan, ungreased, or springform pan with 3-inch (7.5 cm) sides, greased

Crust

1¼ cups	sugar cookie crumbs	300 mL
3 tbsp	unsalted butter, melted	45 mL

Filling

4	packages (each 8 oz/250 g) cream cheese, softened	4
1 cup	sour cream	250 mL
1 cup	granulated sugar	250 mL
3	eggs	3
2	egg yolks	2
¼ cup	all-purpose flour	50 mL
2½ tbsp	freshly squeezed lemon juice	32 mL
1 tbsp	vanilla extract	15 mL
½ cup	strawberries, slightly crushed	125 mL
½ cup	raspberries, cut into quarters	125 mL
½ cup	blackberries, cut into quarters	125 mL

Decoration

½ cup	strawberries, sliced	125 mL
½ cup	raspberries	125 mL
½ cup	blackberries	125 mL
2 tbsp	port wine	25 mL

1. *Crust:* In a bowl, combine cookie crumbs and butter. Press into bottom of cheesecake pan and freeze.

2. *Filling:* In a mixer bowl fitted with paddle attachment, beat cream cheese, sour cream and sugar on medium-high speed until very smooth, for 3 minutes. Add whole eggs and yolks, one at a time, beating after each addition. Stir in flour, lemon juice and vanilla. Fold in berries by hand.

3. Pour batter over frozen crust, smoothing out to sides of pan. Bake in preheated oven until top is light brown and center has a slight jiggle to it, 55 to 65 minutes. Let cool in pan on a wire rack for 2 hours. Cover with plastic wrap and refrigerate for at least 6 hours before decorating or serving.

4. *Decoration:* In a bowl, combine berries and port. Garnish each slice with a spoonful.

Banana Nut Cheesecake

SERVES 10 TO 12

It seems like I always have overripe bananas. Peel and freeze them in plastic bags so they're ready to use in baking recipes.

Tip

Look for dried banana chips in the bulk food section of your supermarket. Do not use fresh bananas for decorating — they will turn black before you can serve the dessert.

Variation

Try almonds or walnuts instead of pecans.

- Preheat oven to 350°F (180°C)
- 9-inch (23 cm) cheesecake pan, ungreased, or springform pan with 3-inch (7.5 cm) sides, greased

Crust

1¼ cup	graham cracker crumbs	300 mL
¼ cup	pecans, toasted (see tip, page 104) and ground	50 mL
3 tbsp	unsalted butter, melted	45 mL

Filling

3	packages (each 8 oz/250 g) cream cheese, softened	3
1 cup	sour cream	250 mL
1¼ cups	mashed ripe bananas (about 3 large)	300 mL
¼ cup	all-purpose flour	50 mL
1 cup	granulated sugar	250 mL
3	eggs	3
½ cup	pecans, toasted and chopped	125 mL
1 tbsp	ground cinnamon	15 mL
1 tsp	freshly grated nutmeg	5 mL
1 tsp	vanilla extract	5 mL

Decoration

	Classic Whipped Cream Topping (see recipe, page 262)	
12	dried banana chips	12

1. *Crust:* In a bowl, combine graham cracker crumbs, ground pecans and butter. Press into cheesecake pan and freeze.
2. *Filling:* In a mixer bowl fitted with paddle attachment, beat cream cheese, sour cream, bananas, flour and sugar on medium-high speed until very smooth, for 3 minutes. Add eggs, one at a time, beating after each addition. Stir in chopped pecans, cinnamon, nutmeg and vanilla.
3. Pour over frozen crust, smoothing out to sides of pan. Bake in preheated oven until the top is light brown and the center has a slight jiggle to it, 45 to 55 minutes. Let cool in pan on a wire rack for 2 hours. Cover with plastic wrap and refrigerate for at least 6 hours before decorating or serving.
4. *Decoration:* Ice top of cake with Classic Whipped Cream Topping or pipe rosettes around top of cake, if desired. Top with banana chips.

Banana Split Cheesecake

SERVES 10 TO 12

The popular ice cream treat invented in 1904 by soda jerk David Strickler of Latrobe, Pennsylvania, is still pleasing today, and it's especially wonderful in cheesecake form.

Tips

To melt bittersweet chocolate in the microwave, break into squares and place in a microwave-safe dish. Microwave on High for 1 to 2 minutes, stirring after 30 seconds.

Dip sliced bananas in lemon juice to avoid browning.

Toasting brings out the natural oils and flavor of nuts. Place nuts in a single layer on a baking sheet and bake at 350°F (180°C) until fragrant, 10 to 12 minutes.

- Preheat oven to 350°F (180°C)
- 9-inch (23 cm) cheesecake pan, ungreased, or springform pan with 3-inch (7.5 cm) sides, greased

Crust

1½ cups	butter cookie crumbs	375 mL
¼ cup	unsalted butter, melted	50 mL

Filling

4	packages (each 8 oz/250 g) cream cheese, softened	4
1 cup	sour cream	250 mL
1¼ cups	granulated sugar	300 mL
4	eggs	4
2 tsp	vanilla extract	10 mL
2 oz	bittersweet chocolate, melted (see page 63 and tip, at left) and cooled	60 g
½ cup	strawberries, mashed	125 mL
1	banana, sliced in ¼-inch (0.5 cm) slices	1

Decoration

	Classic Whipped Cream Topping (see recipe, page 262)	
¼ cup	pineapple topping (store-bought or see recipe, page 264)	50 mL
¼ cup	almonds, toasted (see tip, at left) and sliced	50 mL

1. *Crust:* In a bowl, combine cookie crumbs and butter. Press into bottom of cheesecake pan and freeze.
2. *Filling:* In a mixer bowl fitted with paddle attachment, beat cream cheese, sour cream and sugar on medium-high speed until very smooth, for 3 minutes. Add eggs, one at a time, beating after each addition. Mix in vanilla.
3. Divide batter into three equal portions. Mix chocolate into one-third of the batter. Fold strawberries into one-third of the batter. Keep the last third plain.

Variation

Place maraschino cherries around the top of the cake instead of the rosettes of whipped cream.

4. Spread chocolate batter over frozen crust, smoothing out to sides of pan. Refrigerate for about 5 minutes to firm. Place half the banana slices on top in a single layer. Spread plain batter carefully over bananas. Refrigerate for 5 minutes to firm. Place the remaining banana slices on top in a single layer. Spread strawberry batter carefully over bananas. Bake in preheated oven until top is light brown and center has a slight jiggle to it, 45 to 55 minutes. Let cool in pan on a wire rack for 2 hours. Cover with plastic wrap and refrigerate for at least 6 hours before decorating or serving.

5. *Decoration:* Pipe rosettes around top of cake with Classic Whipped Cream Topping. Fill center with pineapple topping. Sprinkle with almond slices.

Roasted Banana Rum Cheesecake

SERVES 10 TO 12

An island treat! Roasted bananas are simple to make on the barbecue or in the oven.

Tips

Toasting brings out the natural oils and flavor of nuts. Place nuts in a single layer on a baking sheet and bake at 350°F (180°C) until fragrant, 10 to 12 minutes.

You can also barbecue the bananas. Preheat grill to medium and spray the rack so the peels do not stick. Grill for about 5 minutes per side or until peel darkens.

You can roast the bananas, peel them and then freeze in plastic freezer bags for future use. Thaw and let come to room temperature before using.

- Preheat broiler
- 9-inch (23 cm) cheesecake pan, ungreased, or springform pan with 3-inch (7.5 cm) sides, greased
- Baking sheet

Crust

1¼ cups	butter cookie crumbs	300 mL
¼ cup	pecans, toasted (see tip, at left) and ground	50 mL
3 tbsp	unsalted butter, melted	45 mL

Filling

3	firm bananas (unpeeled)	3
½ cup	light rum	125 mL
4	packages (each 8 oz/250 g) cream cheese, softened	4
1¼ cups	granulated sugar	300 mL
½ cup	sour cream	125 mL
¼ cup	liquid honey	50 mL
4	eggs	4
1 tbsp	vanilla extract	15 mL
1 tsp	ground cinnamon	5 mL
½ tsp	ground cloves	2 mL
½ cup	pecans, toasted and chopped	125 mL

Decoration

	Classic Whipped Cream Topping (see recipe, page 262)	
12	dried banana chips	12

1. *Crust:* In a bowl, combine cookie crumbs, ground pecans and butter. Press into bottom of cheesecake pan and freeze.

2. *Filling:* Place unpeeled bananas in a single layer on baking sheet. Roast under preheated broiler for about 5 minutes per side or until peel darkens. Reduce oven temperature to 350°F (180°C). Let bananas cool. Peel, place in a bowl with rum and smash with a fork. Set aside.

3. In a mixer bowl fitted with paddle attachment, beat cream cheese and sugar on medium-high speed until very smooth, for 3 minutes. Mix in sour cream and honey. Add eggs, one at a time, beating after each addition. Stir in vanilla, cinnamon and cloves.

Variation

Substitute apple juice for the rum.

4. Pour half the batter over frozen crust, smoothing out to sides of pan. Spread banana mixture on top and sprinkle with chopped pecans. Pour remaining batter over banana mixture, smoothing out to sides of pan. Bake in preheated oven until top is light brown and center has a slight jiggle to it, 45 to 55 minutes. Let cool in pan on a wire rack for 2 hours. Cover with plastic wrap and refrigerate for at least 6 hours before decorating or serving.

5. *Decoration:* Ice top of cake with Classic Whipped Cream Topping or pipe rosettes around top of cake, if desired. Top with banana chips.

Hummingbird Cheesecake

SERVES 10 TO 12

Although the origin of the name remains a mystery, if you desire a traditional Southern dessert, go with the hummingbird, which features ripe bananas and pineapple.

Tip

Dried banana chips look great as decoration, and you don't have to dip them in lemon juice, as you would fresh bananas.

Variation

Add ½ cup (125 mL) pecans, toasted and chopped, to the batter for crunch.

- Preheat oven to 350°F (180°C)
- 9-inch (23 cm) cheesecake pan, ungreased, or springform pan with 3-inch (7.5 cm) sides, greased

Crust

¾ cup	graham cracker crumbs	175 mL
¾ cup	pecans, toasted (see tip, page 106) and ground	175 mL
¼ cup	unsalted butter, melted	50 mL

Filling

4	packages (each 8 oz/250 g) cream cheese, softened	4
1 cup	packed brown sugar	250 mL
4	eggs	4
¾ cup	mashed ripe bananas (about 2 medium)	175 mL
1 cup	well-drained crushed pineapple (about two 8-oz/227 mL cans)	250 mL
1 tsp	vanilla extract	5 mL

Decoration

	Classic Whipped Cream Topping (see recipe, page 262)	
½ cup	dried banana chips	125 mL

1. *Crust:* In a bowl, combine graham cracker crumbs, pecans and butter. Press into bottom of cheesecake pan and freeze.
2. *Filling:* In a mixer bowl fitted with paddle attachment, beat cream cheese and brown sugar on medium-high speed until very smooth, for 3 minutes. Add eggs, one at a time, beating after each addition. Fold in mashed bananas, pineapple and vanilla by hand.
3. Pour over frozen crust, smoothing out to sides of pan. Bake in preheated oven until top is light brown and center has a slight jiggle to it, 45 to 55 minutes. Let cool in pan on a wire rack for 2 hours. Cover with plastic wrap and refrigerate for at least 6 hours before decorating or serving.
4. *Decoration:* Ice top of cake with Classic Whipped Cream Topping or pipe rosettes around top of cake, if desired. Top with banana chips.

Maui Tropical Cheesecake

SERVES 10 TO 12

Tropical fruits from the islands make this cheesecake feel like a friendly aloha!

Tips

To avoid making macadamia nut butter when grinding the nuts, process with the flour in a food processor fitted with a metal blade.

A non-alcoholic substitute for rum is undiluted orange juice concentrate.

Variation

You can substitute mango or kiwifruit if papaya is not available.

- Preheat oven to 350ºF (180ºC)
- 9-inch (23 cm) cheesecake pan, ungreased, or springform pan with 3-inch (7.5 cm) sides, greased

Crust

1½ cups	macadamia nuts, toasted (see tip, page 106) and ground	375 mL
1 tbsp	all-purpose flour	15 mL
¼ cup	granulated sugar	50 mL

Filling

4	packages (each 8 oz/250 g) cream cheese, softened	4
1½ cups	granulated sugar	375 mL
4	eggs	4
½ cup	well-drained crushed pineapple (about one 8-oz/227 mL can)	125 mL
½ cup	finely chopped papaya (about ½ medium)	125 mL
1 tbsp	rum	15 mL
2 tsp	vanilla extract	10 mL

Decoration

5 to 6	pineapple slices (about one 6-oz/175 mL can)	5 to 6
5 to 6	papaya slices (about ½ medium)	5 to 6

1. *Crust:* In a bowl, combine macadamia nuts, flour and sugar. Press into bottom of cheesecake pan and freeze.

2. *Filling:* In a mixer bowl fitted with paddle attachment, beat cream cheese and sugar on medium-high speed until very smooth, for 3 minutes. Add eggs, one at a time, beating after each addition. Fold in pineapple, papaya, rum and vanilla by hand.

3. Pour over crust, smoothing out to sides of pan. Bake in preheated oven until top is light brown and center has a slight jiggle to it, 45 to 55 minutes. Let cool in pan on a wire rack for 2 hours. Cover with plastic wrap and refrigerate for at least 6 hours before decorating or serving.

4. *Decoration:* Top with alternating pineapple and papaya slices. Chill until ready to serve.

Piña Colada Cheesecake

SERVES 10 TO 12

Cheesecake with an island twist! You can serve this with a rum punch as a dessert for a luau.

Tip

Coconut is often burned by pastry chefs. To avoid crying over burnt coconut, follow this technique. Spread coconut in a single layer on a baking sheet. Bake in a 350°F (180°C) oven for 3 minutes. Check the coconut and stir. Set the timer for another 3 minutes. Repeat until coconut is lightly browned.

- Preheat oven to 350°F (180°C)
- 9-inch (23 cm) cheesecake pan, ungreased, or springform pan with 3-inch (7.5 cm) sides, greased

Crust

1¼ cups	graham cracker crumbs	300 mL
½ cup	flaked sweetened coconut	125 mL
3 tbsp	unsalted butter, melted	45 mL

Filling

1	can (20 oz/567 mL) pineapple chunks, with juice	1
3 tbsp	packed light brown sugar	45 mL
4	packages (each 8 oz/250 g) cream cheese, softened	4
1¼ cups	granulated sugar	300 mL
¼ cup	all-purpose flour	50 mL
4	eggs	4
½ cup	coconut milk	125 mL
2 tsp	vanilla extract	10 mL

Decoration

	Classic Whipped Cream Topping (see recipe, page 262)	
¼ cup	flaked sweetened coconut, toasted (see tip, at left)	50 mL

1. *Crust:* In a bowl, combine graham cracker crumbs, coconut and butter. Press into bottom of cheesecake pan and freeze.

2. *Filling:* In a saucepan on medium heat, cook pineapple, with juice, and brown sugar until soft and syrupy, about 3 minutes. Let stand for 10 minutes, then drain, discarding syrup.

3. In a mixer bowl fitted with paddle attachment, beat cream cheese, sugar and flour on medium-high speed until very smooth, for 3 minutes. Add eggs, one at a time, beating after each addition. Mix in coconut milk and vanilla.

Variation

For a little kick, add
1 tbsp (15 mL) rum
with the vanilla.

4. Pour half the batter over frozen crust, smoothing out to
   sides of pan. Spread pineapple mixture on top. Pour
   remaining batter over pineapple mixture, smoothing out
   to sides of pan. Bake in preheated oven until top is light
   brown and center has a slight jiggle to it, 45 to 55 minutes.
   Let cool in pan on a wire rack for 2 hours. Cover with
   plastic wrap and refrigerate for at least 6 hours before
   decorating or serving.

5. *Decoration:* Ice top of cake with Classic Whipped Cream
   Topping or pipe a ribbon around border, if desired.
   Sprinkle with toasted coconut.

Kiwi Cheesecake

SERVES 10 TO 12

Refreshing with the light sweetness of kiwi and no crust, this cheesecake is perfect for a summer day. Serve with a glass of limeade.

Tips

Fresh kiwis should be firm, like a ripe tomato.

Use freshly squeezed lime juice. Bottled lime juice can have a metallic taste.

- Preheat oven to 350°F (180°C)
- 9-inch (23 cm) cheesecake pan or springform pan with 3-inch (7.5 cm) sides, lined with parchment paper

Filling

2	packages (each 8 oz/250 g) cream cheese, softened	2
1 lb	ricotta cheese, drained (see tip, page 116)	500 g
1 cup	sour cream	250 mL
1½ cups	granulated sugar	375 mL
5	eggs	5
3	kiwifruits, peeled and puréed	3
½ cup	all-purpose flour	125 mL
2 tbsp	freshly squeezed lime juice	25 mL
1 tbsp	vanilla extract	15 mL

Decoration

3	kiwifruits, peeled and thinly sliced	3
½ cup	apricot preserves	125 mL

1. *Filling:* In a mixer bowl fitted with paddle attachment, beat cream cheese, ricotta cheese, sour cream and sugar on medium-high speed until very smooth, for 3 minutes. Add eggs, one at a time, beating after each addition. Stir in kiwi purée, flour, lime juice and vanilla.

2. Pour into prepared pan, smoothing out to sides of pan. Bake in preheated oven until top is light brown and center has a slight jiggle to it, 55 to 65 minutes. Let cool in pan on a wire rack for 2 hours. Cover with plastic wrap and refrigerate for at least 6 hours before decorating or serving.

3. *Decoration:* Arrange sliced kiwis on top of cake. In a small saucepan, bring apricot preserves to a simmer over medium heat. Press through a fine-mesh sieve. Brush on top of kiwis. (This will keep the fruit looking fresh.)

Mangos Diablo Cheesecake

SERVES 10 TO 12

Fresh mangos soaked in tequila make this the perfect dessert to follow spicy foods.

Tips

Toasting brings out the natural oils and flavor of nuts. Place nuts in a single layer on a baking sheet and bake at 350°F (180°C) until fragrant, 10 to 12 minutes.

A ripe mango feels the same as a ripe tomato.

Variation

Substitute freshly squeezed lemon juice for the tequila.

- Preheat oven to 350°F (180°C)
- 9-inch (23 cm) cheesecake pan, ungreased, or springform pan with 3-inch (7.5 cm) sides, greased

Crust

¾ cup	graham cracker crumbs	175 mL
¾ cup	pecans, toasted (see tip, at left) and ground	175 mL
¼ cup	unsalted butter, melted	50 mL

Filling

1 cup	diced mangos (about 2 medium)	250 mL
2 tbsp	tequila	25 mL
3	packages (each 8 oz/250 g) cream cheese, softened	3
1 cup	granulated sugar	250 mL
3	eggs	3
1 tsp	vanilla extract	5 mL

Decoration

Island Fruit Compote (see recipe, page 266)

1. *Crust:* In a bowl, combine graham cracker crumbs, pecans and butter. Press into bottom of cheesecake pan and freeze.
2. *Filling:* In a small bowl, combine mangos and tequila. Set aside.
3. In a mixer bowl fitted with paddle attachment, beat cream cheese and sugar on medium-high speed until very smooth, for 3 minutes. Add eggs, one at a time, beating after each addition. Fold in mango mixture and vanilla by hand.
4. Pour over frozen crust, smoothing out to sides of pan. Bake in preheated oven until top is light brown and center has a slight jiggle to it, 45 to 55 minutes. Let cool in pan on a wire rack for 2 hours. Cover with plastic wrap and refrigerate for at least 6 hours before decorating or serving.
5. *Decoration:* Top each slice with a spoonful of Island Fruit Compote.

Passion Fruit Cheesecake

SERVES 10 TO 12

The seeds from a passion fruit are slightly crunchy and add unique flavor.

Tip

California and Florida produce passion fruit in the winter; imports from climes farther south are available at other times. The fruit is ripe when the skin is deeply wrinkled.

- Preheat oven to 350°F (180°C)
- 9-inch (23 cm) cheesecake pan, ungreased, or springform pan with 3-inch (7.5 cm) sides, greased

Crust

1½ cups	graham cracker crumbs	375 mL
¼ cup	unsalted butter, melted	50 mL

Filling

3	packages (each 8 oz/250 g) cream cheese, softened	3
½ cup	vanilla-flavored yogurt	125 mL
1 cup	granulated sugar	250 mL
3	eggs	3
1 cup	passion fruit seeds and pulp (about 2 to 3 medium)	250 mL
1 tsp	vanilla extract	5 mL

Decoration

Classic Whipped Cream Topping
(see recipe, page 262)

1. *Crust:* In a bowl, combine graham cracker crumbs and butter. Press into bottom of cheesecake pan and freeze.

2. *Filling:* In a mixer bowl fitted with paddle attachment, beat cream cheese, yogurt and sugar on medium-high speed until very smooth, for 3 minutes. Add eggs, one at a time, beating after each addition. Fold in passion fruit seeds and pulp and vanilla by hand.

3. Pour over frozen crust, smoothing out to sides of pan. Bake in preheated oven until top is light brown and center has a slight jiggle to it, 45 to 55 minutes. Let cool in pan on a wire rack for 2 hours. Cover with plastic wrap and refrigerate for at least 6 hours before decorating or serving.

4. *Decoration:* Ice top of cake with Classic Whipped Cream Topping or pipe rosettes around top of cake, if desired.

Citrus Cheesecakes

Orange Honey Ricotta Cheesecake

SERVES 10 TO 12

The flavors of honey and oranges combine to make a great dessert. If you can find orange honey, by all means use that for the honey in the recipe.

Tips

To drain ricotta, place a fine-mesh strainer over a bowl, place the cheese in the strainer and let stand in the refrigerator for at least 1 hour or overnight.

Room temperature egg whites yield a much higher volume than cold whites.

- Preheat oven to 300°F (150°C)
- 9-inch (23 cm) cheesecake pan, ungreased, or springform pan with 3-inch (7.5 cm) sides, greased

Crust

1¼ cups	graham cracker crumbs	300 mL
1 tbsp	unsalted butter, melted	15 mL
2 tsp	liquid honey	10 mL

Filling

1 lb	ricotta cheese, drained (see tip, at left)	500 g
4 oz	cream cheese, softened	125 g
½ cup	liquid honey	125 mL
2	eggs	2
½ cup	plain yogurt	125 mL
1 tbsp	frozen orange juice concentrate, thawed	15 mL
2 tsp	grated orange zest	10 mL
1 tsp	cornstarch	5 ml
¼ tsp	salt	1 mL
3	egg whites	3

Decoration

2	oranges	2
2 tbsp	liquid honey	25 mL

1. *Crust:* In a bowl, combine graham cracker crumbs, butter and honey. Press into bottom of cheesecake pan and freeze.

2. *Filling:* In a mixer bowl fitted with paddle attachment, beat ricotta cheese, cream cheese and honey on medium-high speed until very smooth, for 3 minutes. Add whole eggs, one at a time, beating after each addition. Stir in yogurt, orange juice concentrate, orange zest, cornstarch and salt. Set aside.

3. In a clean mixer bowl fitted with whip attachment, whip egg whites on medium-high speed until stiff but not dry peaks form. Fold into cream cheese mixture carefully so as not to deflate the mixture.

Save extra egg yolks in a small bowl in the refrigerator for up to 2 days by covering them with water and sealing tightly with plastic wrap. To freeze, sprinkle salt or sugar over the yolks in water.

4. Pour over frozen crust, smoothing out to sides of pan. Bake in preheated oven until top is light brown and center has a slight jiggle to it, 50 to 60 minutes. Let cool in pan on a wire rack for 2 hours. Cover with plastic wrap and refrigerate for at least 6 hours before decorating or serving.

5. *Decoration:* Remove white pith and peel from oranges and cut into very thin slices. Arrange slices on top of cake. In a small saucepan over low heat, heat honey. Using a pastry brush, brush hot honey over orange slices. Chill before serving.

Double Orange Cheesecake

An orange-flavored liqueur hints at the taste and aroma of oranges in every bite.

Tip

To drain ricotta, place a fine-mesh strainer over a bowl, place the cheese in the strainer and let stand in the refrigerator for at least 1 hour or overnight.

Variation

Use thawed frozen orange juice concentrate instead of the liqueur.

- Preheat oven to 350°F (180°C)
- 9-inch (23 cm) cheesecake pan, ungreased, or springform pan with 3-inch (7.5 cm) sides, greased

Crust

1½ cups	graham cracker crumbs	375 mL
¼ cup	unsalted butter, melted	50 mL

Filling

1 lb	ricotta cheese, drained (see tip, at left)	500 g
1	package (8 oz/250 g) cream cheese, softened	1
1 cup	granulated sugar	250 mL
4	egg yolks	4
¼ cup	all-purpose flour	50 mL
1 tsp	grated orange zest	5 mL
½ tsp	salt	2 mL
½ cup	whipping (35%) cream	125 mL
½ cup	orange-flavored liqueur	125 mL
4	egg whites	4

Decoration

Classic Whipped Cream Topping
(see recipe, page 262)

1. *Crust:* In a bowl, mix graham cracker crumbs and butter. Press into bottom of cheesecake pan and freeze.

2. *Filling:* In a mixer bowl fitted with paddle attachment, beat ricotta cheese, cream cheese and sugar on medium-high speed until very smooth, for 3 minutes. Add egg yolks, one at a time, beating after each addition. Stir in flour, orange zest, salt, whipping cream and orange liqueur. Set aside.

3. In a clean mixer bowl fitted with whip attachment, whip egg whites on medium-high speed until stiff but not dry peaks form. Fold into cream cheese mixture carefully so as not to deflate the mixture.

4. Pour over frozen crust, smoothing out to sides of pan. Bake in preheated oven until top is light brown and center has a slight jiggle to it, 45 to 55 minutes. Let cool in pan on a wire rack for 2 hours. Cover with plastic wrap and refrigerate for at least 6 hours before decorating or serving.

5. *Decoration:* Ice top of cake with Classic Whipped Cream Topping or pipe a ribbon around border, if desired.

Blood Orange Spiced Cheesecake

SERVES 10 TO 12

These deep red oranges make their way into farmers' markets in the winter months. I freeze the juice for later use.

Tips

I like to zest my oranges one day and juice them the next.

If you cannot find a blood orange, a navel orange is a good alternative, but the cheesecake will not be as sweet.

- Preheat oven to 350°F (180°C)
- 9-inch (23 cm) cheesecake pan, ungreased, or springform pan with 3-inch (7.5 cm) sides, greased

Crust

1¼ cups	butter cookie crumbs	300 mL
¼ cup	unsalted butter, melted	50 mL

Filling

3	packages (each 8 oz/250 g) cream cheese, softened	3
1 cup	sour cream	250 mL
1½ cups	packed brown sugar	375 mL
4	eggs	4
1 tbsp	grated blood orange zest	15 mL
⅓ cup	freshly squeezed blood orange juice	75 mL
2 tsp	ground star anise	10 mL
1 tsp	freshly grated nutmeg	5 mL

Decoration

	Classic Whipped Cream Topping (see recipe, page 262)	
1 tsp	grated blood orange zest	5 mL

1. *Crust:* In a bowl, combine cookie crumbs and butter. Press into bottom of cheesecake pan and freeze.
2. *Filling:* In a mixer bowl fitted with paddle attachment, beat cream cheese, sour cream and brown sugar on medium-high speed until very smooth, for 3 minutes. Add eggs, one at a time, beating after each addition. Stir in orange zest, orange juice, star anise and nutmeg.
3. Pour over frozen crust, smoothing out to sides of pan. Bake in preheated oven until top is light brown and center has a slight jiggle to it, 45 to 55 minutes. Let cool in pan on a wire rack for 2 hours. Cover with plastic wrap and refrigerate for at least 6 hours before decorating or serving.
4. *Decoration:* Ice top of cake with Classic Whipped Cream Topping or pipe rosettes around top of cake, if desired. Sprinkle with orange zest.

Blood Orange Cheesecake

Blood oranges are available in the winter. The outside skin is orange with red splotches. The fruit and juice are a deep red-orange color and very sweet.

Tips

Toasting brings out the natural oils and flavor of nuts. Place nuts in a single layer on a baking sheet and bake at 350°F (180°C) until fragrant, 10 to 12 minutes.

You can substitute a navel orange for the blood orange, but the cheesecake will not be as sweet.

If you find blood oranges, purchase a box and zest them one day and then juice them the next. The juice and zest can be frozen for up to 6 months.

- Preheat oven to 350°F (180°C)
- 9-inch (23 cm) cheesecake pan, ungreased, or springform pan with 3-inch (7.5 cm) sides, greased

Crust
1¼ cups	butter cookie crumbs	300 mL
¼ cup	pecans, toasted (see tip, at left) and ground	50 mL
3 tbsp	unsalted butter, melted	45 mL

Filling
3	packages (each 8 oz/250 g) cream cheese, softened	3
1½ cups	small-curd cottage cheese, drained (see tips, page 148)	375 mL
½ cup	sour cream	125 mL
1½ cups	granulated sugar	375 mL
4	eggs	4
¼ cup	all-purpose flour	50 mL
1 tbsp	grated blood orange zest	15 mL
⅓ cup	freshly squeezed blood orange juice	75 mL
1 tsp	freshly grated nutmeg	5 mL
1 tsp	vanilla extract	5 mL

Topping
½ cup	sour cream	125 mL
¼ cup	granulated sugar	50 mL
1 tbsp	grated blood orange zest	15 mL
2 tbsp	freshly squeezed blood orange juice	25 mL
½ tsp	vanilla extract	2 mL

Decoration
Classic Whipped Cream Topping (see recipe, page 262)

1. *Crust:* In a bowl, combine cookie crumbs, pecans and butter. Press into bottom of cheesecake pan and freeze.
2. *Filling:* In a mixer bowl fitted with paddle attachment, beat cream cheese, cottage cheese, sour cream and sugar on medium-high speed until very smooth, for 3 minutes. Add eggs, one at a time, beating after each addition. Stir in flour, orange zest, orange juice, nutmeg and vanilla.

3. Pour over frozen crust, smoothing out to sides of pan. Bake in preheated oven until top is light brown and center has a slight jiggle to it, 45 to 55 minutes. Let cool on the counter for 10 minutes (do not turn the oven off). The cake will sink slightly.

4. *Topping:* In a small bowl, combine sour cream, sugar, orange zest, orange juice and vanilla. Pour into center of cooled cake and spread out to edges. Bake for 5 minutes more. Let cool in pan on a wire rack for 2 hours. Cover with plastic wrap and refrigerate for at least 6 hours before decorating or serving.

5. *Decoration:* Ice top of cake with Classic Whipped Cream Topping or pipe rosettes around top of cake, if desired.

Mandarin Orange Cheesecake

SERVES 10 TO 12

This cheesecake is a great dessert after spicy Asian food.

Tips

Fresh mandarin oranges are usually available in November and December for the peak holiday baking season. Store in the refrigerator, as they spoil quickly, and wash well before zesting.

If you cannot find fresh mandarin oranges, you can use 1 can (10 oz/300 mL) mandarin orange segments, drained, and use a navel orange for the zest and juice.

- Preheat oven to 350°F (180°C)
- 9-inch (23 cm) cheesecake pan, ungreased, or springform pan with 3-inch (7.5 cm) sides, greased

Crust

1 cup	graham cracker crumbs	250 mL
¾ cup	almonds, toasted (see tip, page 120) and ground	175 mL
¼ cup	unsalted butter, melted	50 mL

Filling

3	packages (each 8 oz/250 g) cream cheese, softened	3
½ cup	unsalted butter, softened	125 mL
1 cup	granulated sugar	250 mL
4	eggs	4
½ cup	sour cream	125 mL
¼ cup	frozen orange juice concentrate, thawed	50 mL
1½ tbsp	grated orange zest, preferably mandarin	22 mL
1 tsp	vanilla extract	5 mL
3	small mandarin oranges, broken into segments	3

Topping

1½ cups	sour cream	375 mL
2 tbsp	granulated sugar	25 mL
2 tbsp	freshly squeezed orange juice, preferably mandarin	25 mL

Decoration

Classic Whipped Cream Topping (see recipe, page 262)

1. *Crust:* In a bowl, combine graham cracker crumbs, almonds and butter. Press into bottom of cheesecake pan and freeze.
2. *Filling:* In a mixer bowl fitted with paddle attachment, beat cream cheese, butter and sugar on medium-high speed until very smooth, for 3 minutes. Add eggs, one at a time, beating after each addition. Stir in sour cream, orange juice concentrate, orange zest and vanilla. Fold in orange segments by hand.

3. Pour over frozen crust, smoothing out to sides of pan. Bake in preheated oven until top is light brown and center has a slight jiggle to it, 45 to 55 minutes. Let cool on the counter for 10 minutes (do not turn the oven off). The cake will sink slightly.

4. *Topping:* In a small bowl, combine sour cream, sugar, and orange juice. Pour into center of cooled cake and spread out to edges. Bake for 5 minutes more. Let cool in pan on a wire rack for 2 hours. Cover with plastic wrap and refrigerate for at least 6 hours before decorating or serving.

5. *Decoration:* Ice top of cake with Classic Whipped Cream Topping or pipe rosettes around top of cake, if desired.

Tangerine (Clementine) Cheesecake

SERVES 10 TO 12

My Tampa, Florida, audience believes that Florida fruit has its own unique taste that is superior to fruit from other states. All I can say is, using fresh fruit in this cheesecake makes a big difference.

Tip

Drain tangerines on paper towels before decorating the cake.

- Preheat oven to 350°F (180°C)
- 9-inch (23 cm) cheesecake pan, ungreased, or springform pan with 3-inch (7.5 cm) sides, greased

Crust

1¼ cups	butter cookie crumbs	300 mL
¼ cup	unsalted butter, melted	50 mL

Filling

3	packages (each 8 oz/250 g) cream cheese, softened	3
1 cup	sour cream	250 mL
½ cup	orange-flavored yogurt	125 mL
1½ cups	packed brown sugar	375 mL
4	eggs	4
¾ cup	chopped tangerine (clementine) segments	175 mL
1 tsp	freshly grated nutmeg	5 mL
1 tsp	vanilla extract	5 mL

Decoration

	Classic Whipped Cream Topping (see recipe, page 262)	
3	tangerines, sliced	3

1. *Crust:* In a bowl, combine cookie crumbs and butter. Press into bottom of cheesecake pan and freeze.

2. *Filling:* In a mixer bowl fitted with paddle attachment, beat cream cheese, sour cream, yogurt and brown sugar on medium-high speed until very smooth, for 3 minutes. Add eggs, one at a time, beating after each addition. Fold in tangerine segments, nutmeg and vanilla by hand.

3. Pour over frozen crust, smoothing out to sides of pan. Bake in preheated oven until top is light brown and center has a slight jiggle to it, 45 to 55 minutes. Let cool in pan on a wire rack for 2 hours. Cover with plastic wrap and refrigerate for at least 6 hours before decorating or serving.

4. *Decoration:* Ice top of cake with Classic Whipped Cream Topping or pipe rosettes around top of cake, if desired. Arrange sliced tangerines in a spiral pattern on top.

Citrus Bliss Cheesecake

SERVES 10 TO 12

Tangy orange and lemon flavors come together in one sublime cheesecake.

Tips

Orange juice concentrate packs a powerful orange flavor that orange juice cannot match.

You'll need about 14 butter cookies (about 6 oz/175 g) to make 1½ cups (375 mL) crumbs.

To make this filling in a mixer instead of a food processor, follow the method for filling in Step 2 of Arizona Sunset Cheesecake (page 126). Proceed with Step 3.

Variation

For a spiced cheesecake, add 1 tsp (5 mL) ground cinnamon with the zest.

- Preheat oven to 325°F (160°C)
- 9-inch (23 cm) cheesecake pan or springform pan with 3-inch (7.5 cm) sides, lined with parchment paper

Crust

1½ cups	butter cookie crumbs	375 mL
¼ cup	unsalted butter, melted	50 mL

Filling

3	packages (each 8 oz/250 g) cream cheese, softened	3
1 cup	sour cream	250 mL
1 cup	granulated sugar	250 mL
4	eggs	4
1 tbsp	grated lemon zest	15 mL
1 tbsp	grated orange zest	15 mL
2 tbsp	freshly squeezed lemon juice	25 mL
2 tbsp	frozen orange juice concentrate, thawed (see tip, at left)	25 mL
2 tsp	vanilla extract	10 mL

1. *Crust:* In a bowl, combine cookie crumbs and butter. Press into bottom of cheesecake pan and freeze.

2. *Filling:* In a food processor fitted with a metal blade, process cream cheese, sour cream and sugar until smooth, about 20 seconds. With the motor running, through the feed tube, add eggs, lemon zest, orange zest, lemon juice, orange juice concentrate and vanilla; process until blended.

3. Pour over frozen crust, smoothing out to sides of pan. Bake in preheated oven until top is light brown and center has a slight jiggle to it, 45 to 55 minutes. Let cool in pan on a wire rack for 2 hours. Cover with plastic wrap and refrigerate for at least 2 hours before serving.

Arizona Sunset Cheesecake

SERVES 10 TO 12

Phoenix is my favorite city without a beach in which to watch wonderful sunsets. I created this recipe while observing the bright hues of orange and yellow over Camelback Mountain.

Tips

Toasting brings out the natural oils and flavor of nuts. Place nuts in a single layer on a baking sheet and bake at 350°F (180°C) until fragrant, 10 to 12 minutes.

Make sure the lemon curd is cool before incorporating it into the batter or the batter may curdle. Good-quality prepared lemon curd is now easy to find at specialty grocers and online vendors if you need to save time.

- Preheat oven to 350°F (180°C)
- 9-inch (23 cm) cheesecake pan, ungreased, or springform pan with 3-inch (7.5 cm) sides, greased

Crust

1¼ cups	butter cookie crumbs	300 mL
¼ cup	pecans, toasted (see tip, at left) and ground	50 mL
¼ cup	unsalted butter, melted	50 mL

Filling

3	packages (each 8 oz/250 g) cream cheese, softened	3
1 cup	sour cream	250 mL
1½ cups	granulated sugar	375 mL
4	eggs	4
1 cup	Fresh Lemon Curd (see recipe, page 265)	250 mL
1 tbsp	grated orange zest	15 mL
2 tsp	vanilla extract	10 mL

Topping

½ cup	sour cream	125 mL
¼ cup	granulated sugar	50 mL
1½ tsp	grated orange zest	7 mL
1½ tsp	grated lemon zest	7 mL
½ tsp	vanilla extract	2 mL

Decoration

	Classic Whipped Cream Topping (see recipe, page 262)	
1 tsp	grated orange zest	5 mL
2 tsp	crushed yellow hard candy	10 mL

1. *Crust:* In a bowl, combine cookie crumbs, pecans and butter. Press into bottom of cheesecake pan and freeze.
2. *Filling:* In a mixer bowl fitted with paddle attachment, beat cream cheese, sour cream and sugar on medium-high speed until very smooth, for 3 minutes. Add eggs, one at a time, beating after each addition. Stir in lemon curd, orange zest and vanilla.
3. Pour over frozen crust, smoothing out to sides of pan. Bake in preheated oven until top is light brown and center has a slight jiggle to it, 45 to 55 minutes. Let cool on the counter for 10 minutes (do not turn the oven off). The cake will sink slightly.

4. *Topping:* In a small bowl, combine sour cream, sugar, orange zest, lemon zest and vanilla. Pour into center of cooling cake and spread out to edges. Bake for 5 minutes more. Let cool in pan on a wire rack for 2 hours. Cover with plastic wrap and refrigerate for at least 6 hours before decorating or serving.

5. *Decoration:* Ice top of cake with Classic Whipped Cream Topping or pipe rosettes around top of cake, if desired. Sprinkle with orange zest and crushed candy.

Cassata Siciliana Cheesecake

SERVES 18 TO 20

I was bowled over by the citrus flavors of a signature gelato produced by Grom, which has seven retail shops in northern Italy. Lucky for all of us, the company is expanding to the New York area, bringing gourmet Italian gelato much closer to home.

Tips

If orange cookies are difficult to find, you can use butter cookies and add 1 tsp (5 mL) grated orange zest to the crust mixture.

Very fresh ricotta is important in this recipe. If you can't find it, omit the ricotta and increase the amount of cream cheese to 5 packages.

If you can't find orange blossom honey, infuse 10 oz (300 g) liquid honey with the zest of 1 orange for 3 weeks.

- Preheat oven to 350°F (180°C)
- 10-inch (25 cm) cheesecake pan, ungreased, or springform pan with 3-inch (7.5 cm) sides, greased

Crust

2½ cups	orange cookie crumbs	625 mL
½ cup	unsalted butter, melted	125 mL

Filling

3	packages (each 8 oz/250 g) cream cheese, softened	3
1 lb	ricotta cheese, drained (see tip, page 118)	500 g
2 cups	granulated sugar	500 mL
5	eggs	5
¼ cup	liquid orange blossom honey	50 mL
¼ cup	candied lemon peel	50 mL
¼ cup	candied orange peel	50 mL
1 tsp	grated orange zest	5 mL

Decoration

	Classic Whipped Cream Topping (see recipe, page 262)	
1 tsp	grated orange zest	5 mL

1. *Crust:* In a bowl, combine cookie crumbs and butter. Press into bottom of cheesecake pan and freeze.
2. *Filling:* In a mixer bowl fitted with paddle attachment, beat cream cheese, ricotta cheese and sugar on medium-high speed until very smooth, for 3 minutes. Add eggs, one at a time, beating after each addition. Fold in honey, lemon peel, orange peel and orange zest by hand.
3. Pour over frozen crust, smoothing out to sides of pan. Bake in preheated oven until top is light brown and center has a slight jiggle to it, 65 to 75 minutes. Let cool in pan on a wire rack for 2 hours. Cover with plastic wrap and refrigerate for at least 6 hours before decorating or serving.
4. *Decoration:* Pipe rosettes around top of cake with Classic Whipped Cream Topping. Sprinkle with orange zest.

Blood Orange Spiced Cheesecake (page 119)
Overleaf: Mandarin Orange Cheesecake (page 122)

Lemon Mist Cheesecake

SERVES 10 TO 12

Tart yet tangy, lemon cheesecake is refreshing with iced tea on a lazy afternoon.

Tips

If you can't find lemon cookies, you can use graham crackers and add ½ tsp (2 mL) lemon zest to the crust mixture.

You'll need about 14 lemon cookies (about 6 oz/175 g) to make 1½ cups (375 mL) crumbs.

To make this filling in a mixer instead of a food processor, follow the method for filling in Step 2 of Blue Ribbon Cheesecake (page 26), beating in lemon zest with juice. Proceed with Step 3.

- Preheat oven to 325°F (160°C)
- 9-inch (23 cm) cheesecake pan or springform pan with 3-inch (7.5 cm) sides, lined with parchment paper

Crust
1½ cups	lemon cookie crumbs	375 mL
¼ cup	unsalted butter, melted	50 mL

Filling
4	packages (each 8 oz/250 g) cream cheese, softened	4
1 cup	granulated sugar	250 mL
3	eggs	3
2 tbsp	grated lemon zest	25 mL
¼ cup	freshly squeezed lemon juice	50 mL
1 tsp	vanilla extract	5 mL

1. *Crust:* In a bowl, combine cookie crumbs and butter. Press into bottom of cheesecake pan and freeze.

2. *Filling:* In a food processor fitted with a metal blade, process cream cheese and sugar until smooth, about 20 seconds. With the motor running, through the feed tube, add eggs, lemon zest, lemon juice and vanilla; process until blended.

3. Pour over frozen crust, smoothing out to sides of pan. Bake in preheated oven until top is light brown and center has a slight jiggle to it, 45 to 55 minutes. Let cool in pan on a wire rack for 2 hours. Cover with plastic wrap and refrigerate for at least 6 hours before serving.

Overleaf: Lemon Soufflé Cheesecake (page 134)

Fresh Raspberry Hazelnut Cheesecake (page 153)

Lemon Curd Swirl Cheesecake

SERVES 10 TO 12

This used to be a favorite cheesecake among brides when I would create the special cake for their day.

Tip

Wash lemons well before zesting. To make lemons easier to juice, roll them firmly on the counter to break up the membranes of the fruit.

- Preheat oven to 325°F (160°C)
- 9-inch (23 cm) cheesecake pan, ungreased, or springform pan with 3-inch (7.5 cm) sides, greased

Crust

1½ cups	lemon cookie crumbs (see tips, page 129)	375 mL
¼ cup	unsalted butter, melted	50 mL

Filling

5	egg yolks	5
⅓ cup	granulated sugar	75 mL
2 tbsp	grated lemon zest	25 mL
5 tbsp	freshly squeezed lemon juice, divided	75 mL
¼ cup	unsalted butter, softened	50 mL
3	packages (each 8 oz/250 g) cream cheese, softened	3
¾ cup	granulated sugar	175 mL
3	eggs	3
1 tsp	vanilla extract	5 mL

Decoration

Classic Whipped Cream Topping (see recipe, page 262)

1. *Crust:* In a bowl, combine cookie crumbs and butter. Press into bottom of cheesecake pan and freeze.

2. *Filling:* Bring water to a simmer in the bottom of a double boiler. In the top of double boiler, away from heat, whisk egg yolks. Sprinkle sugar in while whisking. Pour in 4 tbsp (60 mL) of the lemon juice in a steady stream while whisking. Place top part of double boiler over the simmering water. Cook, stirring constantly, until thick, about 7 minutes. Whisk in butter. Set aside to cool in a bowl.

3. In a mixer bowl fitted with paddle attachment, beat cream cheese and sugar on medium-high speed until very smooth, for 3 minutes. Add whole eggs, one at a time, beating after each addition. Stir in lemon zest, the remaining lemon juice and vanilla. Reserve half the cooled lemon mixture for decoration. Swirl remaining half into batter.

4. Pour over frozen crust, smoothing out to sides of pan. Bake in preheated oven until top is light brown and center has a slight jiggle to it, 45 to 55 minutes. Let cool in pan on a wire rack for 2 hours. Cover with plastic wrap and refrigerate for at least 6 hours before decorating or serving.

5. *Decoration:* Pipe rosettes around top of cake with Classic Whipped Cream Topping. Fill center with remaining lemon mixture.

Meyer Lemon Cheesecake

SERVES 10 TO 12

Meyer lemons are found in Southern California and the south of France. A cross between a lemon and a mandarin orange, Meyers have a slight floral essence and delicate lemon flavor.

Tips

If you can't find Meyer lemons, mix equal parts orange and lemon zest and juice to try to approximate their sweet fragrance and flavor.

Treat yourself to a box of Meyer lemons and make zest and juice to keep handy in the freezer.

Variation

Top cake with fresh blueberries.

- Preheat oven to 325°F (160°C)
- 9-inch (23 cm) cheesecake pan, ungreased, or springform pan with 3-inch (7.5 cm) sides, greased

Crust

1½ cups	lemon cookie crumbs (see tips, page 129)	375 mL
¼ cup	unsalted butter, melted	50 mL

Filling

2	packages (each 8 oz/250 g) cream cheese, softened	2
¾ cup	granulated sugar	175 mL
3	eggs	3
2 tbsp	grated Meyer lemon zest	25 mL
2 tbsp	freshly squeezed Meyer lemon juice (see tip, at left)	25 mL
1 tsp	vanilla extract	5 mL

Topping

½ cup	sour cream	125 mL
¼ cup	granulated sugar	50 mL
1 tbsp	freshly squeezed Meyer lemon juice	15 mL
½ tsp	vanilla extract	2 mL

1. *Crust:* In a bowl, combine cookie crumbs and butter. Press into bottom of cheesecake pan and freeze.

2. *Filling:* In a mixer bowl fitted with paddle attachment, beat cream cheese and sugar on medium-high speed until very smooth, for 3 minutes. Add eggs, one at a time, beating after each addition. Stir in lemon zest, lemon juice and vanilla.

3. Pour over frozen crust, smoothing out to sides of pan. Bake in preheated oven until top is light brown and center has a slight jiggle to it, 45 to 55 minutes. Let cool on the counter for 10 minutes (do not turn the oven off). The cake will sink slightly.

4. *Topping:* In a small bowl, combine sour cream, sugar, lemon juice and vanilla. Pour into center of cooled cake and spread out to edges. Bake for 5 minutes more. Let cool in pan on a wire rack for 2 hours. Cover with plastic wrap and refrigerate for at least 6 hours before serving.

Lemon Meringue Cheesecake

SERVES 10 TO 12

My sister Monica never wanted a cake for her birthday. She always asked for Lemon Meringue Pie, which inspired this recipe. It's just like the pie, but it's a cheesecake!

Tips

Toasting brings out the natural oils and flavor of nuts. Place nuts in a single layer on a baking sheet and bake at 350°F (180°C) until fragrant, 10 to 12 minutes.

Room temperature egg whites yield a much higher volume than cold whites.

You can use a kitchen torch instead of the oven to brown the meringue.

- Preheat oven to 350°F (180°C)
- 9-inch (23 cm) cheesecake pan, ungreased, or springform pan with 3-inch (7.5 cm) sides, greased

Crust

1	package (6 oz/175 g) flaked sweetened coconut, toasted (see tip, page 135)	1
¼ cup	pecans, toasted (see tip, at left) and ground	50 mL
3 tbsp	unsalted butter, melted	45 mL

Filling

2	packages (each 8 oz/250 g) cream cheese, softened	2
⅓ cup	granulated sugar	75 mL
3	egg yolks	3
¼ cup	freshly squeezed lemon juice	50 mL
1 tsp	vanilla extract	5 mL

Topping

3	egg whites	3
Pinch	salt	Pinch
1	jar (7 oz/198 g) marshmallow cream (fluff)	1
½ cup	pecans, toasted and chopped	125 mL

1. *Crust:* In a bowl, combine coconut, ground pecans and butter. Press into bottom of cheesecake pan and freeze.
2. *Filling:* In a mixer bowl fitted with paddle attachment, beat cream cheese and sugar on medium-high speed until very smooth, for 3 minutes. Add eggs yolks, one at a time, beating after each addition. Mix in lemon juice and vanilla.
3. Pour over frozen crust, smoothing out to sides of pan. Bake in preheated oven until top is light brown and center has a slight jiggle to it, 40 to 50 minutes. Let cool in pan on a wire rack while you prepare the topping. Position oven rack as far away from heat source as possible. Set the oven to broil.
4. *Topping:* In a clean mixer bowl fitted with whip attachment, whip egg whites and salt on medium speed until foamy. Gradually add marshmallow cream, beating until stiff peaks form. Sprinkle top of cake with chopped pecans. Spread marshmallow mixture on top of pecans. Place on lowest oven rack and broil until meringue is light brown.

South of France Lemon Cheesecake

SERVES 10 TO 12

This is the simplest cheesecake ever! You don't even need to bring out a mixer. It reminds me of my annual tours of Provence.

Tips

It is very important to drain the ricotta overnight. Otherwise, you will have too much liquid.

This cheesecake has quite a different texture from the others in this book. Don't look for doneness by browning or a jiggly center.

Make a dessert cheese course by serving fresh fruit on the side.

- Preheat oven to 300°F (150°C)
- 9-inch (23 cm) cheesecake pan or springform pan with 3-inch (7.5 cm) sides, lined with parchment paper

2 lbs	ricotta cheese, drained (see tip, page 118)	1 kg
2/3 cup	granulated sugar	150 mL
1/3 cup	all-purpose flour	75 mL
6	eggs	6
2 tsp	grated orange zest	10 mL
2 tsp	grated lemon zest	10 mL
1 tbsp	freshly squeezed lemon juice	15 mL
1/4 tsp	ground cinnamon	1 mL
2 tsp	vanilla extract	10 mL

1. In a large bowl, stir ricotta cheese with a rubber spatula until creamy. Stir in sugar and flour until blended. Add eggs, one at a time, stirring after each addition. Stir in orange zest, lemon zest, lemon juice, cinnamon and vanilla.

2. Pour into prepared pan, smoothing out to sides of pan. Bake in preheated oven until tip of knife inserted in center comes out clean, 75 to 90 minutes. Let cool in pan on a wire rack for 2 hours. Cover with plastic wrap and refrigerate for at least 6 hours before serving.

Lemon Soufflé Cheesecake

*While dining in
Los Angeles at Ciudad,
I had a wonderful
cheesecake that was so
light and airy, I had to
create my own version
in homage to Chefs
Mary Sue Milliken
and Susan Feniger.*

Tips

Room temperature egg
whites yield a much
higher volume than
cold whites.

Save extra egg yolks
in a small bowl in the
refrigerator for up to
2 days by covering them
with water and sealing
tightly with plastic wrap.
To freeze, sprinkle salt
or sugar over the yolks
in water.

- Preheat oven to 325°F (160°C)
- 9-inch (23 cm) cheesecake pan, ungreased, or springform pan with 3-inch (7.5 cm) sides, greased

Crust

1½ cups	butter cookie crumbs	375 mL
¼ cup	unsalted butter, melted	50 mL

Filling

4	packages (each 8 oz/250 g) cream cheese, softened	4
½ cup	sour cream	125 mL
1½ cups	granulated sugar	375 mL
4	egg yolks	4
1 tbsp	grated lemon zest	15 mL
3 tbsp	freshly squeezed lemon juice	45 mL
1½ tsp	vanilla extract	7 mL
6	egg whites	6
¼ tsp	cream of tartar	1 mL

Decoration

¼ cup	confectioner's (icing) sugar	50 mL

1. *Crust:* In a bowl, combine cookie crumbs and butter. Press into bottom of cheesecake pan and freeze.

2. *Filling:* In a mixer bowl fitted with paddle attachment, beat cream cheese, sour cream and sugar on medium-high speed until very smooth, for 3 minutes. Add egg yolks, one at a time, beating after each addition. Stir in lemon zest, lemon juice and vanilla. Set aside.

3. In a clean mixer bowl fitted with whip attachment, whip egg whites and cream of tartar on low speed for 1 minute. Increase speed to medium-high and whip until stiff but not dry peaks form. Fold into cream cheese mixture carefully so as not to deflate the mixture.

4. Pour over frozen crust, smoothing out to sides of pan. Bake in preheated oven until top is light brown and center has a slight jiggle to it, 45 to 55 minutes. Let cool in pan on a wire rack for 2 hours. Cover with plastic wrap and refrigerate for at least 6 hours before decorating or serving.

5. *Decoration:* Using a sugar dredger or flour sifter, dust top of cake with confectioner's sugar.

Lemon Lime Cheesecake

SERVES 8 TO 10

Double citrus flavors make this cake a refreshing dessert on a hot day.

Tip

Coconut is often burned by pastry chefs. To avoid crying over burnt coconut, follow this technique. Spread coconut in a single layer on a baking sheet. Bake in a 350°F (180°C) oven for 3 minutes. Check the coconut and stir. Set the timer for another 3 minutes. Repeat until coconut is lightly browned.

Variation

Replace the lime oil with grapefruit oil.

- Preheat oven to 350°F (180°C)
- 8-inch (20 cm) cheesecake pan, ungreased, or springform pan with 3-inch (7.5 cm) sides, greased

Crust

1 cup	graham cracker crumbs	250 mL
¼ cup	flaked sweetened coconut, toasted (see tip, at left)	50 mL
¼ cup	unsalted butter, melted	50 mL

Filling

2	packages (each 8 oz/250 g) cream cheese, softened	2
½ cup	vanilla-flavored yogurt	125 mL
1 cup	granulated sugar	250 mL
3	eggs	3
1 cup	Fresh Lemon Curd (see recipe, page 265)	250 mL
1 tbsp	grated lime zest	15 mL
1 tsp	lime oil (see page 19)	5 mL
1 tsp	vanilla extract	5 mL

Decoration

	Classic Whipped Cream Topping (see recipe, page 262)	
1 cup	Fresh Lemon Curd	250 mL
½ tsp	grated lemon zest	2 mL
½ tsp	grated lime zest	2 mL

1. *Crust:* In a bowl, combine graham cracker crumbs, coconut and butter. Press into bottom of cheesecake pan and freeze.

2. *Filling:* In a mixer bowl fitted with paddle attachment, beat cream cheese, yogurt and sugar on medium-high speed until very smooth, for 3 minutes. Add eggs, one at a time, beating after each addition. Stir in lemon curd, lime zest, lime oil and vanilla.

3. Pour over frozen crust, smoothing out to sides of pan. Bake in preheated oven until top is light brown and center has a slight jiggle to it, 35 to 45 minutes. Let cool in pan on a wire rack for 2 hours. Cover with plastic wrap and refrigerate for at least 6 hours before decorating or serving.

4. *Decoration:* Pipe rosettes around top of cake with Classic Whipped Cream Topping. Fill center with lemon curd and sprinkle with lemon and lime zests.

Citrus Daiquiri Cheesecake

SERVES 10 TO 12

What a great way to enjoy the tart taste of lemons and limes! Lucky me, I get to pick the fruit from the trees in my backyard whenever I need them.

Tips

Zest lemons and limes before juicing.

To save time, purchase shelled pistachios. Shelled pistachios can be stored in the refrigerator for up to 3 months, but are not a good candidate for freezing. The more economical unshelled nuts can be stored for 3 months in the refrigerator or for up to 1 year in the freezer. Buy green pistachios, not the dyed red ones.

- Preheat oven to 350°F (180°C)
- 9-inch (23 cm) cheesecake pan, ungreased, or springform pan with 3-inch (7.5 cm) sides, greased

Crust

1 cup	graham cracker crumbs	250 mL
¼ cup	pistachios, ground	50 mL
¼ cup	unsalted butter, melted	50 mL

Filling

4	packages (each 8 oz/250 g) cream cheese, softened	4
1 cup	granulated sugar	250 mL
4	eggs	4
¼ cup	rum	50 mL
2 tsp	grated lime zest	10 mL
2 tsp	grated lemon zest	10 mL
3 tbsp	freshly squeezed lime juice	45 mL
2 tbsp	freshly squeezed lemon juice	25 mL
1 tbsp	cornstarch	15 mL

Topping

½ cup	sour cream	125 mL
1½ tbsp	granulated sugar	22 mL
½ tsp	grated lime zest	2 mL
½ tsp	grated lemon zest	2 mL

Decoration

⅓ cup	pistachios, chopped	75 mL

1. *Crust:* In a bowl, combine graham cracker crumbs, ground pistachios and butter. Press into bottom of cheesecake pan and freeze.

2. *Filling:* In a mixer bowl fitted with paddle attachment, beat cream cheese and sugar on medium-high speed until very smooth, for 3 minutes. Add eggs, one at a time, beating after each addition. Stir in rum, lime zest, lemon zest, lime juice, lemon juice and cornstarch.

You can use ¼ tsp (1 mL) rum extract instead of the rum. A non-alcoholic substitute for the rum is frozen orange juice concentrate.

3. Pour over frozen crust, smoothing out to sides of pan. Bake in preheated oven until top is light brown and center has a slight jiggle to it, 45 to 55 minutes. Let cool on the counter for 10 minutes (do not turn the oven off). The cake will sink slightly.

4. *Topping:* In a bowl, combine sour cream, sugar, lime zest and lemon zest. Pour into center of cooled cake and spread out to edges. Bake for 5 minutes more. Let cool in pan on a wire rack for 2 hours. Cover with plastic wrap and refrigerate for at least 6 hours before decorating or serving.

5. *Decoration:* Sprinkle chopped pistachios in a 1-inch (2.5 cm) border around top of cake.

Florida Key Lime Cheesecake

SERVES 10 TO 12

Key limes are very small, about half the size of the most common Persian variety.

Tips

Key limes are sometimes difficult to find in local grocery stores. If they are unavailable, substitute half Persian lime juice and half lemon juice for the amount of juice called for in the recipe and use Persian lime zest.

A thin, twisted slice of lime makes an easy, pretty garnish for a last-minute touch.

- Preheat oven to 325°F (160°C)
- 9-inch (23 cm) cheesecake pan, ungreased, or springform pan with 3-inch (7.5 cm) sides, greased

Crust

1½ cups	butter cookie crumbs	375 mL
¼ cup	unsalted butter, melted	50 mL

Filling

4	packages (each 8 oz/250 g) cream cheese, softened	4
1½ cups	granulated sugar	375 mL
2	eggs	2
2	egg yolks	2
1 tbsp	grated Key lime zest	15 mL
¼ cup	freshly squeezed Key lime juice	50 mL
1 tsp	vanilla extract	5 mL

Topping

½ cup	sour cream	125 mL
¼ cup	granulated sugar	50 mL
1 tsp	grated Key lime zest	5 mL
1 tbsp	freshly squeezed Key lime juice	15 mL
½ tsp	vanilla extract	2 mL

1. *Crust:* In a bowl, combine cookie crumbs and butter. Press into bottom of cheesecake pan and freeze.
2. *Filling:* In a mixer bowl fitted with paddle attachment, beat cream cheese and sugar on medium-high speed until very smooth, for 3 minutes. Add whole eggs and egg yolks, one at a time, beating after each addition. Stir in lime zest, lime juice and vanilla.
3. Pour over frozen crust, smoothing out to sides of pan. Bake in preheated oven until top is light brown and center has a slight jiggle to it, 45 to 55 minutes. Let cool on the counter for 10 minutes (do not turn the oven off). The cake will sink slightly.
4. *Topping:* In a bowl, combine sour cream, sugar, lime zest, lime juice and vanilla. Pour into center of cooled cake and spread out to edges. Bake for 5 minutes more. Let cool in pan on a wire rack for 2 hours. Cover with plastic wrap and refrigerate for at least 6 hours before serving.

Lime Curd Cheesecake

SERVES 10 TO 12

The tart lime paired with the sweet filling creates a refreshing taste for a spring dessert.

Tip

Extra egg whites can be stored in the refrigerator for up to 4 days or frozen for up to 6 months.

- Preheat oven to 325°F (160°C)
- 9-inch (23 cm) cheesecake pan, ungreased, or springform pan with 3-inch (7.5 cm) sides, greased

Crust

1½ cups	butter cookie crumbs	375 mL
¼ cup	unsalted butter, melted	50 mL

Filling

5	egg yolks	5
⅓ cup	granulated sugar	75 mL
2 tbsp	grated lime zest	25 mL
5 tbsp	freshly squeezed lime juice, divided	75 mL
¼ cup	unsalted butter, softened	50 mL
3	packages (each 8 oz/250 g) cream cheese, softened	3
¾ cup	granulated sugar	175 mL
3	eggs	3
1 tsp	vanilla extract	5 mL

Decoration

Classic Whipped Cream Topping
(see recipe, page 262)

1. *Crust:* In a bowl, combine cookie crumbs and butter. Press into bottom of cheesecake pan and freeze.

2. *Filling:* Bring water to a simmer in the bottom of a double boiler. In the top of double boiler, away from heat, whisk egg yolks. Sprinkle sugar in while whisking. Pour in 4 tbsp (60 mL) of the lime juice in a steady stream while whisking. Place top part of double boiler over the simmering water. Cook, stirring constantly, until thick, about 7 minutes. Whisk in butter. Set aside to cool in a bowl.

3. In a mixer bowl fitted with paddle attachment, beat cream cheese and sugar on medium-high speed until very smooth, for 3 minutes. Add whole eggs, one at a time, beating after each addition. Stir in lime zest, the remaining lime juice and vanilla. Reserve half of the cooled lime mixture for decoration. Swirl remaining half into batter.

4. Pour over frozen crust, smoothing out to sides of pan. Bake in preheated oven until top is light brown and center has a slight jiggle to it, 45 to 55 minutes. Let cool in pan on a wire rack for 2 hours. Cover with plastic wrap and refrigerate for at least 6 hours before decorating or serving.

5. *Decoration:* Pipe rosettes around top of cake with Classic Whipped Cream Topping. Fill center with remaining lime mixture.

Lime Soufflé Cheesecake

SERVES 10 TO 12

The lime flavor is very aromatic, both tart and sweet all at once.

Tips

Room temperature egg whites yield a much higher volume than cold whites.

Save extra egg yolks in a small bowl in the refrigerator for up to 2 days by covering them with water and sealing tightly with plastic wrap. To freeze, sprinkle salt or sugar over the yolks in water.

- Preheat oven to 325°F (160°C)
- 9-inch (23 cm) cheesecake pan, ungreased, or springform pan with 3-inch (7.5 cm) sides, greased

Crust

1½ cups	butter cookie crumbs	375 mL
¼ cup	unsalted butter, melted	50 mL

Filling

4	packages (each 8 oz/250 g) cream cheese, softened	4
½ cup	sour cream	125 mL
1½ cups	granulated sugar	375 mL
4	egg yolks	4
1 tbsp	grated lime zest	15 mL
2 tbsp	freshly squeezed lime juice	25 mL
1½ tsp	vanilla extract	7 mL
6	egg whites	6
¼ tsp	cream of tartar	1 mL

Decoration

¼ cup	confectioner's (icing) sugar	50 mL

1. *Crust:* In a bowl, combine cookie crumbs and butter. Press into bottom of cheesecake pan and freeze.

2. *Filling:* In a mixer bowl fitted with paddle attachment, beat cream cheese, sour cream and sugar on medium-high speed until very smooth, for 3 minutes. Add egg yolks, one at a time, beating after each addition. Stir in lime zest, lime juice and vanilla. Set aside.

3. In a clean mixer bowl fitted with whip attachment, whip egg whites and cream of tartar on low speed for 1 minute. Increase speed to medium-high and whip until stiff but not dry peaks form. Fold into cream cheese mixture carefully so as not to deflate the mixture.

4. Pour over frozen crust, smoothing out to sides of pan. Bake in preheated oven until top is light brown and center has a slight jiggle to it, 45 to 55 minutes. Let cool in pan on a wire rack for 2 hours. Cover with plastic wrap and refrigerate for at least 6 hours before decorating or serving.

5. *Decoration:* Using a sugar dredger or flour sifter, dust top of cake with confectioner's sugar.

Nut Cheesecakes

Peanut Butter Cheesecake

SERVES 10 TO 12

My mom is such a fan of my cheesecakes that she hoards them. Once, at a party, she took the first bite and said, "I'm taking the rest home with me."

Tip

Natural peanut butters have too much oil for this recipe.

Variation

Omit the sour cream topping and sprinkle the top of the cooled cake with ½ cup (125 mL) semisweet chocolate chips.

- Preheat oven to 350°F (180°C)
- 9-inch (23 cm) cheesecake pan, ungreased, or springform pan with 3-inch (7.5 cm) sides, greased

Crust

1½ cups	peanut butter sandwich cookie crumbs	375 mL
¼ cup	dry-roasted peanuts, crushed	50 mL
¼ cup	all-purpose flour	50 mL
¼ cup	unsalted butter, melted	50 mL

Filling

3	packages (each 8 oz/250 g) cream cheese, softened	3
1 cup	sour cream	250 mL
¼ cup	creamy peanut butter	50 mL
1½ cups	granulated sugar	375 mL
4	eggs	4
1 tsp	vanilla extract	5 mL

Topping

½ cup	sour cream	125 mL
¼ cup	granulated sugar	50 mL
¼ cup	creamy peanut butter	50 mL
1 tbsp	freshly squeezed lemon juice	15 mL
½ tsp	vanilla extract	2 mL
¼ cup	dry-roasted peanuts	50 mL

1. *Crust:* In a bowl, combine cookie crumbs, peanuts, flour and butter. Press into bottom of cheesecake pan and freeze.

2. *Filling:* In a mixer bowl fitted with paddle attachment, beat cream cheese, sour cream, peanut butter and sugar on medium-high speed until very smooth, for 3 minutes. Add eggs, one at a time, beating after each addition. Mix in vanilla.

3. Pour over frozen crust, smoothing out to sides of pan. Bake in preheated oven until top is light brown and center has a slight jiggle to it, 45 to 55 minutes. Let cool on the counter for 10 minutes (do not turn the oven off). The cake will sink slightly.

4. *Topping:* In a small bowl, combine sour cream, sugar, peanut butter, lemon juice and vanilla. Pour into center of cooled cake and spread out to edges. Sprinkle top with peanuts. Bake for 5 minutes more. Let cool in pan on a wire rack for 2 hours. Cover with plastic wrap and refrigerate for at least 6 hours before serving.

Peanut Brittle Cheesecake

SERVES 10 TO 12

Your guests will always ask, "What kind of crunchy peanuts are in this cheesecake?" Never tell.

Tip
Use fresh peanut brittle, which is easy to find at holiday time.

Variation
If you can find other brittle, such as almond or macadamia, use it by all means.

- Preheat oven to 350°F (180°C)
- 9-inch (23 cm) cheesecake pan, ungreased, or springform pan with 3-inch (7.5 cm) sides, greased

Crust

1½ cups	butter cookie crumbs	375 mL
¼ cup	unsalted butter, melted	50 mL

Filling

4	packages (each 8 oz/250 g) cream cheese, softened	4
1¼ cups	granulated sugar	300 mL
4	eggs	4
1 cup	sour cream	250 mL
¼ cup	all-purpose flour	50 mL
1 tbsp	vanilla extract	15 mL
3 oz	peanut brittle, crushed into bite-size pieces	90 g

Decoration

	Classic Whipped Cream Topping (see recipe, page 262)	
3 oz	peanut brittle, crushed into bite-size pieces	90 g

1. *Crust:* In a bowl, combine cookie crumbs and butter. Press into bottom of cheesecake pan and freeze.

2. *Filling:* In a mixer bowl fitted with paddle attachment, beat cream cheese and sugar on medium-high speed until very smooth, for 3 minutes. Add eggs, one at a time, beating after each addition. Stir in sour cream, flour and vanilla. Fold in peanut brittle by hand.

3. Pour over frozen crust, smoothing out to sides of pan. Bake in preheated oven until top is light brown and center has a slight jiggle to it, 45 to 55 minutes. Let cool in pan on a wire rack for 2 hours. Cover with plastic wrap and refrigerate for at least 6 hours before decorating or serving.

4. *Decoration:* Ice top of cake with Classic Whipped Cream Topping or pipe rosettes around top of cake, if desired. Top with pieces of peanut brittle.

Buckeye Cheesecake

SERVES 10 TO 12

I was introduced to buckeyes, great chocolate candies packed with peanut butter, on my first teaching trip to Ohio. They inspired this cheesecake.

Tips

To melt chocolate in the microwave, break into squares and place in a microwave-safe dish. Microwave on High for 1 to 2 minutes, stirring the mixture after 30 seconds.

To make lemons easier to juice, roll them firmly on the counter to break up the membranes of the fruit.

- Preheat oven to 350°F (180°C)
- 9-inch (23 cm) cheesecake pan, ungreased, or springform pan with 3-inch (7.5 cm) sides, greased

Crust
1½ cups	peanut butter sandwich cookie crumbs	375 mL
¼ cup	all-purpose flour	50 mL
¼ cup	unsalted butter, melted	50 mL

Filling
4 oz	bittersweet chocolate, chopped	125 g
¼ cup	creamy peanut butter	50 mL
3	packages (each 8 oz/250 g) cream cheese, softened	3
1 cup	sour cream	250 mL
1½ cups	granulated sugar	375 mL
4	eggs	4
1 tsp	vanilla extract	5 mL

Topping
½ cup	sour cream	125 mL
¼ cup	granulated sugar	50 mL
¼ cup	creamy peanut butter	50 mL
1 tbsp	freshly squeezed lemon juice	15 mL
½ tsp	vanilla extract	2 mL

1. *Crust:* In a bowl, combine cookie crumbs, flour and butter. Press into bottom of cheesecake pan and freeze.
2. *Filling:* Melt chocolate in the top of a double boiler over hot, not boiling water. When fully melted, add peanut butter and stir until blended. Set aside to cool slightly.
3. In a mixer bowl fitted with paddle attachment, beat cream cheese, sour cream and sugar on medium-high speed until very smooth, for 3 minutes. Add eggs, one at a time, beating after each addition. Mix in vanilla. Swirl in melted chocolate mixture.

4. Pour over frozen crust, smoothing out to sides of pan. Bake in preheated oven until top is light brown and center has a slight jiggle to it, 45 to 55 minutes. Let cool on the counter for 10 minutes (do not turn the oven off). The cake will sink slightly.

5. *Topping:* In a small bowl, combine sour cream, sugar, peanut butter, lemon juice and vanilla. Pour into center of cooled cake and spread out to edges. Bake for 5 minutes more. Let cool in pan on a wire rack for 2 hours. Cover with plastic wrap and refrigerate for at least 6 hours before serving.

Creamy Peanut Cheesecake

SERVES 10 TO 12

This cheesecake has a double hit of flavor, with dry-roasted peanuts and creamy peanut butter for perfect balance.

Tips

If the cottage cheese has a wet look to it, drain it through a fine-mesh sieve. Too much moisture will change the texture of the cheesecake.

If small-curd cottage cheese is not available, purée cottage cheese in a food processor before adding to the cream cheese.

- Preheat oven to 350°F (180°C)
- 9-inch (23 cm) cheesecake pan, ungreased, or springform pan with 3-inch (7.5 cm) sides, greased

Crust

1½ cups	peanut butter sandwich cookie crumbs	375 mL
¼ cup	all-purpose flour	50 mL
¼ cup	unsalted butter, melted	50 mL

Filling

4	packages (each 8 oz/250 g) cream cheese, softened	4
1 cup	small-curd cottage cheese, drained (see tips, at left)	250 mL
1¼ cups	granulated sugar	300 mL
1 cup	creamy peanut butter	250 mL
4	eggs	4
3 tbsp	freshly squeezed lemon juice	45 mL
1 tsp	vanilla extract	5 mL
1 cup	dry-roasted peanuts, chopped	250 mL

Topping

½ cup	sour cream	125 mL
¼ cup	granulated sugar	50 mL
¼ cup	creamy peanut butter	50 mL
1 tbsp	freshly squeezed lemon juice	15 mL
½ tsp	vanilla extract	2 mL

Decoration

Classic Whipped Cream Topping (see recipe, page 262)

1. *Crust:* In a bowl, combine cookie crumbs, flour and butter. Press into bottom of cheesecake pan and freeze.
2. *Filling:* In a mixer bowl fitted with paddle attachment, beat cream cheese, cottage cheese and sugar on medium-high speed until very smooth, for 3 minutes. Beat in peanut butter on medium-high speed for 2 minutes. Add eggs, one at a time, beating after each addition. Mix in lemon juice and vanilla. Fold in peanuts by hand.

Tip

To make lemons easier to juice, roll them firmly on the counter to break up the membranes of the fruit.

3. Pour over frozen crust, smoothing out to sides of pan. Bake in preheated oven until top is light brown and center has a slight jiggle to it, 45 to 55 minutes. Let cool on the counter for 10 minutes (do not turn the oven off). The cake will sink slightly.

4. *Topping:* In a small bowl, combine sour cream, sugar, peanut butter, lemon juice and vanilla. Pour into center of cooled cake and spread out to edges. Bake for 5 minutes more. Let cool in pan on a wire rack for 2 hours. Cover with plastic wrap and refrigerate for at least 6 hours before decorating or serving.

5. *Decoration:* Ice top of cake with Classic Whipped Cream Topping or pipe rosettes around top of cake, if desired.

Butter Toffee Peanut Cheesecake

SERVES 10 TO 12

When I was about seven years old, I used to sell cans of butter toffee peanuts to raise money for my baseball team. I was an excellent salesman, selling cases and cases of them. Now they are easily found in the grocery store.

Tip

When making cookie crumbs, you do not have to scrape the cream filling out of the cookies; just place them whole into the food processor and pulse.

- Preheat oven to 350°F (180°C)
- 9-inch (23 cm) cheesecake pan, ungreased, or springform pan with 3-inch (7.5 cm) sides, greased

Crust

1¼ cups	peanut butter sandwich cookie crumbs	300 mL
¼ cup	unsalted butter, melted	50 mL

Filling

4	packages (each 8 oz/250 g) cream cheese, softened	4
1½ cups	granulated sugar	375 mL
½ cup	creamy peanut butter	125 mL
3	eggs	3
2	egg yolks	2
1 cup	butter toffee peanuts, crushed	250 mL
1 tsp	vanilla extract	5 mL

Decoration

	Classic Whipped Cream Topping (see recipe, page 262)	
¼ cup	butter toffee peanuts, crushed	50 mL

1. *Crust:* In a bowl, combine cookie crumbs and butter. Press into bottom of cheesecake pan and freeze.

2. *Filling:* In a mixer bowl fitted with paddle attachment, beat cream cheese and sugar on medium-high speed until very smooth, for 3 minutes. Beat in peanut butter on medium-high speed for 2 minutes. Add whole eggs and egg yolks, one at a time, beating after each addition. Fold in butter toffee peanuts and vanilla by hand.

3. Pour over frozen crust, smoothing out to sides of pan. Bake in preheated oven until top is light brown and center has a slight jiggle to it, 45 to 55 minutes. Let cool in pan on a wire rack for 2 hours. Cover with plastic wrap and refrigerate for at least 6 hours before decorating or serving.

4. *Decoration:* Ice top of cake with Classic Whipped Cream Topping or pipe rosettes around top of cake, if desired. Sprinkle with butter toffee peanuts.

Toasted Almond Cheesecake

SERVES 10 TO 12

Here's the perfect cheesecake for almond lovers. It has layers of almond flavor in the crust, filling and decoration.

Tip

To quickly prepare cookie crumbs, place whole cookies in a food processor fitted with a metal blade and pulse a few times. You can add the butter to the food processor and pulse until blended. When mixed with the butter, the crumbs should feel like wet sand.

Variation

An orange-flavored liqueur is a good flavor accent to the almonds in place of the almond-flavored liqueur.

- Preheat oven to 350ºF (180ºC)
- 9-inch (23 cm) cheesecake pan, ungreased, or springform pan with 3-inch (7.5 cm) sides, greased

Crust

1½ cups	almond cookie crumbs	375 mL
¼ cup	unsalted butter, melted	50 mL

Filling

2 tbsp	instant coffee powder or granules	25 mL
1 tbsp	hot water	15 mL
4	packages (each 8 oz/250 g) cream cheese, softened	4
1¼ cups	granulated sugar	300 mL
4	eggs	4
½ cup	almonds, toasted (see tip, page 158) and chopped	125 mL
3 tbsp	almond-flavored liqueur	45 mL
1 tsp	vanilla extract	5 mL

Decoration

	Classic Whipped Cream Topping (see recipe, page 262)	
12	whole almonds, toasted	12

1. *Crust:* In a bowl, combine cookie crumbs and butter. Press into bottom of cheesecake pan and freeze.
2. *Filling:* In a small bowl, dissolve coffee powder in hot water. Set aside.
3. In a mixer bowl fitted with paddle attachment, beat cream cheese and sugar on medium-high speed until very smooth, for 3 minutes. Add eggs, one at a time, beating after each addition. With the mixer running, pour in coffee in a steady stream. Fold in chopped almonds, liqueur and vanilla by hand.
4. Pour over frozen crust, smoothing out to sides of pan. Bake in preheated oven until top is light brown and center has a slight jiggle to it, 45 to 55 minutes. Let cool in pan on a wire rack for 2 hours. Cover with plastic wrap and refrigerate for at least 6 hours before decorating or serving.
5. *Decoration:* Ice top of cake with Classic Whipped Cream Topping or pipe rosettes around top of cake, if desired. Top with whole almonds.

Kentucky Almond Bourbon Cheesecake

SERVES 10 TO 12

Kentucky, home of the Kentucky Derby and flavorful bourbons served in sterling silver cups, inspired this charming cheesecake with a sweet almond crunch.

Tip

Save time by purchasing blanched (skinless) almonds to toast. Save money by purchasing them with the skins on; the skins can be removed by rubbing the almonds in a dish towel while they're still hot from toasting.

Variation

Pecans also go well with Kentucky flavors.

- Preheat oven to 350°F (180°C)
- 9-inch (23 cm) cheesecake pan, ungreased, or springform pan with 3-inch (7.5 cm) sides, greased

Crust

1½ cups	almonds, toasted (see tip, page 158) and ground	375 mL
¼ cup	all-purpose flour	50 mL
¼ cup	unsalted butter, melted	50 mL

Filling

4	packages (each 8 oz/250 g) cream cheese, softened	4
1¼ cups	granulated sugar	300 mL
2	eggs	2
3	egg yolks	3
1 cup	almonds, toasted and chopped	250 mL
3 tbsp	Kentucky bourbon	45 mL
1 tsp	vanilla extract	5 mL

Decoration

Classic Whipped Cream Topping (see recipe, page 262)

1. *Crust:* In a bowl, combine ground almonds, flour and butter. Press into bottom of cheesecake pan and freeze.

2. *Filling:* In a mixer bowl fitted with paddle attachment, beat cream cheese and sugar on medium-high speed until very smooth, for 3 minutes. Add whole eggs and egg yolks, one at a time, beating after each addition. Fold in chopped almonds, bourbon and vanilla by hand.

3. Pour over frozen crust, smoothing out to sides of pan. Bake in preheated oven until top is light brown and center has a slight jiggle to it, 45 to 55 minutes. Let cool in pan on a wire rack for 2 hours. Cover with plastic wrap and refrigerate for at least 6 hours before decorating or serving.

4. *Decoration:* Ice top of cake with Classic Whipped Cream Topping or pipe rosettes around top of cake, if desired.

Honey Cashew Cheesecake

SERVES 10 TO 12

I adore the sweetness and the crunch of honey cashews and can eat an entire bag at one sitting. No surprise, they make a fabulous cheesecake.

Tip

Extra egg whites can be stored in the refrigerator for up to 4 days or frozen for up to 6 months.

- Preheat oven to 350°F (180°C)
- 9-inch (23 cm) cheesecake pan, ungreased, or springform pan with 3-inch (7.5 cm) sides, greased

Crust

1 cup	graham cracker crumbs	250 mL
¼ cup	honey cashews, ground	50 mL
¼ cup	unsalted butter, melted	50 mL

Filling

3	packages (each 8 oz/250 g) cream cheese, softened	3
½ cup	sour cream	125 mL
½ cup	vanilla-flavored yogurt	125 mL
1½ cups	granulated sugar	375 mL
3	eggs	3
2	egg yolks	2
1 cup	honey cashews, chopped	250 mL
1 tsp	vanilla extract	5 mL

Decoration

	Classic Whipped Cream Topping (see recipe, page 262)	
¼ cup	honey cashews, chopped	50 mL

1. *Crust:* In a bowl, combine graham cracker crumbs, ground cashews and butter. Press into bottom of cheesecake pan and freeze.

2. *Filling:* In a mixer bowl fitted with paddle attachment, beat cream cheese, sour cream, yogurt and sugar on medium-high speed until very smooth, for 3 minutes. Add whole eggs and egg yolks, one at a time, beating after each addition. Fold in chopped cashews and vanilla by hand.

3. Pour over frozen crust, smoothing out to sides of pan. Bake in preheated oven until top is light brown and center has a slight jiggle to it, 45 to 55 minutes. Let cool in pan on a wire rack for 2 hours. Cover with plastic wrap and refrigerate for at least 6 hours before decorating or serving.

4. *Decoration:* Ice top of cake with Classic Whipped Cream Topping or pipe rosettes around top of cake, if desired. Sprinkle with chopped cashews.

Hazelnut Cheesecake

SERVES 10 TO 12

Hazelnuts, once available only at holiday time, are now easy to find year-round. This simple cheesecake lets the hazelnut flavor shine through.

Tips

Toast hazelnuts in a 350°F (180°C) oven for 10 to 12 minutes, stirring a few times, until lightly browned and fragrant. You can use them with the skins on, if desired.

A few slices of fresh fruit on each serving plate will turn this dessert into a cheese course — it's rich, but not too sweet.

- Preheat oven to 350°F (180°C)
- 9-inch (23 cm) cheesecake pan, ungreased, or springform pan with 3-inch (7.5 cm) sides, greased

Crust

1½ cups	butter cookie crumbs	375 mL
¼ cup	unsalted butter, melted	50 mL

Filling

3	packages (each 8 oz/250 g) cream cheese, softened	3
1 cup	small-curd cottage cheese, drained (see tips, page 146)	250 mL
1 cup	plain yogurt	250 mL
1¼ cups	granulated sugar	300 mL
2	eggs	2
2	egg yolks	2
3 tbsp	freshly squeezed lemon juice	45 mL
1 tsp	vanilla extract	5 mL
1 cup	hazelnuts, toasted (see tip, at left) and chopped	250 mL

Decoration

Classic Whipped Cream Topping (see recipe, page 262)

1. *Crust:* In a bowl, combine cookie crumbs and butter. Press into bottom of cheesecake pan and freeze.

2. *Filling:* In a mixer bowl fitted with paddle attachment, beat cream cheese, cottage cheese, yogurt and sugar on medium-high speed until very smooth, for 3 minutes. Add whole eggs and egg yolks, one at a time, beating after each addition. Mix in lemon juice and vanilla. Fold in hazelnuts by hand.

3. Pour over frozen crust, smoothing out to sides of pan. Bake in preheated oven until top is light brown and center has a slight jiggle to it, 45 to 55 minutes. Let cool in pan on a wire rack for 2 hours. Cover with plastic wrap and refrigerate for at least 6 hours before decorating or serving.

4. *Decoration:* Ice top of cooled cake with Classic Whipped Cream Topping or pipe rosettes around top of cake, if desired.

Fresh Raspberry Hazelnut Cheesecake

SERVES 10 TO 12

Fresh raspberries and toasted hazelnuts are a taste sensation!

Tip

If you can't find hazelnuts, you can use almonds instead.

Variation

Hazelnut-flavored liqueur adds another dimension of nutty flavor. Add 2 tbsp (25 mL) with the vanilla (don't eliminate any of the other liquids).

- Preheat oven to 350°F (180°C)
- 9-inch (23 cm) cheesecake pan, ungreased, or springform pan with 3-inch (7.5 cm) sides, greased

Crust

1 1/4 cups	sugar cookie crumbs	300 mL
1/2 cup	hazelnuts, toasted (see tip, page 152) and ground	125 mL
3 tbsp	unsalted butter, melted	45 mL

Filling

4	packages (each 8 oz/250 g) cream cheese, softened	4
3/4 cup	sour cream	175 mL
1 1/4 cups	granulated sugar	300 mL
4	eggs	4
1/4 cup	all-purpose flour	50 mL
2 1/2 tbsp	freshly squeezed lemon juice	32 mL
1 tbsp	vanilla extract	15 mL
1 cup	raspberries, cut into quarters, if large	250 mL
1/2 cup	hazelnuts, toasted and coarsely ground	125 mL

Decoration

1/2 cup	raspberries	125 mL
1/4 cup	hazelnuts, toasted and chopped	50 mL
	Whipped cream (optional)	

1. *Crust:* In a bowl, combine cookie crumbs, ground hazelnuts and butter. Press into bottom of cheesecake pan and freeze.
2. *Filling:* In a mixer bowl fitted with paddle attachment, beat cream cheese, sour cream and sugar on medium-high speed until very smooth, for 3 minutes. Add eggs, one at a time, beating after each addition. Stir in flour, lemon juice and vanilla. Fold in raspberries and ground hazelnuts by hand.
3. Pour over frozen crust, smoothing out to sides of pan. Bake in preheated oven until top is light brown and center has a slight jiggle to it, 45 to 55 minutes. Let cool in pan on a wire rack for 2 hours. Cover with plastic wrap and refrigerate for at least 6 hours before decorating or serving.
4. *Decoration:* Sprinkle top of cake with raspberries and chopped hazelnuts. Serve with a dollop of whipped cream on the side, if desired.

White Chocolate Macadamia Nut Cheesecake

SERVES 10 TO 12

Macadamia nuts on their own are a gourmet delicacy; encasing them in white chocolate takes elegance to a whole new level and makes this a special birthday party cheesecake.

Tips

I like to have the baking pan with water already in the oven before mixing my cheesecake batter.

To melt white chocolate, bring water to a boil in the bottom of a double boiler and turn the heat off. Place chopped white chocolate in the top portion of the double boiler and stir until melted. The steam is hot enough to melt white chocolate. Do not use the microwave to melt white chocolate, as it has a lower melting point than other chocolates. If you don't have a double boiler, a saucepan with a metal bowl loosely fitted on top will also work. After the chocolate has melted, remove it from the bottom boiler and let cool until tepid.

- Preheat oven to 400°F (200°F)
- 9-inch (23 cm) cheesecake pan, ungreased, or springform pan with 3-inch (7.5 cm) sides, greased
- 13- by 9-inch (3 L) baking pan, filled with 2 inches (5 cm) boiling water

Crust
1¼ cups	butter cookie crumbs	300 mL
¼ cup	unsalted butter, melted	50 mL

Filling
3	packages (each 8 oz/250 g) cream cheese, softened	3
1 cup	sour cream	250 mL
½ cup	plain yogurt	125 mL
½ cup	granulated sugar	125 mL
4	eggs	4
12 oz	white chocolate, melted (see tip, at left) and cooled	375 g
1 cup	macadamia nuts, toasted (see tip, page 158) and chopped	250 mL
1 tbsp	vanilla extract	15 mL
½ tsp	salt	2 mL

Decoration
	Classic Whipped Cream Topping (see recipe, page 262)	
¼ cup	macadamia nuts, toasted and chopped	50 mL

1. *Crust:* In a bowl, combine cookie crumbs and butter. Press into bottom of cheesecake pan and freeze.

2. *Filling:* In a mixer bowl fitted with paddle attachment, beat cream cheese, sour cream, yogurt and sugar on medium-high speed until very smooth, for 3 minutes. Add eggs, one at a time, beating after each addition. With the mixer running, pour in melted chocolate in a steady stream. Fold in macadamia nuts, vanilla and salt by hand.

Variation

Use store-bought chocolate-covered macadamia nuts to double the chocolate flavors.

3. Pour into cheesecake pan, smoothing out to sides of pan. Center cheesecake pan on the middle rack in the oven with a baking pan of boiling water on the lower rack. Bake at 400°F (200°C) for 10 minutes. Reduce oven temperature to 350°F (180°C) and bake until top is light brown and center has a slight jiggle to it, 45 to 55 minutes. Let cool in pan on a wire rack for 2 hours. Cover with plastic wrap and refrigerate for at least 6 hours before decorating or serving.

4. *Decoration:* Pipe rosettes around top of cake with Classic Whipped Cream Topping. Sprinkle center with macadamia nuts.

Aloha Cheesecake

SERVES 10 TO 12

On a chilly winter day, when you're dreaming of a tropical paradise, this cheesecake will evoke visions of balmy days and swaying palm trees.

Tip

It takes a larger can of pineapple than you would think to get 1/2 cup (125 mL) of fruit, because the juice is part of the weight. Use the drained pineapple juice in a fruit smoothie for a snack.

Variation

Add 1 tsp (5 mL) rum extract with the vanilla to punch up the flavor.

• Preheat oven to 350°F (180°C)
• 9-inch (23 cm) cheesecake pan, ungreased, or springform pan with 3-inch (7.5 cm) sides, greased

Crust

1 cup	graham cracker crumbs	250 mL
1/4 cup	macadamia nuts, toasted (see tip, page 158) and ground	50 mL
1/4 cup	packed brown sugar	50 mL
1/4 cup	unsalted butter, melted	50 mL

Filling

3	packages (each 8 oz/250 g) cream cheese, softened	3
1 cup	sour cream	250 mL
1 cup	packed brown sugar	250 mL
4	eggs	4
1/2 cup	well-drained crushed pineapple (about one 8-oz/227 mL can)	125 mL
1/2 cup	macadamia nuts, toasted and ground	125 mL
1 tsp	vanilla extract	5 mL

Decoration

5 to 6	well-drained pineapple slices (about one 6-oz/175 mL can)	5 to 6
1/4 cup	whole macadamia nuts, toasted	50 mL

1. *Crust:* In a bowl, combine graham cracker crumbs, ground macadamia nuts, brown sugar and butter. Press into bottom of cheesecake pan and freeze.

2. *Filling:* In a mixer bowl fitted with paddle attachment, beat cream cheese, sour cream and brown sugar on medium-high speed until very smooth, for 3 minutes. Add eggs, one at a time, beating after each addition. Fold in crushed pineapple, ground macadamia nuts and vanilla by hand.

3. Pour over frozen crust, smoothing out to sides of pan. Bake in preheated oven until top is light brown and center has a slight jiggle to it, 45 to 55 minutes. Let cool in pan on a wire rack for 2 hours. Cover with plastic wrap and refrigerate for at least 6 hours before decorating or serving.

4. *Decoration:* Arrange pineapple slices on top of cake and sprinkle with whole macadamia nuts.

Toasted Pecan Cheesecake

SERVES 10 TO 12

When I was teaching in Whistler, British Columbia, one spring, a student announced that this cheesecake should be proclaimed a national treasure.

Tip

Store raw nuts in the freezer and toast right before using.

Variation

For the decoration, substitute 12 glazed pecans (see Pecan Praline Cheesecake, page 158) for the chopped pecans.

- Preheat oven to 350°F (180°C)
- 9-inch (23 cm) cheesecake pan, ungreased, or springform pan with 3-inch (7.5 cm) sides, greased

Crust

1½ cups	pecans, toasted (see tip, page 158) and ground	375 mL
¼ cup	all-purpose flour	50 mL
¼ cup	unsalted butter, melted	50 mL

Filling

3	packages (each 8 oz/250 g) cream cheese, softened	3
1 cup	plain yogurt	250 mL
1¼ cups	granulated sugar	300 mL
4	eggs	4
1 cup	pecans, toasted and chopped	250 mL
1 tsp	vanilla extract	5 mL

Decoration

	Classic Whipped Cream Topping (see recipe, page 262)	
¼ cup	pecans, toasted and chopped	50 mL

1. *Crust:* In a bowl, combine ground pecans, flour and butter. Press into bottom of cheesecake pan and freeze.

2. *Filling:* In a mixer bowl fitted with paddle attachment, beat cream cheese, yogurt and sugar on medium-high speed until very smooth, for 3 minutes. Add eggs, one at a time, beating after each addition. Fold in chopped pecans and vanilla by hand.

3. Pour over frozen crust, smoothing out to sides of pan. Bake in preheated oven until top is light brown and center has a slight jiggle to it, 45 to 55 minutes. Let cool in pan on a wire rack for 2 hours. Cover with plastic wrap and refrigerate for at least 6 hours before decorating or serving.

4. *Decoration:* Ice top of cake with Classic Whipped Cream Topping or pipe rosettes around top of cake, if desired. Sprinkle with chopped pecans.

Pecan Praline Cheesecake

SERVES 10 TO 12

If you love pralines and cream ice cream as much as I do, you'll love this cheesecake.

Tips

You can make the glazed pecans weeks ahead. Just store in an airtight container. I like to use glazed pecans in salads with a blue cheese crumble and an oil-and-vinegar dressing.

Toasting brings out the natural oils and flavor of nuts. Place nuts in a single layer on a baking sheet and bake at 350°F (180°C) until fragrant, 10 to 12 minutes.

To drain ricotta, place a fine-mesh strainer over a bowl, place the cheese in the strainer and let stand in the refrigerator for at least 1 hour or overnight.

- Preheat oven to 350°F (180°C)
- 13- by 9-inch (3 L) baking pan, lined with parchment paper
- 9-inch (23 cm) cheesecake pan, ungreased, or springform pan with 3-inch (7.5 cm) sides, greased

Crust
1¼ cups	pecans, toasted (see tip, at left) and ground	300 mL
¼ cup	all-purpose flour	50 mL
3 tbsp	unsalted butter	45 mL

Filling
1	egg white	1
¼ cup	granulated sugar	50 mL
1½ cups	pecan halves	375 mL
1 lb	ricotta cheese, drained (see tip, at left)	500 g
4 oz	cream cheese, softened	125 g
½ cup	liquid honey	125 mL
2	eggs	2
1 tsp	vanilla extract	5 mL
½ cup	plain yogurt	125 mL
⅓ cup	cornstarch	75 mL

Decoration
Classic Whipped Cream Topping (see recipe, page 262)

1. *Crust:* In a bowl, combine ground pecans, flour and butter. Press into bottom of cheesecake pan and freeze.
2. *Filling:* In a bowl, whisk egg white and sugar. Add pecans, stirring to coat evenly. Spread out evenly in prepared baking pan. Bake in preheated oven until light brown, for 10 to 18 minutes (do not turn the oven off). Reserve 12 pecans for decoration; coarsely chop remaining pecans. Set aside.

3. In a mixer bowl fitted with paddle attachment, beat ricotta cheese, cream cheese and honey on medium-high speed until very smooth, for 3 minutes. Add eggs, one at a time, beating after each addition. Mix in vanilla. Stir in yogurt and cornstarch. Gently fold in chopped pecans by hand.

4. Pour over frozen crust, smoothing out to sides of pan. Bake in preheated oven until top is light brown and center has a slight jiggle to it, 45 to 55 minutes. Let cool in pan on a wire rack for 2 hours. Cover with plastic wrap and refrigerate for at least 6 hours before decorating or serving.

5. *Decoration:* Ice top of cake with Classic Whipped Cream Topping or pipe rosettes around top of cake, if desired. Top with reserved glazed pecans.

New Orleans Pecan Cheesecake

SERVES 10 TO 12

The Crescent City would never produce a merely ordinary pecan dessert — there is always something extra that makes it New Orleans–style. In this case, it's cane syrup.

Tip

To quickly prepare cookie crumbs, place whole cookies in a food processor fitted with a metal blade and pulse a few times. You can add the butter to the food processor and pulse until blended. When mixed with the butter, the crumbs should feel like wet sand.

Variation

You can use ½ cup (125 mL) light (fancy) molasses in place of the cane syrup.

- Preheat oven to 350°F (180°C)
- 9-inch (23 cm) cheesecake pan, ungreased, or springform pan with 3-inch (7.5 cm) sides, greased

Crust

1¼ cups	pecan cookie crumbs	300 mL
¼ cup	unsalted butter, melted	50 mL

Filling

4	packages (each 8 oz/250 g) cream cheese, softened	4
½ cup	all-purpose flour	125 mL
¾ cup	pure cane syrup (see page 277)	175 mL
4	eggs	4
1 cup	pecans, toasted (see tip, page 158) and chopped	250 mL
2 tsp	rum extract	10 mL
1 tsp	freshly squeezed lemon juice	5 mL

Decoration

	Classic Whipped Cream Topping (see recipe, page 262)	
¼ cup	pecan halves, toasted	50 mL

1. *Crust:* In a bowl, combine cookie crumbs and butter. Press into bottom of cheesecake pan and freeze.
2. *Filling:* In a mixer bowl fitted with paddle attachment, beat cream cheese, flour and cane syrup until very smooth, for 2 minutes. Add eggs, one at a time, beating after each addition. Fold in pecans, rum extract and lemon juice by hand.
3. Pour over frozen crust, smoothing out to sides of pan. Bake in preheated oven until top is light brown and center has a slight jiggle to it, 45 to 55 minutes. Let cool in pan on a wire rack for 2 hours. Cover with plastic wrap and refrigerate for at least 6 hours before decorating or serving.
4. *Decoration:* Pipe rosettes around top of cake with Classic Whipped Cream Topping. Sprinkle center with pecan halves.

Caramel Pecan Cheesecake (page 161)

Overleaf: Pistachio Cheesecake (page 162)

Caramel Pecan Cheesecake

SERVES 10 TO 12

A childhood fondness for turtle candies, with crunchy pecans wrapped in rich caramel, inspired this decadent cheesecake.

Tip

It's best not to spread the melted caramel mixture right to the edge of the pan. If you do, it might stick and make it difficult to remove the cake from the pan.

Variation

Pecan lovers will enjoy pecan shortbread cookie crumbs in the crust instead of the chocolate sandwich cookies.

Overleaf: Chocolate Mocha Chunk Cheesecake (page 172)

Berry Berry Berry Cheesecake (page 175)

- Preheat oven to 350°F (180°C)
- 9-inch (23 cm) cheesecake pan, ungreased, or springform pan with 3-inch (7.5 cm) sides, greased

Crust

1¼ cups	chocolate sandwich cookie crumbs	300 mL
¼ cup	pecans, toasted (see tip, page 158) and ground	50 mL
¼ cup	unsalted butter, melted	50 mL

Filling

1 cup	soft caramels	250 mL
2 tbsp	evaporated milk or whipping (35%) cream	25 mL
6 oz	bittersweet chocolate chunks	175 g
2	packages (each 8 oz/250 g) cream cheese, softened	2
1 cup	sour cream	250 mL
½ cup	granulated sugar	125 mL
3	eggs	3
1 tsp	vanilla extract	5 mL
1 cup	pecans, toasted and chopped	250 mL

1. *Crust:* In a bowl, combine cookie crumbs, ground pecans and butter. Press into bottom of cheesecake pan and freeze.

2. *Filling:* In a small saucepan over low heat, melt caramels in evaporated milk, stirring frequently, until smooth. Reserve about 3 tbsp (45 mL); cover and refrigerate. Pour remaining caramel mixture over frozen crust, spreading evenly and leaving a ½-inch (1 cm) border uncovered. Sprinkle chocolate chunks over caramel. Set aside.

3. In a mixer bowl fitted with paddle attachment, beat cream cheese, sour cream and sugar on medium-high speed until very smooth, for 3 minutes. Add eggs, one at a time, beating after each addition. Mix in vanilla. Fold in chopped pecans by hand.

4. Pour over frozen crust, smoothing out to sides of pan. Bake in preheated oven until top is light brown and center has a slight jiggle to it, 45 to 55 minutes. Let cool in pan on a wire rack for 2 hours. Cover with plastic wrap and refrigerate for at least 6 hours before decorating or serving.

5. *Decoration:* Reheat reserved caramel mixture in the microwave (or in a small saucepan over low heat) until melted. Drizzle over cake.

Pistachio Cheesecake

SERVES 10 TO 12

Pistachios are a great addition to cheesecakes — both in the filling and as decoration.

Tip

Use fresh lime juice; bottled sometimes has a metallic taste.

Variations

Garnish each slice with Fresh Raspberry Sauce (see recipe, page 271) during the holidays for a green and red effect.

Use chocolate sandwich cookies instead of the butter cookies for the crust. It's a delicious alternative.

- Preheat oven to 350°F (180°C)
- 9-inch (23 cm) cheesecake pan, ungreased, or springform pan with 3-inch (7.5 cm) sides, greased

Crust

1½ cups	butter cookie crumbs	375 mL
¼ cup	unsalted butter, melted	50 mL

Filling

2	packages (each 8 oz/250 g) cream cheese, softened	2
1 lb	ricotta cheese, drained (see tip, page 158)	500 g
1 cup	sour cream	250 mL
1½ cups	granulated sugar	375 mL
5	eggs	5
1 cup	pistachios, finely ground	250 mL
½ cup	all-purpose flour	125 mL
2 tbsp	freshly squeezed lime juice	25 mL
1 tbsp	vanilla extract	15 mL

Decoration

	Classic Whipped Cream Topping (see recipe, page 262)	
¼ cup	pistachios, ground	50 mL

1. *Crust:* In a bowl, combine cookie crumbs and butter. Press into bottom of cheesecake pan and freeze.
2. *Filling:* In a mixer bowl fitted with paddle attachment, beat cream cheese, ricotta cheese, sour cream and sugar on medium-high speed until very smooth, for 3 minutes. Add eggs, one at a time, beating after each addition. Stir in pistachios, flour, lime juice and vanilla.
3. Pour over frozen crust, smoothing out to sides of pan. Bake in preheated oven until top is light brown and center has a slight jiggle to it, 45 to 55 minutes. Let cool in pan on a wire rack for 2 hours. Cover with plastic wrap and refrigerate for at least 6 hours before decorating or serving.
4. *Decoration:* Ice top of cake with Classic Whipped Cream Topping or pipe rosettes around top of cake, if desired. Top with a dusting of ground pistachios.

Black Walnut Cheesecake

SERVES 8 TO 10

California grows the majority of walnuts from the U.S. The fall harvest makes them abundant for holiday cooking.

Tip

Toasting brings out the natural oils and flavor of nuts. Place nuts in a single layer on a baking sheet and bake at 350°F (180°C) until fragrant, 10 to 12 minutes.

- Preheat oven to 325°F (160°C)
- 8-inch (20 cm) cheesecake pan, ungreased, or springform pan with 3-inch (7.5 cm) sides, greased

Crust

1¼ cups	butter cookie crumbs	300 mL
3 tbsp	unsalted butter, melted	45 mL

Filling

2	packages (each 8 oz/250 g) cream cheese, softened	2
¾ cup	granulated sugar	175 mL
2	eggs	2
½ cup	black walnuts, toasted (see tip, at left) and chopped	125 mL
1 tsp	maple extract	5 mL
1 tsp	vanilla extract	5 mL

Decoration

	Classic Whipped Cream Topping (see recipe, page 262)	
½ cup	black walnuts, toasted and chopped	125 mL

1. *Crust:* In a bowl, combine cookie crumbs and butter. Press into bottom of cheesecake pan and freeze.

2. *Filling:* In a mixer bowl fitted with paddle attachment, beat cream cheese and sugar on medium-high speed until very smooth, for 3 minutes. Add eggs, one at a time, beating after each addition. Fold in black walnuts, maple extract and vanilla by hand.

3. Pour over frozen crust, smoothing out to sides of pan. Bake in preheated oven until top is light brown and center has a slight jiggle to it, 35 to 45 minutes. Let cool in pan on a wire rack for 2 hours. Cover with plastic wrap and refrigerate for at least 6 hours before decorating or serving.

4. *Decoration:* Pipe rosettes around top of cake with Classic Whipped Cream Topping. Fill center with black walnuts.

Walnut Date Cheesecake

SERVES 10 TO 12

Walnuts and dates go hand in hand, just like chocolate and peanut butter.

Tip

When measuring honey, lightly spray the measuring cup with a nonstick spray so the honey will release easily.

Variation

Substitute chopped prunes for the dates if you have them on hand.

- Preheat oven to 350°F (180°C)
- 9-inch (23 cm) cheesecake pan, ungreased, or springform pan with 3-inch (7.5 cm) sides, greased

Crust

1½ cups	walnuts, toasted (see tip, page 163) and ground	375 mL
¼ cup	all-purpose flour	50 mL
¼ cup	unsalted butter, melted	50 mL

Filling

3	packages (each 8 oz/250 g) cream cheese, softened	3
1 cup	sour cream	250 mL
¼ cup	liquid honey	50 mL
1¼ cups	granulated sugar	300 mL
4	eggs	4
1 cup	walnuts, toasted and chopped	250 mL
½ cup	chopped pitted dates	125 mL
1 tsp	vanilla extract	5 mL

Decoration

	Classic Whipped Cream Topping (see recipe, page 262)	
¼ cup	walnut halves	50 mL

1. *Crust:* In a bowl, combine ground walnuts, flour and butter. Press into bottom of cheesecake pan and freeze.

2. *Filling:* In a mixer bowl fitted with paddle attachment, beat cream cheese, sour cream, honey and sugar on medium-high speed until very smooth, for 3 minutes. Add eggs, one at a time, beating after each addition. Fold in chopped walnuts, dates and vanilla by hand.

3. Pour over frozen crust, smoothing out to sides of pan. Bake in preheated oven until top is light brown and center has a slight jiggle to it, 45 to 55 minutes. Let cool in pan on a wire rack for 2 hours. Cover with plastic wrap and refrigerate for at least 6 hours before decorating or serving.

4. *Decoration:* Ice top of cake with Classic Whipped Cream Topping or pipe rosettes around top of cake, if desired. Sprinkle with walnut halves.

Maple Walnut Cheesecake

SERVES 10 TO 12

Canada is well known for its maple syrup. Authentic maple flavor with crunchy walnuts reminds me of a cheesecake I had in Quebec a few years back.

Tip

Look for grade B or medium maple syrup for baking. The flavor is bolder and it is often less expensive.

Variation

Black walnuts work well in this recipe too.

- Preheat oven to 350°F (180°C)
- 9-inch (23 cm) cheesecake pan, ungreased, or springform pan with 3-inch (7.5 cm) sides, greased

Crust

1 cup	graham cracker crumbs	250 mL
¼ cup	walnuts, toasted (see tip, page 163) and ground	50 mL
¼ cup	unsalted butter, melted	50 mL

Filling

3	packages (each 8 oz/250 g) cream cheese, softened	3
1 cup	vanilla-flavored yogurt	250 mL
1 cup	granulated sugar	250 mL
¼ cup	pure maple syrup	50 mL
3	eggs	3
1½ cups	walnuts, toasted and chopped	375 mL
1 tsp	vanilla extract	5 mL
½ tsp	salt	2 mL

Decoration

½ cup	walnuts, toasted and chopped	125 mL
½ cup	pure maple syrup	125 mL

1. *Crust:* In a bowl, combine graham cracker crumbs, ground walnuts and butter. Press into bottom of cheesecake pan and freeze.

2. *Filling:* In a mixer bowl fitted with paddle attachment, beat cream cheese, yogurt and sugar on medium-high speed until very smooth, for 3 minutes. Mix in maple syrup. Add eggs, one at a time, beating after each addition. Fold in chopped walnuts, vanilla and salt by hand.

3. Pour over frozen crust, smoothing out to sides of pan. Bake in preheated oven until top is light brown and center has a slight jiggle to it, 45 to 55 minutes. Let cool in pan on a wire rack for 2 hours. Cover with plastic wrap and refrigerate for at least 6 hours before decorating or serving.

4. *Decoration:* In a bowl, combine walnuts and maple syrup. Drizzle over top of cake.

Three-Nut Cheesecake

SERVES 10 TO 12

A rich, nutty taste permeates this creamy cheesecake.

Tips

If you process nuts alone, you may get nut butter; adding a little flour to the nuts prevents this by drying the oils.

Wash lemons well before zesting. To make lemons easier to juice, roll them firmly on the counter to break up the membranes of the fruit.

- Preheat oven to 350°F (180°C)
- 9-inch (23 cm) cheesecake pan or springform pan with 3-inch (7.5 cm) sides, lined with parchment paper

Crust

1½ cups	pecan halves	375 mL
¼ cup	all-purpose flour	50 mL
¼ cup	unsalted butter, melted	50 mL

Filling

1 cup	walnut halves	250 mL
¾ cup	unsalted cashews	175 mL
2 tsp	all-purpose flour	10 mL
4	packages (each 8 oz/250 g) cream cheese, softened	4
1⅓ cups	granulated sugar	325 mL
4	eggs	4
1 tbsp	grated lemon zest	15 mL
2 tbsp	freshly squeezed lemon juice	25 mL
1 tsp	vanilla extract	5 mL
¼ tsp	maple extract	1 mL

1. *Crust:* In a food processor fitted with metal blade, process pecans and flour until finely ground. Transfer to a bowl and mix in butter. Press into bottom of cheesecake pan. Bake in preheated oven for 10 minutes (do not turn the oven off). Set aside.

2. *Filling:* In same work bowl fitted with metal blade, pulse walnuts, cashews and flour until coarsely chopped, about 15 times. Transfer to a bowl and set aside.

3. In same work bowl fitted with metal blade, process cream cheese and sugar until smooth, about 20 seconds. With the motor running, through the feed tube, add eggs, lemon zest, lemon juice, vanilla and maple extract; process until blended.

4. Pour half the batter over baked crust, smoothing out to sides of pan. Sprinkle half of the chopped nuts over top. Spread remaining batter over nut layer and sprinkle with remaining nuts. Bake in preheated oven until top is light brown and center has a slight jiggle to it, 45 to 55 minutes. Let cool in pan on a wire rack for 2 hours. Cover with plastic wrap and refrigerate for at least 6 hours before serving.

No-Bake Cheesecakes

Holiday Rum Eggnog Cheesecake

SERVES 10 TO 12

Here's a perfect dessert to make when the turkey is taking up all the room in the oven.

Tip

If gingersnaps are difficult to find, you can use graham crackers with 1 tsp (5 mL) ground ginger blended in.

Variation

Unsweetened apple juice is a non-alcoholic substitute for rum.

- 9-inch (23 cm) cheesecake pan, ungreased, or springform pan with 3-inch (7.5 cm) sides, greased

Crust

1 1/4 cups	gingersnap cookie crumbs	300 mL
3 tbsp	unsalted butter, melted	45 mL

Filling

2	packets (each 1/4 oz/7.5 g) powdered unflavored gelatin	2
1/4 cup	milk	50 mL
2	packages (each 8 oz/250 g) cream cheese, softened	2
1/4 cup	granulated sugar	50 mL
1 cup	eggnog	250 mL
1/4 cup	light rum	50 mL
1 1/2 tsp	vanilla extract	7 mL
1/2 tsp	freshly grated nutmeg	2 mL
1 cup	whipping (35%) cream, whipped	250 mL

Decoration

	Classic Whipped Cream Topping (see recipe, page 262)	
1/4 tsp	freshly grated nutmeg	1 mL

1. *Crust:* In a bowl, combine cookie crumbs and butter. Press into bottom of cheesecake pan and freeze.
2. *Filling:* Sprinkle gelatin over milk in a small saucepan and let stand for 1 minute. Stir over low heat until gelatin is completely dissolved. Set aside to cool slightly.
3. In a mixer bowl fitted with paddle attachment, beat cream cheese and sugar on medium-high speed until very smooth, for 3 minutes. Slowly mix in dissolved gelatin. Mix in eggnog, rum, vanilla and nutmeg. Fold in whipped cream by hand.
4. Pour over frozen crust, smoothing out to sides of pan. Cover with plastic wrap and refrigerate for at least 6 hours before decorating or serving. Run a hot knife around edge of pan to loosen.
5. *Decoration:* Ice top of cake with Classic Whipped Cream Topping or pipe rosettes around top of cake, if desired. Dust with nutmeg.

Irish Cream Cheesecake

SERVES 10 TO 12

A hint of whiskey will warm you up on a cold winter day.

Tip

Alcohol ignites easily, so use caution in warming the liquid to dissolve the gelatin.

Variation

Fold in ½ cup (125 mL) semisweet chocolate chunks with the whipped cream.

- 9-inch (23 cm) cheesecake pan, ungreased, or springform pan with 3-inch (7.5 cm) sides, greased

Crust
1½ cups	graham cracker crumbs	375 mL
3 tbsp	unsalted butter, melted	45 mL

Filling
1	packet (¼ oz/7.5 g) powdered unflavored gelatin	1
½ cup	Irish whiskey or bourbon	125 mL
2	packages (each 8 oz/250 g) cream cheese, softened	2
1 cup	granulated sugar	250 mL
2 tbsp	unsweetened Dutch-process cocoa powder, sifted	25 mL
1 tbsp	freshly squeezed lemon juice	15 mL
2 tsp	vanilla extract	10 mL
1 cup	whipping (35%) cream, whipped	250 mL

Decoration
	Classic Whipped Cream Topping (see recipe, page 262)	
1 tbsp	unsweetened Dutch-process cocoa powder, sifted	15 mL

1. *Crust:* In a bowl, combine graham cracker crumbs and butter. Press into bottom of cheesecake pan and freeze.

2. *Filling:* Sprinkle gelatin over whiskey in a small saucepan and let stand for 1 minute. Stir over low heat until gelatin is completely dissolved (see tip, at left). Set aside to cool slightly.

3. In a mixer bowl fitted with paddle attachment, beat cream cheese, sugar and cocoa on medium-high speed until very smooth, for 3 minutes. Slowly mix in dissolved gelatin. Mix in lemon juice and vanilla. Fold in whipped cream by hand.

4. Pour over frozen crust, smoothing out to sides of pan. Cover with plastic wrap and refrigerate for at least 6 hours before decorating or serving. Run a hot knife around edge of pan to loosen.

5. *Decoration:* Ice top of cake with Classic Whipped Cream Topping or pipe rosettes around top of cake, if desired. Dust with cocoa powder.

Cookies and Cream Cheesecake

SERVES 10 TO 12

The cookies and cream combination started a sensation in ice cream, then cake, and now cheesecake.

Tip

Make sure your cream cheese is at room temperature before making this cheesecake.

Variation

Any type of cookie works well in this recipe.

- 9-inch (23 cm) cheesecake pan, ungreased, or springform pan with 3-inch (7.5 cm) sides, greased

Crust

1¼ cups	chocolate sandwich cookie crumbs	300 mL
3 tbsp	unsalted butter, melted	45 mL

Filling

1	packet (¼ oz/7.5 g) powdered unflavored gelatin	1
¼ cup	milk	50 mL
2	packages (each 8 oz/250 g) cream cheese, softened	2
¾ cup	granulated sugar	175 mL
1½ tsp	vanilla extract	7 mL
2 cups	slightly crushed chocolate sandwich cookies (about 16)	500 mL
1 cup	whipping (35%) cream, whipped	250 mL

Decoration

	Classic Whipped Cream Topping (see recipe, page 262)	
12	chocolate sandwich cookies	12

1. *Crust:* In a bowl, combine cookie crumbs and butter. Press into bottom of cheesecake pan and freeze.

2. *Filling:* Sprinkle gelatin over milk in a small saucepan and let stand for 1 minute. Stir over low heat until gelatin is completely dissolved. Set aside to cool slightly.

3. In a mixer bowl fitted with paddle attachment, beat cream cheese and sugar on medium-high speed until very smooth, for 3 minutes. Slowly mix in dissolved gelatin. Mix in vanilla. Fold in crushed cookies and whipped cream by hand.

4. Pour over frozen crust, smoothing out to sides of pan. Cover with plastic wrap and refrigerate for at least 6 hours before decorating or serving. Run a hot knife around edge of pan to loosen.

5. *Decoration:* Ice top of cake with Classic Whipped Cream Topping or pipe rosettes around top of cake, if desired. Crumble cookies on top.

Mint Cheesecake

Mint is a flavor that refreshes with every bite. Try this cheesecake with an espresso.

Tip

When making cookie crumbs, you do not have to scrape the cream filling out of the cookies; just place them whole into the food processor and pulse.

Variation

Substitute 1 tbsp (15 mL) crème de menthe liqueur for the mint extract.

- 9-inch (23 cm) cheesecake pan, ungreased, or springform pan with 3-inch (7.5 cm) sides, greased

Crust

1¼ cups	chocolate sandwich cookie crumbs	300 mL
3 tbsp	unsalted butter, melted	45 mL

Filling

2	packets (each ¼ oz/7.5 g) powdered unflavored gelatin	2
¼ cup	cold water	50 mL
4	packages (each 8 oz/250 g) cream cheese, softened	4
1 cup	granulated sugar	250 mL
½ cup	milk	125 mL
1 tsp	vanilla extract	5 mL
¼ tsp	mint extract	1 mL
2 cups	whipping (35%) cream, whipped	500 mL
6 oz	milk chocolate chunks	175 g

Decoration

	Classic Whipped Cream Topping (see recipe, page 262)	
6	sprigs mint	6

1. *Crust:* In a bowl, combine cookie crumbs and butter. Press into bottom of cheesecake pan and freeze.

2. *Filling:* Sprinkle gelatin over water in a small saucepan and let stand for 1 minute. Stir over low heat until gelatin is completely dissolved. Set aside to cool slightly.

3. In a mixer bowl fitted with paddle attachment, beat cream cheese and sugar on medium-high speed until very smooth, for 3 minutes. Slowly mix in dissolved gelatin. Mix in milk, vanilla and mint extract. Fold in whipped cream and chocolate chunks by hand.

4. Pour over frozen crust, smoothing out to sides of pan. Cover with plastic wrap and refrigerate for at least 6 hours before decorating or serving. Run a hot knife around edge of pan to loosen.

5. *Decoration:* Ice top of cake with Classic Whipped Cream Topping or pipe rosettes around top of cake, if desired. Garnish with mint sprigs.

Chocolate Mocha Chunk Cheesecake

SERVES 10 TO 12

You get just a hint of mocha flavor in this elegant cheesecake.

Tips

Using Dutch-process cocoa powder creates a richer cheesecake.

You can whip the cream up to 2 hours before making the cheesecake so it is ready when you need it. Keep in the refrigerator until ready to use.

- 9-inch (23 cm) cheesecake pan, ungreased, or springform pan with 3-inch (7.5 cm) sides, greased

Crust
1¼ cups	chocolate sandwich cookie crumbs	300 mL
3 tbsp	unsalted butter, melted	45 mL

Filling
2	packets (each ¼ oz/7.5 g) powdered unflavored gelatin	2
½ cup	milk	125 mL
¼ cup	instant coffee powder or granules	50 mL
1 tbsp	hot water	15 mL
4	packages (each 8 oz/250 g) cream cheese, softened	4
1½ cups	granulated sugar	375 mL
⅔ cup	unsweetened Dutch-process cocoa powder, sifted	150 mL
1 tsp	vanilla extract	5 mL
2 cups	whipping (35%) cream, whipped	500 mL
12 oz	bittersweet chocolate chunks	375 g

Decoration
	Classic Whipped Cream Topping (see recipe, page 262)	
2 oz	bittersweet chocolate	60 g

1. *Crust:* In a bowl, combine cookie crumbs and butter. Press into bottom of cheesecake pan and freeze.
2. *Filling:* Sprinkle gelatin over milk in a small saucepan and let stand for 1 minute. Stir over low heat until gelatin is dissolved. Set aside to cool slightly.
3. In a small bowl, dissolve coffee powder in hot water. Set aside.

Add 2 tbsp (25 mL)
coffee-flavored liqueur
with the vanilla for an
extra mocha punch.

4. In a mixer bowl fitted with paddle attachment, beat
   cream cheese and sugar on medium-high speed until very
   smooth, for 3 minutes. Slowly mix in dissolved gelatin.
   With the mixer running, pour in coffee in a steady stream.
   Stir in cocoa and vanilla. Fold in whipped cream and
   chocolate chunks by hand.

5. Pour over frozen crust, smoothing out to sides of pan.
   Cover with plastic wrap and refrigerate for at least 6 hours
   before decorating or serving. Run a hot knife around edge
   of pan to loosen.

6. *Decoration:* Ice top of cake with Classic Whipped Cream
   Topping or pipe rosettes around top of cake, if desired.
   Grate chocolate over cake.

Raspberry Cream Cheesecake

SERVES 10 TO 12

You don't have to heat up the oven for this no-bake, perfect treat. Enjoy it with friends on a hot summer day.

Tip

It's easier to get the marshmallow cream out of the jar with a hot spatula. Run hot water over the spatula to warm it.

Variation

Try strawberries or blueberries in place of the raspberries.

- 9-inch (23 cm) cheesecake pan, ungreased, or springform pan with 3-inch (7.5 cm) sides, greased

Crust

1½ cups	butter cookie crumbs	375 mL
3 tbsp	unsalted butter, melted	45 mL

Filling

1	packet (¼ oz/7.5 g) powdered unflavored gelatin	1
¼ cup	milk	50 mL
2	packages (each 8 oz/250 g) cream cheese, softened	2
1	jar (7 oz/198 g) marshmallow cream (fluff)	1
1 tbsp	freshly squeezed lemon juice	15 mL
2 tsp	vanilla extract	10 mL
1 cup	whipping (35%) cream	250 mL
¼ cup	granulated sugar	50 mL
2 cups	fresh raspberries, crushed	500 mL

Decoration

	Classic Whipped Cream Topping (see recipe, page 262)	
1 cup	fresh raspberries	250 mL

1. *Crust:* In a bowl, combine cookie crumbs and butter. Press into bottom of cheesecake pan and freeze.
2. *Filling:* Sprinkle gelatin over milk in a small saucepan and let stand for 1 minute. Stir over low heat until gelatin is completely dissolved. Set aside to cool slightly.
3. In a mixer bowl fitted with paddle attachment, beat cream cheese and marshmallow cream on medium-high speed until very smooth, for 3 minutes. Slowly mix in dissolved gelatin. Mix in lemon juice and vanilla. Set aside.
4. In a clean, well-chilled mixer bowl fitted with whip attachment, whip cream on medium-high speed until soft peaks form. With the mixer running, sprinkle with sugar and whip until stiff peaks form. Fold into batter by hand. Fold in crushed raspberries.
5. Pour over frozen crust, smoothing out to sides of pan. Cover with plastic wrap and refrigerate for at least 6 hours before decorating or serving. Run a hot knife around edge of pan to loosen.
6. *Decoration:* Ice top of cake with Classic Whipped Cream Topping or pipe rosettes around top of cake, if desired. Garnish with raspberries.

Berry Berry Berry Cheesecake

SERVES 10 TO 12

This cheesecake bursts with the flavor of three different kinds of berries folded into the batter.

Tips

Wash and dry berries completely before using.

If you must substitute frozen berries, fold them in while still frozen.

- 9-inch (23 cm) cheesecake pan, ungreased, or springform pan with 3-inch (7.5 cm) sides, greased

Crust

1½ cups	butter cookie crumbs	375 mL
3 tbsp	unsalted butter, melted	45 mL

Filling

1	packet (¼ oz/7.5 g) powdered unflavored gelatin	1
¼ cup	milk	50 mL
2	packages (each 8 oz/250 g) cream cheese, softened	2
1 cup	granulated sugar	250 mL
1 tbsp	freshly squeezed lemon juice	15 mL
2 tsp	vanilla extract	10 mL
1 cup	whipping (35%) cream, whipped	250 mL
1 cup	fresh strawberries, crushed	250 mL
1 cup	fresh blackberries, crushed	250 mL
1 cup	fresh raspberries, crushed	250 mL

Decoration

	Classic Whipped Cream Topping (see recipe, page 262)	
1 cup	mixed berries (such as strawberries, blackberries and raspberries)	250 mL

1. *Crust:* In a bowl, combine cookie crumbs and butter. Press into bottom of cheesecake pan and freeze.

2. *Filling:* Sprinkle gelatin over milk in a small saucepan and let stand for 1 minute. Stir over low heat until gelatin is completely dissolved. Set aside to cool slightly.

3. In a mixer bowl fitted with paddle attachment, beat cream cheese and sugar on medium-high speed until very smooth, for 3 minutes. Slowly mix in dissolved gelatin. Mix in lemon juice and vanilla. Fold in whipped cream by hand. Fold in crushed berries.

4. Pour over frozen crust, smoothing out to sides of pan. Cover with plastic wrap and refrigerate for at least 6 hours before decorating or serving. Run a hot knife around edge of pan to loosen.

5. *Decoration:* Ice top of cake with Classic Whipped Cream Topping or pipe rosettes around top of cake, if desired. Garnish with berries.

Orange Citrus Cheesecake

I'm lucky to live near some of the last remaining orange groves in Southern California, where the aroma of the blossoms is intoxicating.

Tips

Orange juice does not have as much flavor as concentrate. If you have juice but not concentrate, use double the amount and reduce it by half over low heat to intensify the flavor.

Variation

Add 2 tbsp (25 mL) orange-flavored liqueur with the vanilla to further highlight the citrus flavor.

• 9-inch (23 cm) cheesecake pan, ungreased, or springform pan with 3-inch (7.5 cm) sides, greased

Crust

1¼ cups	butter cookie crumbs	300 mL
3 tbsp	unsalted butter, melted	45 mL

Filling

1	packet (¼ oz/7.5 g) powdered unflavored gelatin	1
½ cup	frozen orange juice concentrate, thawed	125 mL
3	packages (each 8 oz/250 g) cream cheese, softened	3
¾ cup	granulated sugar	175 mL
1 tsp	vanilla extract	5 mL
¼ tsp	grated orange zest	1 mL
1 cup	whipping (35%) cream, whipped	250 mL

Decoration

	Classic Whipped Cream Topping (see recipe, page 262)	
¼ tsp	grated orange zest	1 mL

1. *Crust:* In a bowl, combine cookie crumbs and butter. Press into bottom of cheesecake pan and freeze.

2. *Filling:* Sprinkle gelatin over orange juice concentrate in a small saucepan and let stand for 1 minute. Stir over low heat until gelatin is completely dissolved. Set aside to cool slightly.

3. In a mixer bowl fitted with paddle attachment, beat cream cheese and sugar on medium-high speed until very smooth, for 3 minutes. Slowly mix in dissolved gelatin. Stir in vanilla and orange zest. Fold in whipped cream by hand.

4. Pour over frozen crust, smoothing out to sides of pan. Cover with plastic wrap and refrigerate for at least 6 hours before decorating or serving. Run a hot knife around edge of pan to loosen.

5. *Decoration:* Ice top of cake with Classic Whipped Cream Topping or pipe rosettes around top of cake, if desired. Sprinkle with orange zest.

Lemon Cheesecake

SERVES 10 TO 12

Creamy lemon no-bake cheesecake is perfect when it's too hot to turn on the oven.

Tip

Make sure the gelatin is cooled before mixing it into the cream cheese mixture; otherwise, the cake will take a long time to firm up.

Variation

Substitute orange- or lime-flavored gelatin and orange or lime juice for the lemon-flavored gelatin and lemon juice.

- 13- by 9-inch (3 L) baking pan, lined with foil, leaving a slight overhang

Crust

2½ cups	graham cracker crumbs	625 mL
½ cup	unsalted butter, melted	125 mL

Filling

1	box (4-serving size) lemon-flavored gelatin	1
1 cup	boiling water	250 mL
1	package (8 oz/250 g) cream cheese, softened	1
1 cup	granulated sugar	250 mL
1½ cups	evaporated milk	375 mL
3 tbsp	freshly squeezed lemon juice	45 mL
1 tsp	vanilla extract	5 mL

1. *Crust:* In a bowl, combine graham cracker crumbs and butter. Press into bottom of baking pan and freeze.
2. *Filling:* In a small bowl, dissolve gelatin in boiling water. Set aside to cool completely.
3. In a mixer bowl fitted with paddle attachment, beat cream cheese and sugar on medium-high speed until very smooth, for 3 minutes. Slowly mix in dissolved gelatin. Mix in evaporated milk, lemon juice and vanilla.
4. Pour over frozen crust, smoothing out to sides of pan. Cover with plastic wrap and refrigerate for at least 6 hours before serving. Use the foil as a handle to lift the cake from the pan.

Lime Cheesecake

While traveling in Florida, my friend Neil and I came across a tart cheesecake. This perfect cool lime cheesecake is reminiscent of that delectable find.

Tips

To quickly prepare cookie crumbs, place whole cookies in a food processor fitted with a metal blade and pulse a few times. You can add the butter to the food processor and pulse until blended. When mixed with the butter, the crumbs should feel like wet sand.

Zest limes before juicing. Leftover zest and juice freeze well for future recipes.

- 9-inch (23 cm) cheesecake pan, ungreased, or springform pan with 3-inch (7.5 cm) sides, greased

Crust

1¼ cups	butter cookie crumbs	300 mL
3 tbsp	unsalted butter, melted	45 mL

Filling

1	packet (¼ oz/7.5 g) powdered unflavored gelatin	1
¼ tsp	grated lime zest	1 mL
½ cup	freshly squeezed lime juice	125 mL
3	packages (each 8 oz/250 g) cream cheese, softened	3
¾ cup	granulated sugar	175 mL
1 tsp	vanilla extract	5 mL
1 cup	whipping (35%) cream, whipped	250 mL

Decoration

	Classic Whipped Cream Topping (see recipe, page 262)	
¼ tsp	grated lime zest	1 mL

1. *Crust:* In a bowl, combine cookie crumbs and butter. Press into bottom of cheesecake pan and freeze.

2. *Filling:* Sprinkle gelatin over lime juice in a small saucepan and let stand for 1 minute. Stir over low heat until gelatin is completely dissolved. Set aside to cool slightly.

3. In a mixer bowl fitted with paddle attachment, beat cream cheese and sugar on medium-high speed until very smooth, for 3 minutes. Slowly mix in dissolved gelatin. Stir in vanilla and lime zest. Fold in whipped cream by hand.

4. Pour over frozen crust, smoothing out to sides of pan. Cover with plastic wrap and refrigerate for at least 6 hours before decorating or serving. Run a hot knife around edge of pan to loosen.

5. *Decoration:* Ice top of cake with Classic Whipped Cream Topping or pipe rosettes around top of cake, if desired. Sprinkle with lime zest.

Small Cheesecakes
and Bars

Mojito Cheesecake

About 20 years ago, on a summer day, a friend who had just come back from Cuba introduced me to a refreshing drink, the mojito. He said it was going to be a big hit in the States. He was correct, and years later I have developed a cheesecake with the same flavors.

Tip

Keep the caps on the extract bottles until you are ready to use them, as the flavors dissipate when the extracts are exposed to air.

Variation

You can substitute 2 tbsp (25 mL) dark rum for the rum extract.

- Preheat oven to 350°F (180°C)
- 6-inch (15 cm) cheesecake pan, ungreased, or springform pan with 3-inch (7.5 cm) sides, greased

Crust

1 cup	butter cookie crumbs	250 mL
2 tbsp	unsalted butter, melted	25 mL

Filling

2	packages (each 8 oz/250 g) cream cheese, softened	2
½ cup	small-curd cottage cheese (see tips, page 146)	125 mL
¾ cup	granulated sugar	175 mL
2	eggs	2
1 tbsp	grated lime zest	15 mL
½ tsp	mint extract	2 mL
½ tsp	rum extract	2 mL

Decoration

	Classic Whipped Cream Topping (see recipe, page 262)	
8	mint leaves	8

1. *Crust:* In a bowl, combine cookie crumbs and butter. Press into bottom of cheesecake pan and freeze.
2. *Filling:* In a mixer bowl fitted with paddle attachment, beat cream cheese, cottage cheese and sugar on medium-high speed until very smooth, for 3 minutes. Add eggs, one at a time, beating after each addition. Stir in lime zest, mint extract and rum extract.
3. Pour over frozen crust, smoothing out to sides of pan. Bake in preheated oven until top is light brown and center has a slight jiggle to it, 35 to 45 minutes. Let cool in pan on a wire rack for 2 hours. Cover with plastic wrap and refrigerate for at least 6 hours before decorating or serving.
4. *Decoration:* Pipe 8 rosettes around top of cake with Classic Whipped Cream. Top each rosette with a mint leaf.

Quadruple-Chocolate Cheesecake

- Preheat oven to 325°F (160°C)
- 6-inch (15 cm) cheesecake pan, ungreased, or springform pan with 3-inch (7.5 cm) sides, greased

Crust

¾ cup	chocolate sandwich cookie crumbs	175 mL
2 tbsp	unsalted butter, melted	25 mL

Filling

2 tbsp	unsweetened Dutch-process cocoa powder	25 mL
2 tsp	hot brewed espresso	10 mL
2	packages (each 8 oz/250 g) cream cheese, softened	2
¾ cup	granulated sugar	175 mL
2	eggs	2
4 oz	white chocolate chunks	125 g
2 oz	bittersweet chocolate chunks	60 g
2 oz	milk chocolate chunks	60 g
1 tsp	vanilla extract	5 mL

Decoration

Classic Whipped Cream Topping
(see recipe, page 262)

1. *Crust:* In a bowl, combine cookie crumbs and butter. Press into bottom of cheesecake pan and freeze.
2. *Filling:* In a small bowl, dissolve cocoa powder in hot espresso. Set aside.
3. In a mixer bowl fitted with paddle attachment, beat cream cheese and sugar on medium-high speed until very smooth, for 3 minutes. Add eggs, one at a time, beating after each addition. Fold in white, bittersweet and milk chocolate chunks, vanilla and dissolved cocoa by hand.
4. Pour over frozen crust, smoothing out to sides of pan. Bake in preheated oven until top is light brown and center has a slight jiggle to it, 25 to 35 minutes. Let cool in pan on a wire rack for 2 hours. Cover with plastic wrap and refrigerate for at least 6 hours before decorating or serving.
5. *Decoration:* Ice top of cake with Classic Whipped Cream Topping or pipe rosettes around top of cake, if desired.

Deep Dark Chocolate Fudge Cheesecake

SERVES 4 TO 6

My students in West Lafayette, Indiana, are chocolate lovers who appreciate dark, darker, darkest.

Tips

It is best to use a chocolate bar and cut it into chunks instead of using chips.

A small whisk is perfect for the small, but important, job of dissolving cocoa powder in hot water.

- Preheat oven to 325°F (160°C)
- 6-inch (15 cm) cheesecake pan, ungreased, or springform pan with 3-inch (7.5 cm) sides, greased

Crust

¾ cup	chocolate sandwich cookie crumbs	175 mL
2 tbsp	unsalted butter, melted	25 mL

Filling

2 tbsp	unsweetened Dutch-process cocoa powder	25 mL
2 tsp	hot water	10 mL
2	packages (each 8 oz/250 g) cream cheese, softened	2
¾ cup	granulated sugar	175 mL
2	eggs	2
8 oz	bittersweet chocolate chunks	250 g
1 tsp	vanilla extract	5 mL

Decoration

Classic Whipped Cream Topping (see recipe, page 262)
Truffle Fudge Topping (see recipe, page 263)

1. *Crust:* In a bowl, combine cookie crumbs and butter. Press into bottom of cheesecake pan and freeze.

2. *Filling:* In a small bowl, dissolve cocoa powder in hot water. Set aside.

3. In a mixer bowl fitted with paddle attachment, beat cream cheese and sugar on medium-high speed until very smooth, for 3 minutes. Add eggs, one at a time, beating after each addition. Fold in chocolate chunks, vanilla and dissolved cocoa by hand.

4. Pour over frozen crust, smoothing out to sides of pan. Bake in preheated oven until top is firm to the touch and center has a slight jiggle to it, 25 to 35 minutes. Let cool in pan on a wire rack for 2 hours. Cover with plastic wrap and refrigerate for at least 6 hours before decorating or serving.

5. *Decoration:* Ice top of cake with Classic Whipped Cream Topping or pipe rosettes around top of cake, if desired. Top each slice with a spoonful of Truffle Fudge Topping.

Blackout Cheesecake

SERVES 4 TO 6

Deep, dark chocolate cheesecake is simple, but elegant enough for a small dinner party.

Tips

Buy the best-quality chocolate bar and cut into chunks instead of using chips.

A small whisk is perfect for the small, but important, job of dissolving cocoa powder in hot water.

Variation

Add 1 tbsp (15 mL) hazelnut-flavored liqueur with the vanilla for extra depth and zing.

- Preheat oven to 325°F (160°C)
- 6-inch (15 cm) cheesecake pan, ungreased, or springform pan with 3-inch (7.5 cm) sides, greased

Crust

¾ cup	chocolate sandwich cookie crumbs	175 mL
2 tbsp	unsalted butter, melted	25 mL

Filling

2 tbsp	unsweetened Dutch-process cocoa powder	25 mL
1 tbsp	hot water	15 mL
2	packages (each 8 oz/250 g) cream cheese, softened	2
¾ cup	granulated sugar	175 mL
2	eggs	2
1	egg yolk	1
	Truffle Fudge Topping (see recipe, page 263)	
6 oz	bittersweet chocolate chunks	175 g
1 tsp	vanilla extract	5 mL

1. *Crust:* In a bowl, combine cookie crumbs and butter. Press into bottom of cheesecake pan and freeze.

2. *Filling:* In a small bowl, dissolve cocoa powder in hot water. Set aside.

3. In a mixer bowl fitted with paddle attachment, beat cream cheese and sugar on medium-high speed until very smooth, for 3 minutes. Add whole eggs and egg yolk, one at a time, beating after each addition. Fold in dissolved cocoa, half of the Truffle Fudge Topping, chocolate chunks and vanilla by hand.

4. Pour over frozen crust, smoothing out to sides of pan. Bake in preheated oven until top is light brown and center has a slight jiggle to it, 30 to 40 minutes. Let cool in pan on a wire rack for 2 hours. Cover with plastic wrap and refrigerate for at least 6 hours before decorating and serving.

5. *Decoration:* Top each slice with a dollop of the remaining Truffle Fudge Topping.

Tin Roof Cheesecake

SERVES 4 TO 6

On my first trip to the gold rush area of central California, I struck gold in an old-fashioned ice cream parlor, where they made a dessert called Tin Roof, packed with chocolate-covered peanuts.

Tip

Place chocolate peanuts in a sealable plastic bag and roll a rolling pin over them a few times until crushed to desired coarseness.

- Preheat oven to 325°F (160°C)
- 6-inch (15 cm) cheesecake pan, ungreased, or springform pan with 3-inch (7.5 cm) sides, greased

Crust

¾ cup	chocolate sandwich cookie crumbs	175 mL
2 tbsp	unsalted butter, melted	25 mL

Filling

2	packages (each 8 oz/250 g) cream cheese, softened	2
½ cup	packed brown sugar	125 mL
2	eggs	2
½ cup	chocolate-covered peanuts, coarsely crushed (see tip, at left)	125 mL
1 tsp	vanilla extract	5 mL
1 tsp	freshly squeezed lemon juice	5 mL

Decoration

	Classic Whipped Cream Topping (see recipe, page 262)	
2 tbsp	chocolate-covered peanuts, coarsely crushed	25 mL

1. *Crust:* In a bowl, combine cookie crumbs and butter. Press into bottom of cheesecake pan and freeze.

2. *Filling:* In a mixer bowl fitted with paddle attachment, beat cream cheese and brown sugar on medium-high speed until very smooth, for 3 minutes. Add eggs, one at a time, beating after each addition. Fold in peanuts, vanilla and lemon juice by hand.

3. Pour over frozen crust, smoothing out to sides of pan. Bake in preheated oven until top is firm to the touch and center has a slight jiggle to it, 25 to 35 minutes. Let cool in pan on a wire rack for 2 hours. Cover with plastic wrap and refrigerate for at least 6 hours before decorating or serving.

4. *Decoration:* Ice top of cake with Classic Whipped Cream Topping or pipe rosettes around top of cake, if desired. Sprinkle top with chocolate-covered peanuts.

Strawberry Swirl Cheesecake

SERVES 4 TO 6

This cheesecake may be small, but it's packed with flavor.

Tips

Use preserves or jam, rather than jelly, for the seeds and texture.

If preserves are thick, add ¼ cup (50 mL) batter to loosen before swirling them in.

Variation

Try any flavor of preserves.

- Preheat oven to 325°F (160°C)
- 6-inch (15 cm) cheesecake pan, ungreased, or springform pan with 3-inch (7.5 cm) sides, greased

Crust

¾ cup	graham cracker crumbs	175 mL
2 tbsp	unsalted butter, melted	25 mL

Filling

2	packages (each 8 oz/250 g) cream cheese, softened	2
¾ cup	granulated sugar	175 mL
2	eggs	2
⅓ cup	strawberry preserves or jam	75 mL
1 tsp	vanilla extract	5 mL

1. *Crust:* In a bowl, combine graham cracker crumbs and butter. Press into bottom of cheesecake pan and freeze.

2. *Filling:* In a mixer bowl fitted with paddle attachment, beat cream cheese and sugar on medium-high speed until very smooth, for 3 minutes. Add eggs one at a time, beating after each addition. Stir in vanilla. Swirl in strawberry preserves.

3. Pour over frozen crust, smoothing out to sides of pan. Bake in preheated oven until top is light brown and center has a slight jiggle to it, 30 to 35 minutes. Let cool in pan on a wire rack for 2 hours. Cover with plastic wrap and refrigerate for at least 6 hours before serving.

Orange Blossom Cheesecake

SERVES 4 TO 6

The orange flower water creates a floral fragrance at the table when this cheesecake is served.

Tips

If orange cookies are difficult to find, you can use butter cookies and add ½ tsp (2 mL) grated orange zest to the crust mixture.

Orange flower water can be found at specialty gourmet food stores or spice purveyors.

If you can't find orange blossom honey, infuse 10 oz (300 g) liquid honey with the zest of 1 orange for 3 weeks.

- Preheat oven to 350°F (180°C)
- 6-inch (15 cm) cheesecake pan, ungreased, or springform pan with 3-inch (7.5 cm) sides, greased

Crust

1 cup	orange cookie crumbs	250 mL
2 tbsp	unsalted butter, melted	25 mL

Filling

2	packages (each 8 oz/250 g) cream cheese, softened	2
½ cup	vanilla-flavored yogurt	125 mL
½ cup	granulated sugar	125 mL
2	eggs	2
2 tbsp	liquid orange blossom honey	25 mL
1 tbsp	orange flower water	15 mL
1 tsp	grated orange zest	5 mL

Decoration

	Classic Whipped Cream Topping (see recipe, page 262)	
1 tsp	grated orange zest	5 mL

1. *Crust:* In a bowl, combine cookie crumbs and butter. Press into bottom of cheesecake pan and freeze.
2. *Filling:* In a mixer bowl fitted with paddle attachment, beat cream cheese, yogurt and sugar on medium-high speed until very smooth, for 3 minutes. Add eggs, one at a time, beating after each addition. Stir in honey, orange flower water and orange zest.
3. Pour over frozen crust, smoothing out to sides of pan. Bake in preheated oven until top is light brown and center has a slight jiggle to it, 35 to 45 minutes. Let cool in pan on a wire rack for 2 hours. Cover with plastic wrap and refrigerate for at least 6 hours before decorating or serving.
4. *Decoration:* Pipe rosettes around top of cake with Classic Whipped Cream Topping. Sprinkle with orange zest.

Almond Cheesecake

SERVES 4 TO 6

Here's the perfect size cheesecake for a small dinner party.

Tip

To be economical, purchase almonds whole with the skins on. To toast, place in a 350°F (180°C) oven until fragrant, 10 to 12 minutes. Rub hot nuts in a dishtowel to remove the skins. Don't chop nuts until they have cooled.

Variation

For an even silkier texture, use mascarpone instead of regular cream cheese.

- Preheat oven to 300°F (150°C)
- 6-inch (15 cm) cheesecake pan, ungreased, or springform pan with 3-inch (7.5 cm) sides, greased

Crust

¾ cup	almond cookie crumbs	175 mL
2 tbsp	unsalted butter, melted	25 mL

Filling

2	packages (each 8 oz/250 g) cream cheese, softened	2
¾ cup	granulated sugar	175 mL
2	eggs	2
¼ cup	blanched almonds, toasted (see tip, at left) and chopped	50 mL
2 tbsp	almond-flavored liqueur	25 mL
1 tsp	vanilla extract	5 mL

Decoration

	Classic Whipped Cream Topping (see recipe, page 262)	
6	whole blanched almonds, toasted	6

1. *Crust:* In a bowl, combine cookie crumbs and butter. Press into bottom of cheesecake pan and freeze.

2. *Filling:* In a mixer bowl fitted with paddle attachment, beat cream cheese and sugar on medium-high speed until very smooth, for 3 minutes. Add eggs, one at a time, beating after each addition. Fold in chopped almonds, liqueur and vanilla by hand.

3. Pour over frozen crust, smoothing out to sides of pan. Bake in preheated oven until top is light brown and center has a slight jiggle to it, 40 to 45 minutes. Let cool in pan on a wire rack for 2 hours. Cover with plastic wrap and refrigerate for at least 6 hours before decorating or serving.

4. *Decoration:* Ice top of cake with Classic Whipped Cream Topping or pipe rosettes around top of cake, if desired. Top with whole almonds.

Individual Lemon Cheesecakes

These delicious bites of lemon cream are great for a party or lunch. Bake a batch and freeze the leftovers.

Tips

To freeze, let cool completely. Wrap each cake in plastic wrap, then in foil.

You can divide this recipe in half and make 12 mini cheesecakes using a regular muffin tin.

Variation

Add up to 1 tbsp (15 mL) jam on top of each cake and create an array of flavors.

- Preheat oven to 300°F (150°C)
- Texas-size muffin tin with at least 16 cups (about 1⅝ inches/4 cm deep) or 24 regular-size muffin cups (about 1¼ inches/3 cm deep), lined with paper muffin cups

Crust

2½ cups	graham cracker crumbs	625 mL
½ cup	unsalted butter, melted	125 mL

Filling

4	packages (each 8 oz/250 g) cream cheese, softened	4
1¼ cups	granulated sugar	300 mL
4	eggs	4
3 tbsp	freshly squeezed lemon juice	45 mL
1 tsp	vanilla extract	5 mL

Topping

1 cup	sour cream	250 mL
½ cup	granulated sugar	125 mL
1 tbsp	freshly squeezed lemon juice	15 mL
1 tsp	vanilla extract	5 mL

1. *Crust:* In a bowl, combine graham cracker crumbs and butter. Press evenly into bottom of each muffin cup and freeze.
2. *Filling:* In a mixer bowl fitted with paddle attachment, beat cream cheese and sugar on medium-high speed until very smooth, for 3 minutes. Add eggs, one at a time, beating after each addition. Mix in lemon juice and vanilla.
3. Fill each cup about three-quarters full. Bake in preheated oven until cheesecakes puff up a bit and centers have a slight jiggle to them, 20 to 25 minutes. Let cool on a wire rack for 10 minutes (do not turn the oven off).
4. *Topping:* In a small bowl, combine sour cream, sugar, lemon juice and vanilla. Pour into center of each cooled cake and spread out to edges. Bake for 5 minutes more. Let cool in tin on a wire rack for 2 hours. Cover with plastic wrap and refrigerate for at least 6 hours before serving.

Two-Bite Cheesecakes

MAKES 24 MINI CHEESECAKES

I like to serve these for lunch or brunch, when just a bite is all you need.

Tip

Toasting brings out the natural oils and flavor of nuts. Place nuts in a single layer on a baking sheet and bake at 350°F (180°C) until fragrant, 10 to 12 minutes.

Variation

If you have a few extra minutes, dollop a bit of berry jam on top of each cheesecake.

- Preheat oven to 325°F (160°C)
- 24-cup mini muffin tin, lined with paper muffin cups

Crust

¾ cup	graham cracker crumbs	175 mL
¼ cup	pecans, toasted (see tip, at left) and ground	50 mL
¼ cup	unsalted butter, melted	50 mL

Filling

2	packages (each 8 oz/250 g) cream cheese, softened	2
¾ cup	granulated sugar	175 mL
2	eggs	2
1½ tsp	vanilla extract	7 mL
½ tsp	almond extract	2 mL

1. *Crust:* In a bowl, combine graham cracker crumbs, pecans and butter. Press 2 tsp (10 mL) into bottom of each muffin cup and freeze.

2. *Filling:* In a mixer bowl fitted with paddle attachment, beat cream cheese and sugar on medium-high speed until very smooth, for 3 minutes. Add eggs, one at a time, beating after each addition. Mix in vanilla and almond extract.

3. Fill each cup about three-quarters full. Bake in preheated oven until cheesecakes puff up a bit, 18 to 22 minutes. Let cool on a wire rack for 10 minutes before removing from tin. Serve immediately or cool, cover and refrigerate for up to 1 day.

Apple Spice Mini Cheesecakes

MAKES 24 MINI CHEESECAKES

This simple apple cheesecake is perfect for lunch or brunch.

Tip

If you plan to freeze the mini cakes for entertaining in the future, let them cool completely in pan, then place the entire pan in freezer for 2 hours. They will easily pop out for storage in a resealable plastic bag.

Variation

Substitute a pear for the apple.

- Preheat oven to 325°F (160°C)
- 24-cup mini muffin tin, lined with paper muffin cups

Crust

1 cup	gingersnap cookie crumbs	250 mL
1/4 cup	pecans, toasted (see tip, page 189) and ground	50 mL
1/4 cup	unsalted butter, melted	50 mL

Filling

2	packages (each 8 oz/250 g) cream cheese, softened	2
3/4 cup	granulated sugar	175 mL
2	eggs	2
1	baking apple (such as Granny Smith or Pippin), peeled and finely chopped	1
1 1/2 tsp	vanilla extract	7 mL
1/2 tsp	ground cinnamon	2 mL
1/4 tsp	freshly grated nutmeg	1 mL

1. *Crust:* In a bowl, combine cookie crumbs, pecans and butter. Press 2 1/2 tsp (12 mL) into bottom of each muffin cup and freeze.
2. *Filling:* In a mixer bowl fitted with paddle attachment, beat cream cheese and sugar on medium-high speed until very smooth, for 3 minutes. Add eggs, one at a time, beating after each addition. Fold in apple, vanilla, cinnamon and nutmeg by hand.
3. Divide filling evenly among muffin cups. Bake in preheated oven until cheesecakes puff up a bit, 18 to 22 minutes. Let cool on a wire rack for 10 minutes before removing from tin. Serve immediately or cool, cover and refrigerate for up to 1 day.

Cherry Bomb
Mini Cheesecakes

**MAKES 24 MINI
CHEESECAKES**

*When you need a two-
bite dessert for a buffet
table, these fit the bill.
They pair well with
cookies or brownie
squares.*

Variation

Soak cherries for at least
1 day in 1 cup (250 mL)
almond-flavored liqueur.
Drain before use and
reserve the liqueur for
another use, such as a
batch of cocktails calling
for almond-flavored
liqueur and cherry syrup.

- Preheat oven to 325°F (160°C)
- 24-cup mini muffin tin, lined with paper muffin cups

Crust

1 cup	graham cracker crumbs	250 mL
¼ cup	unsalted butter, melted	50 mL

Filling

2	packages (each 8 oz/250 g) cream cheese, softened	2
¾ cup	granulated sugar	175 mL
2	eggs	2
1½ tsp	vanilla extract	7 mL
½ tsp	almond extract	2 mL
24	maraschino cherries, drained and patted dry	24

1. *Crust:* In a bowl, combine graham cracker crumbs and butter. Press 2 tsp (10 mL) into bottom of each muffin cup and freeze.

2. *Filling:* In a mixer bowl fitted with paddle attachment, beat cream cheese and sugar on medium-high speed until very smooth, for 3 minutes. Add eggs, one at a time, beating after each addition. Mix in vanilla and almond extract.

3. Place one cherry in each muffin cup. Divide filling evenly among muffin cups. Bake in preheated oven until cheesecakes puff up a bit, 18 to 22 minutes. Let cool on a wire rack for 10 minutes before removing from tin. Serve immediately or cool, cover and refrigerate for up to 1 day.

Blackberry Mini Cheesecakes

MAKES 24 MINI CHEESECAKES

Pair these with Cherry Bomb Mini Cheesecakes (page 191) to complete your buffet table.

Tip

If blackberries are large, cut them in half to fit into muffin cups and just use one half per cup.

Variation

Fold in ½ cup (125 mL) almonds, toasted (see tip, page 189) and chopped, with the vanilla.

- Preheat oven to 325°F (160°C)
- 24-cup mini muffin tin, lined with paper muffin cups

Crust

1 cup	graham cracker crumbs	250 mL
¼ cup	unsalted butter, melted	50 mL

Filling

2	packages (each 8 oz/250 g) cream cheese, softened	2
1 cup	sour cream	250 mL
¾ cup	granulated sugar	175 mL
2	eggs	2
1½ tsp	vanilla extract	7 mL
24	fresh blackberries (see tip, at left)	24

1. *Crust:* In a bowl, combine graham cracker crumbs and butter. Press 2½ tsp (12 mL) into bottom of each muffin cup and freeze.

2. *Filling:* In a mixer bowl fitted with paddle attachment, beat cream cheese, sour cream and sugar on medium-high speed until very smooth, for 3 minutes. Add eggs, one at a time, beating after each addition. Mix in vanilla.

3. Place a blackberry in each muffin cup. Divide filling evenly among muffin cups. Bake in preheated oven until cheesecakes puff up a bit, 18 to 22 minutes. Let cool on a wire rack for 10 minutes before removing from tin. Serve immediately or cool, cover and refrigerate for up to 1 day.

Orange Blossom Cheesecake (page 186)

Overleaf: Chocolate Peanut Butter Cheese Bars (page 198) and Individual Lemon Cheesecakes (page 188)

Ice Cream Cone Cheesecakes

MAKES 12 MINI CHEESECAKES

These mini cheesecakes are housed in ice cream cones — perfect for a kids' birthday party! You can ice the tops to make them look like real ice cream.

Tip

These ice cream cone cheesecakes freeze for up to 4 months, wrapped in plastic wrap and then foil. There's no need to thaw them — just decorate and serve.

Variation

Substitute canned buttercream icing for the Classic Whipped Cream Topping.

- Preheat oven to 325°F (160°C)
- 12-cup muffin tin

12	flat-bottomed ice cream cones	12

Filling

3	packages (each 8 oz/250 g) cream cheese, softened	3
1 cup	granulated sugar	250 mL
3	eggs	3
12 oz	semisweet chocolate chunks	375 g
1 tsp	vanilla extract	5 mL
1 tsp	freshly squeezed lemon juice	5 mL

Decoration

Classic Whipped Cream Topping
(see recipe, page 262)
Assorted sprinkles

1. Fill muffin tin with ice cream cones.
2. *Filling:* In a mixer bowl fitted with paddle attachment, beat cream cheese and sugar on medium-high speed until very smooth, for 3 minutes. Add eggs, one at a time, beating after each addition. Fold in chocolate chunks, vanilla and lemon juice by hand.
3. Fill each cone about three-quarters full. Bake in preheated oven until tops are light brown and slightly cracked, 35 to 40 minutes. Let cool in tin on a wire rack for 2 hours. Cover with plastic wrap and refrigerate for at least 2 hours before decorating or serving.
4. *Decoration:* Pipe large rosettes of Classic Whipped Cream Topping on top of each cone. Decorate with sprinkles.

Spumoni Cheesecake Bars
(page 203)

Dulce de Leche Cheesecake Bars

MAKES 12 TO 18 BARS

Enjoy creamy, light cheesecake the Latin American way, with a hint of caramel inside and on top.

Tip

To quickly prepare graham cracker crumbs, place whole graham crackers in a food processor fitted with a metal blade and pulse a few times. You can add the butter to the food processor and pulse until blended. When mixed with the butter, the crumbs should feel like wet sand.

- Preheat oven to 325°F (160°C)
- 13- by 9-inch (3 L) metal baking pan, lined with foil

Crust

2½ cups	graham cracker crumbs	625 mL
⅓ cup	unsalted butter, melted	75 mL

Filling

1	can (14 oz/396 g or 300 mL) sweetened condensed milk	1
3	packages (each 8 oz/250 g) cream cheese, softened	3
¾ cup	packed brown sugar	175 mL
3	eggs	3
1 tsp	vanilla extract	5

1. *Crust:* In a bowl, combine graham cracker crumbs and butter. Press into bottom of prepared pan and freeze.

2. *Filling:* In a heatproof bowl set over a saucepan of lightly simmering water, heat condensed milk, stirring occasionally, until light caramel in color and thick, 60 to 70 minutes. Check water periodically and add more as necessary to keep the water level just below the bottom of the bowl.

3. In a mixer bowl fitted with paddle attachment, beat cream cheese and brown sugar on medium-high speed until very smooth, for 3 minutes. Add eggs, one at a time, beating after each addition. Fold in vanilla and half the caramelized milk by hand. Cover the remaining caramelized milk and set aside.

4. Pour over frozen crust, smoothing out to sides of pan. Bake in preheated oven until top is light brown and center has a slight jiggle to it, 45 to 55 minutes. Let cool in pan on a wire rack for 2 hours. Cover with plastic wrap and refrigerate for at least 6 hours before topping.

5. *Topping:* Return reserved caramelized milk to double boiler and heat gently until thin enough to pour easily. Pour over cooled cheesecake. Cut into bars.

Italian Zabaglione Cheesecake Bars

MAKES 12 TO 18 BARS

Any good Italian menu deserves a special Italian dessert.

Tip

Some almond cookies are very moist. The crumb mixture should feel like wet sand. If the crumbs alone seem moist enough, don't add the butter.

- Preheat oven to 325°F (160°C)
- 13- by 9-inch (3 L) metal baking pan, lined with foil

Crust

2½ cups	almond cookie crumbs	625 mL
½ cup	unsalted butter, melted	125 mL

Filling

2	packages (each 8 oz/250 g) cream cheese, softened	2
1 lb	mascarpone cheese	500 g
1 cup	granulated sugar	250 mL
¼ cup	all-purpose flour	50 mL
3	eggs	3
2	egg yolks	2
¼ cup	Marsala wine	50 mL
2 tsp	vanilla extract	10 mL

1. *Crust:* In a bowl, combine cookie crumbs and butter. Press into bottom of prepared pan and freeze.

2. *Filling:* In a mixer bowl fitted with paddle attachment, beat cream cheese, mascarpone cheese, sugar and flour until very smooth, for 3 minutes. Add whole eggs and egg yolks, one at a time, beating after each addition. Mix in wine and vanilla.

3. Pour over frozen crust, smoothing out to sides of pan. Bake in preheated oven until top is light brown and center has a slight jiggle to it, 45 to 55 minutes. Let cool in pan on a wire rack for 2 hours. Cover with plastic wrap and refrigerate for at least 6 hours before cutting into bars.

Devil's Food Cheese Bars

Columbus, Ohio, has a wonderful Jazz and Ribs Fest every summer, a great combination — just like these bars.

Tips

When making cookie crumbs, you do not have to scrape the cream filling out of the cookies; just place them whole into the food processor and pulse.

A small whisk is perfect for the small, but important, job of dissolving cocoa powder in hot water.

- Preheat oven to 325°F (160°C)
- 13- by 9-inch (3 L) metal baking pan, lined with foil

Crust

2½ cups	chocolate sandwich cookie crumbs	625 mL
⅓ cup	unsalted butter, melted	75 mL

Filling

¼ cup	unsweetened Dutch-process cocoa powder	50 mL
3 tbsp	hot water	45 mL
4	packages (each 8 oz/250 g) cream cheese, softened	4
1 cup	sour cream	250 mL
1½ cups	granulated sugar	375 mL
3	eggs	3
1	egg yolk	1
1 tbsp	liquid red food coloring	15 mL
1 tbsp	vanilla extract	15 mL

1. *Crust:* In a bowl, combine cookie crumbs and butter. Press into bottom of prepared pan and freeze.
2. *Filling:* In a small bowl, dissolve cocoa powder in hot water. Set aside.
3. In a mixer bowl fitted with paddle attachment, beat cream cheese, sour cream and sugar on medium-high speed until very smooth, for 3 minutes. Add whole eggs and egg yolk, one at a time, beating after each addition. Mix in food coloring, vanilla and dissolved cocoa.
4. Pour over frozen crust, smoothing out to sides of pan. Bake in preheated oven until top is light brown and center has a slight jiggle to it, 45 to 55 minutes. Let cool in pan on a wire rack for 2 hours. Cover with plastic wrap and refrigerate for at least 6 hours before cutting into bars.

Chocolate Raspberry Cheese Bars

MAKES 12 TO 18 BARS

These fudgey raspberry bars with chunks of chocolate are for those who really love berries and chocolate.

Tip

If using frozen raspberries, make sure they are completely thawed and drained before adding them to the batter.

Variation

For a dramatic red, white and black version, substitute white chocolate chunks for the semisweet chocolate.

- Preheat oven to 325°F (160°C)
- 13- by 9-inch (3 L) metal baking pan, lined with foil

Crust

2½ cups	chocolate sandwich cookie crumbs	625 mL
⅓ cup	unsalted butter, melted	75 mL

Filling

3	packages (each 8 oz/250 g) cream cheese, softened	3
1 cup	granulated sugar	250 mL
3	eggs	3
3 oz	bittersweet chocolate, melted (see page 63) and cooled	90 g
1 cup	raspberries, quartered	250 mL
1 cup	semisweet or bittersweet chocolate chunks	250 mL
2 tsp	vanilla extract	10 mL

1. *Crust:* In a bowl, combine cookie crumbs and butter. Press into bottom of prepared pan and freeze.

2. *Filling:* In a mixer bowl fitted with paddle attachment, beat cream cheese and sugar on medium-high speed until very smooth, for 3 minutes. Add eggs, one at a time, beating after each addition. With the mixer running, pour in melted chocolate in a steady stream. Fold in raspberries, chocolate chunks and vanilla by hand.

3. Pour over frozen crust, smoothing out to sides of pan. Bake in preheated oven until top is light brown and center has a slight jiggle to it, 45 to 55 minutes. Let cool in pan on a wire rack for 2 hours. Cover with plastic wrap and refrigerate for at least 6 hours before cutting into bars.

Chocolate Peanut Butter Cheese Bars

MAKES 10 TO 12 BARS

I created this recipe for one of my oldest students, Catherine, who was 95 when she passed away. She never stopped learning, and I think of her every time I make these.

Tips

To melt bittersweet chocolate in the microwave, break into squares and place in a microwave-safe dish. Microwave on High for 1 to 2 minutes, stirring after 30 seconds.

Natural peanut butters have too much oil for this recipe.

To make lemons easier to juice, roll them firmly on the counter to break up the membranes of the fruit.

- Preheat oven to 325°F (160°C)
- 13- by 9-inch (3 L) metal baking pan, lined with foil

Crust

2½ cups	peanut butter sandwich cookie crumbs	625 mL
½ cup	all-purpose flour	125 mL
½ cup	unsalted butter, melted	125 mL

Filling

4	packages (each 8 oz/250 g) cream cheese, softened	4
1¼ cups	granulated sugar	300 mL
4	eggs	4
8 oz	bittersweet chocolate, melted (see page 63 and tip, at left) and cooled	250 g
1 cup	creamy peanut butter	250 mL
3 tbsp	freshly squeezed lemon juice	45 mL
1 tsp	vanilla extract	5 mL
2 cups	semisweet chocolate chunks	500 mL

Topping

1 cup	sour cream	250 mL
½ cup	granulated sugar	125 mL
⅓ cup	creamy peanut butter	75 mL
1 tbsp	freshly squeezed lemon juice	15 mL
1 tsp	vanilla extract	5 mL
½ cup	semisweet chocolate chunks	125 mL

1. *Crust:* In a bowl, combine cookie crumbs, flour and butter. Press into bottom of prepared pan and freeze.
2. *Filling:* In a mixer bowl fitted with paddle attachment, beat cream cheese and sugar on medium-high speed until very smooth, for 3 minutes. Add eggs, one at a time, beating after each addition. With the mixer running, pour in melted chocolate in a steady stream. Mix in peanut butter, lemon juice and vanilla. Fold in chocolate chunks by hand.

Variation

You can use milk
chocolate chunks
instead of semisweet
chocolate in the topping.

3. Pour over frozen crust, smoothing out to sides of pan. Bake in preheated oven until top is light brown and center has a slight jiggle to it, 35 to 45 minutes. Let cool on the counter for 10 minutes (do not turn the oven off). The cake will sink slightly.

4. *Topping:* In a bowl, combine sour cream, sugar, peanut butter, lemon juice and vanilla. Pour into center of cooled cake and spread out to edges. Sprinkle with chocolate chunks. Bake for 5 minutes more. Let cool in pan on a wire rack for 2 hours. Cover with plastic wrap and refrigerate for at least 6 hours before cutting into bars.

Grasshopper Cheese Bars

**MAKES 12 TO
18 BARS**

*No grasshoppers in
these bars — just
the cool sensation of
chocolate and mint.*

Variation

Omit the peppermint
extract and semisweet
chocolate, and fold
1 cup (250 mL) mint
chips into the batter
by hand.

- Preheat oven to 325°F (160°C)
- 13- by 9-inch (3 L) metal baking pan, lined with foil, sprayed
  with nonstick spray

Crust

2½ cups	chocolate sandwich cookie crumbs	625 mL
⅓ cup	unsalted butter, melted	75 mL

Filling

3	packages (each 8 oz/250 g) cream cheese, softened	3
¾ cup	granulated sugar	175 mL
3	eggs	3
¼ cup	all-purpose flour	50 mL
½ cup	sour cream	125 mL
1 tsp	vanilla extract	5 mL
¼ tsp	peppermint extract	1 mL
3 oz	semisweet chocolate, melted (see page 63) and cooled	90 g

Decoration

Classic Whipped Cream Topping
(see recipe, page 262)

1. *Crust:* In a bowl, combine cookie crumbs and butter.
   Press into bottom of prepared pan and freeze.
2. *Filling:* In a mixer bowl fitted with paddle attachment,
   beat cream cheese and sugar on medium-high speed until
   very smooth, for 3 minutes. Add eggs, one at a time, beating
   after each addition. Mix in flour, sour cream, vanilla and
   peppermint. With the mixer running, pour in melted
   chocolate in a steady stream.
3. Pour over frozen crust, smoothing out to sides of pan.
   Bake in preheated oven until top is light brown and center
   has a slight jiggle to it, 45 to 55 minutes. Let cool in pan
   on a wire rack for 2 hours. Cover with plastic wrap and
   refrigerate for at least 6 hours before decorating.
4. *Decoration:* Cut into bars and top each with Classic
   Whipped Cream Topping.

Dutch Apple Cheesecake Bars

*These cheesecake bars
are very rich, with crisp
apples lining the top
and center.*

Tip

You can prepare these
bars up to 3 weeks
ahead. When chilled,
wrap the pan in plastic
wrap, then in foil, and
freeze. Thaw in the
refrigerator for 24 hours
before serving.

Variation

Fold the sliced apple
topping into the batter
in addition to the
chopped apples.

- Preheat oven to 325°F (160°C)
- 13- by 9-inch (3 L) metal baking pan, lined with foil, sprayed with nonstick spray

Crust

2½ cups	graham cracker crumbs	625 mL
½ cup	unsalted butter, melted	125 mL

Filling

3	packages (each 8 oz/250 g) cream cheese, softened	3
1 cup	sour cream	250 mL
1½ cups	packed light brown sugar	375 mL
4	eggs	4
1 tbsp	vanilla extract	15 mL
1 tsp	freshly squeezed lemon juice	5 mL
1 tsp	ground cinnamon	5 mL
½ tsp	freshly grated nutmeg	2 mL
¼ tsp	ground cloves	1 mL
1	baking apple (such as Granny Smith or Pippin), peeled and finely chopped	1

Topping

3 tbsp	cold unsalted butter	45 mL
¼ cup	all-purpose flour	50 mL
¼ cup	packed light brown sugar	50 mL
½ tsp	ground cinnamon	2 mL
¼ tsp	ground cloves	1 mL
18	thin apple slices (about 1½ medium)	18

1. *Crust:* In a bowl, combine graham cracker crumbs and butter. Press into bottom of prepared pan and freeze.
2. *Filling:* In a mixer bowl fitted with paddle attachment, beat cream cheese, sour cream and brown sugar on medium-high speed until very smooth, for 3 minutes. Add eggs, one at a time, beating after each addition. Mix in vanilla and lemon juice. Stir in cinnamon, nutmeg and cloves. Fold in chopped apple by hand. Pour over frozen crust, smoothing out to sides of pan.
3. *Topping:* In a bowl, using a pastry fork or two knives, cut butter into flour. Add sugar, cinnamon and cloves. Add apple slices and toss to coat. Arrange in rows over batter.
4. Bake in preheated oven until apples are light brown and center of filling has a slight jiggle to it, 40 to 50 minutes. Let cool in pan on a wire rack for 2 hours. Cover with plastic wrap and refrigerate for at least 6 hours before cutting into squares.

Berry Cheese Bars

**MAKES 12 TO
18 BARS**

*Our local farmers'
market carries little
French-style berries.
I love making this
cheesecake with their
artisan berries, but
you can use any type
of berries you have
on hand.*

Tip

I like to place a dollop
of whipped cream on
the plate beside each bar.

- Preheat oven to 325°F (160°C)
- 13- by 9-inch (3 L) metal baking pan, lined with foil

Crust

2½ cups	butter cookie crumbs	625 mL
⅓ cup	unsalted butter, melted	75 mL

Filling

3	packages (each 8 oz/250 g) cream cheese, softened	3
1 cup	sour cream	250 mL
1 cup	granulated sugar	250 mL
3	eggs	3
1 cup	fresh berries, cut into small pieces	250 mL
2 tsp	vanilla extract	10 mL

1. *Crust:* In a bowl, combine cookie crumbs and butter.
   Press into bottom of prepared pan and freeze.

2. *Filling:* In a mixer bowl fitted with paddle attachment,
   beat cream cheese, sour cream and sugar on medium-high
   speed until very smooth, for 3 minutes. Add eggs, one
   at a time, beating after each addition. Fold in berries and
   vanilla by hand.

3. Pour over frozen crust, smoothing out to sides of pan.
   Bake in preheated oven until top is light brown and center
   has a slight jiggle to it, 45 to 55 minutes. Let cool in pan
   on a wire rack for 2 hours. Cover with plastic wrap and
   refrigerate for at least 6 hours before cutting into bars.

Spumoni Cheesecake Bars

**MAKES 12 TO
18 BARS**

*The colorful layers
look hard to create,
but they're not — and
these bars are perfect
for a crowd.*

Tip

Toasting brings out the
natural oils and flavor
of nuts. Place nuts in a
single layer on a baking
sheet and bake at 350°F
(180°C) until fragrant,
10 to 12 minutes.

- Preheat oven to 325°F (160°C)
- 13- by 9-inch (3 L) metal baking pan, lined with foil

Crust

2½ cups	butter cookie crumbs	625 mL
⅓ cup	unsalted butter, melted	75 mL

Filling

2	packages (each 8 oz/250 g) cream cheese, softened	2
1 lb	mascarpone cheese	500 g
1¼ cups	granulated sugar	300 mL
4	eggs	4
2 tsp	vanilla extract	10 mL
½ cup	fresh strawberries, mashed	125 mL
½ cup	pistachios, toasted (see tip, at left) and chopped	125 mL
1	jar (8 oz/250 mL) green maraschino cherries, drained and finely chopped	1
½ cup	pecans, toasted and chopped	125 mL

Decoration

Classic Whipped Cream Topping
(see recipe, page 262)

1. *Crust:* In a bowl, combine cookie crumbs and butter. Press into bottom of prepared pan and freeze.

2. *Filling:* In a mixer bowl fitted with paddle attachment, beat cream cheese, mascarpone and sugar on medium-high speed until very smooth, for 3 minutes. Add eggs, one at a time, beating after each addition. Mix in vanilla.

3. Divide batter into three equal portions. Fold strawberries into one-third of the batter. Fold pistachios into one-third of the batter. Fold cherries into remaining third.

4. Spread strawberry batter over frozen crust, smoothing out to sides of pan. Refrigerate for about 5 minutes to firm. Spread pistachio batter carefully over strawberry layer, covering it completely. Refrigerate for 5 minutes to firm. Spread cherry batter over pistachio layer. Sprinkle with pecans. Bake in preheated oven until top is light brown and center has a slight jiggle to it, 40 to 50 minutes. Let cool in pan on a wire rack for 2 hours. Cover with plastic wrap and refrigerate for at least 6 hours before decorating.

5. *Decoration:* Cut into bars and top each with Classic Whipped Cream Topping.

Lemon Shortbread Cheese Bars

MAKES 12 TO 18 BARS

Pucker up for these sweet and tart cheese bars.

Tip

Top these bars with Port Wine Berry Compote (page 266) for contrast.

Variation

Substitute blood orange zest and juice for the lemon zest and juice.

- Preheat oven to 325°F (160°C)
- 13- by 9-inch (3 L) metal baking pan, lined with foil

Crust

2½ cups	lemon shortbread cookie crumbs	625 mL
⅓ cup	unsalted butter, melted	75 mL

Filling

3	packages (8 oz/250 g) cream cheese, softened	3
1 cup	granulated sugar	250 mL
3	eggs	3
2 tbsp	grated lemon zest	25 mL
2 tbsp	freshly squeezed lemon juice	25 mL
1 tsp	vanilla extract	5 mL

1. *Crust:* In a bowl, combine cookie crumbs and butter. Press into bottom of prepared pan and freeze.

2. *Filling:* In a mixer bowl fitted with paddle attachment, beat cream cheese and sugar on medium-high speed until very smooth, for 3 minutes. Add eggs, one at a time, beating after each addition. Stir in lemon zest, lemon juice and vanilla.

3. Pour over frozen crust, smoothing out to sides of pan. Bake in preheated oven until top is light brown and center has a slight jiggle to it, 45 to 55 minutes. Let cool in pan on a wire rack for 2 hours. Cover with plastic wrap and refrigerate for at least 6 hours before cutting into bars.

Cheese Pies

Cappuccino Cheese Pie

The rich flavors of cappuccino and a chocolate crust will enhance any dinner.

Tip

You can also use 2 shots of espresso to substitute for the powder and hot water.

Variation

Fold in ½ cup (125 mL) chopped chocolate-covered peanut butter cups with the espresso mixture.

- Preheat oven to 325°F (160°C)
- 9-inch (23 cm) deep-dish pie plate, ungreased

Crust

1¼ cups	chocolate sandwich cookie crumbs	300 mL
3 tbsp	unsalted butter, melted	45 mL

Filling

1 tbsp	instant espresso powder	15 mL
1 tbsp	hot water	15 mL
2 tsp	vanilla extract	10 mL
2	packages (each 8 oz/250 g) cream cheese, softened	2
8 oz	mascarpone cheese	250 g
¾ cup	packed brown sugar	175 mL
2	eggs	2

Decoration

Classic Whipped Cream Topping (see recipe, page 262)

1. *Crust:* In a bowl, combine cookie crumbs and butter. Press into bottom and sides of pie plate and freeze.

2. *Filling:* In a small bowl, dissolve espresso powder in hot water and vanilla. Set aside.

3. In a mixer bowl fitted with paddle attachment, beat cream cheese, mascarpone cheese and sugar on medium-high speed until very smooth, for 3 minutes. Add eggs, one at a time, beating after each addition. Mix in espresso mixture.

4. Pour over frozen crust, smoothing out to sides of pie plate. Bake in preheated oven until top is light brown and center has a slight jiggle to it, 30 to 40 minutes. Let cool in pan on a wire rack for 2 hours. Cover with plastic wrap and refrigerate for at least 6 hours before decorating or serving.

5. *Decoration:* Ice top of pie with Classic Whipped Cream Topping or pipe rosettes around top of pie, if desired.

Puerto Rican Rum Cheese Pie

· ·

SERVES 5 TO 6

A tour of the rum factories is a must when you visit the beautiful island of Puerto Rico. Definitely bring a bottle back home to cook with.

Tip

Light, or clear, rum is colorless and a little lighter in flavor than dark rum. Substituting dark rum in the pie will enhance the rum flavor and may make the color a bit darker.

Variation

Fold ¼ cup (50 mL) chopped toasted hazelnuts into the filling for flavor and crunch.

- Preheat oven to 325°F (160°C)
- 9-inch (23 cm) pie plate, ungreased

Crust

1¼ cups	butter cookie crumbs	300 mL
3 tbsp	unsalted butter, melted	45 mL

Filling

2	packages (each 8 oz/250 g) cream cheese, softened	2
½ cup	packed light brown sugar	125 mL
2	eggs	2
1 tbsp	light rum	15 mL
1 tsp	ground cinnamon	5 mL
½ tsp	vanilla extract	2 mL

Decoration

Classic Whipped Cream Topping
(see recipe, page 262)

1. *Crust:* In a bowl, combine cookie crumbs and butter. Press into bottom and sides of pie plate and freeze.
2. *Filling:* In a mixer bowl fitted with paddle attachment, beat cream cheese and brown sugar on medium-high speed until very smooth, for 3 minutes. Add eggs, one at a time, beating after each addition. Stir in rum, cinnamon and vanilla.
3. Pour over frozen crust, smoothing out to sides of pie plate. Bake in preheated oven until top is light brown and center has a slight jiggle to it, 25 to 35 minutes. Let cool in pan on a wire rack for 2 hours. Cover with plastic wrap and refrigerate for at least 6 hours before decorating or serving.
4. *Decoration:* Ice top of pie with Classic Whipped Cream Topping or pipe rosettes around top of pie, if desired.

Chocolate Chunk Cheese Pie

SERVES 5 TO 6

*Port would be perfect
served with this rich pie.*

Tips

Toasting brings out the
natural oils and flavor
of nuts. Place nuts in a
single layer on a baking
sheet and bake at 350°F
(180°C) until fragrant,
10 to 12 minutes.

A small whisk is
perfect for the small,
but important, job
of dissolving cocoa
powder in hot water.

To stay crisp, the crust
needs to cool completely
before it is filled.

Variation

Use white chocolate
chunks instead of the
bittersweet chocolate
for a different look.

- Preheat oven to 350°F (180°C)
- 9-inch (23 cm) pie plate, ungreased

Crust

1 cup	pecans, toasted (see tip, at left) and ground	250 mL
3 tbsp	all-purpose flour	45 mL
2 tbsp	unsalted butter, melted	25 mL

Filling

2 tbsp	unsweetened Dutch-process cocoa powder	25 mL
1½ tbsp	hot water	22 mL
2	packages (each 8 oz/250 g) cream cheese, softened	2
¾ cup	granulated sugar	175 mL
2	eggs	2
1 tbsp	freshly squeezed lemon juice	15 mL
1 tsp	vanilla extract	5 mL
4 oz	bittersweet chocolate chunks	125 g

Decoration

Fresh Raspberry Sauce (see recipe, page 271)

1. *Crust:* In a bowl, combine pecans, flour and butter. Press into bottom and sides of pie plate and bake in preheated oven for 6 minutes. Let cool until filling is ready. Reduce oven temperature to 325°F (160°C).
2. *Filling:* In a small bowl, dissolve cocoa in hot water. Set aside.
3. In a mixer bowl fitted with paddle attachment, beat cream cheese and sugar on medium-high speed until very smooth, for 3 minutes. Add eggs, one at a time, beating after each addition. Mix in lemon juice and vanilla. Fold in dissolved cocoa and chocolate chunks by hand.
4. Pour over baked crust, smoothing out to sides of pie plate. Bake in preheated oven until top is light brown and center has a slight jiggle to it, 25 to 35 minutes. Let cool in pan on a wire rack for 2 hours. Cover with plastic wrap and refrigerate for at least 6 hours before decorating or serving.
5. *Decoration:* Top each slice with a spoonful of Fresh Raspberry Sauce.

Deep Fudge Cheese Pie

SERVES 5 TO 6

The triple combination of the crust, the cocoa and the fudge topping creates the complexity you want in a deep, dark chocolate pie.

Tip

Make sure your cocoa is free of lumps before adding the hot water. Sift it if necessary.

Variation

Fold in ½ cup (125 mL) bittersweet chocolate chunks with the cocoa mixture.

- Preheat oven to 325°F (160°C)
- 9-inch (23 cm) pie plate, ungreased

Crust

1¼ cups	chocolate sandwich cookie crumbs	300 mL
3 tbsp	unsalted butter, melted	45 mL

Filling

2 tbsp	unsweetened Dutch-process cocoa powder	25 mL
1 tbsp	hot water	15 mL
2 tsp	vanilla extract	10 mL
2	packages (each 8 oz/250 g) cream cheese, softened	2
¾ cup	packed brown sugar	175 mL
3	egg yolks	3

Decoration

Truffle Fudge Topping (see recipe, page 263)

1. *Crust:* In a bowl, combine cookie crumbs and butter. Press into bottom and sides of pie plate and freeze.
2. *Filling:* In a small bowl, dissolve cocoa in hot water and vanilla. Set aside.
3. In a mixer bowl fitted with paddle attachment, beat cream cheese and brown sugar on medium-high speed until very smooth, for 3 minutes. Add egg yolks, one at a time, beating after each addition. Mix in dissolved cocoa.
4. Pour over frozen crust, smoothing out to sides of pie plate. Bake in preheated oven until top is light brown and center has a slight jiggle to it, 25 to 35 minutes. Let cool in pan on a wire rack for 2 hours. Cover with plastic wrap and refrigerate for at least 6 hours before decorating or serving.
5. *Decoration:* Spread Truffle Fudge Topping over top of pie.

Brownie Cheese Pie

SERVES 5 TO 6

Two layers, one a rich brownie, the other a sweet vanilla, make this a great choice for summer picnics.

Tip

Having a second mixer bowl saves washing dishes mid-recipe.

Variation

Top with Fresh Raspberry Sauce (page 271).

- Preheat oven to 325°F (160°C)
- 9-inch (23 cm) pie plate, ungreased

Crust
1 cup	chocolate sandwich cookie crumbs	250 mL
3 tbsp	unsalted butter, melted	45 mL

Brownie Filling
⅓ cup	unsalted butter, softened	75 mL
⅓ cup	granulated sugar	75 mL
2	eggs	2
5 oz	semisweet chocolate, melted (see page 63) and cooled	150 g
1¼ tsp	vanilla extract	6 mL
Pinch	salt	Pinch
⅓ cup	all-purpose flour	75 mL

Vanilla Filling
1	package (8 oz/250 g) cream cheese, softened	1
2 tbsp	unsalted butter, softened	25 mL
½ cup	granulated sugar	125 mL
1	egg	1
1 tbsp	all-purpose flour	15 mL
2 tbsp	sour cream	25 mL
1 tsp	vanilla extract	5 mL

1. *Crust:* In a bowl, combine cookie crumbs and butter. Press into bottom and sides of pie plate and freeze.

2. *Brownie filling:* In a mixer bowl fitted with paddle attachment, beat butter and sugar on medium-high speed until light and fluffy, for 3 minutes. Add eggs, one at a time, beating after each addition. With the mixer running, pour in melted chocolate in a steady stream. Mix in vanilla and salt. Quickly beat in flour. Spread over bottom of frozen crust. Refrigerate while preparing vanilla filling.

3. *Vanilla filling:* In a clean mixer bowl fitted with paddle attachment, beat cream cheese, butter and sugar on medium-high speed until very smooth, for 3 minutes. Add egg, mixing until blended. Stir in flour, sour cream and vanilla.

4. Spread vanilla filling evenly over brownie filling. Bake in preheated oven until top is light brown and center has a slight jiggle to it, 25 to 35 minutes. Let cool in pan on a wire rack for 2 hours. Cover with plastic wrap and

Apple Nutmeg Cheese Pie

SERVES 5 TO 6

Just like apple pie, but with a cheese base, this recipe may replace your traditional apple pie.

Tip

To keep apples from turning brown after you dice them, soak the pieces in lemon juice and water while preparing the rest of the recipe. If you are out of lemons, you can break up a vitamin C tablet in the water. Drain apples well before adding to the filling.

Variation

For a different twist, use a ripe pear instead of the apple.

- Preheat oven to 325°F (160°C)
- 9-inch (23 cm) pie plate, ungreased

Crust

1¼ cups	butter cookie crumbs	300 mL
3 tbsp	unsalted butter, melted	45 mL
1 tsp	freshly grated nutmeg	5 mL

Filling

2	packages (each 8 oz/250 g) cream cheese, softened	2
¼ cup	sour cream	50 mL
½ cup	packed light brown sugar	125 mL
2	eggs	2
1	baking apple (such as Granny Smith or Pippin), peeled and diced	1
1 tsp	freshly grated nutmeg	5 mL
½ tsp	ground cinnamon	2 mL
¼ tsp	ground allspice	1 mL
½ tsp	vanilla extract	2 mL

1. *Crust:* In a bowl, combine cookie crumbs, butter and nutmeg. Press into bottom and sides of pie plate and freeze.

2. *Filling:* In a mixer bowl fitted with paddle attachment, beat cream cheese, sour cream and brown sugar on medium-high speed until very smooth, for 3 minutes. Add eggs, one at a time, beating after each addition. Fold in diced apple, nutmeg, cinnamon, allspice and vanilla by hand.

3. Pour over frozen crust, smoothing out to sides of pie plate. Bake in preheated oven until top is light brown and center has a slight jiggle to it, 25 to 35 minutes. Let cool in pan on a wire rack for 2 hours. Cover with plastic wrap and refrigerate for at least 6 hours before serving.

Pear Nutmeg Cheese Pie

SERVES 5 TO 6

Ohio Bartlett pears are marvelous but have such a short season at the end of the summer. If I can't get them for my classes, I use canned pears for this recipe.

Tip

If you use canned pears, drain before adding to the filling. Canned pear juice is a versatile sweetener for cocktails, fruit salad or savory sauces for roasted meats.

Variation

Canned or fresh peaches work well too.

- Preheat oven to 325°F (160°C)
- 9-inch (23 cm) pie plate, ungreased

Crust

1¼ cups	butter cookie crumbs	300 mL
3 tbsp	unsalted butter, melted	45 mL

Filling

1	package (8 oz/250 g) cream cheese, softened	1
1 cup	small-curd cottage cheese, drained (see tips, page 214)	250 mL
¾ cup	granulated sugar	175 mL
2	eggs	2
¾ cup	chopped pear (about 1 medium)	175 mL
2 tsp	freshly grated nutmeg	10 mL
2 tsp	vanilla extract	10 mL

Decoration

Classic Whipped Cream Topping (see recipe, page 262)

1. *Crust:* In a bowl, combine cookie crumbs and butter. Press into bottom and sides of pie plate and freeze.

2. *Filling:* In a mixer bowl fitted with paddle attachment, beat cream cheese, cottage cheese and sugar on medium-high speed until very smooth, for 3 minutes. Add eggs, one at a time, beating after each addition. Fold in pear, nutmeg and vanilla by hand.

3. Pour over frozen crust, smoothing out to sides of pie plate. Bake in preheated oven until top is light brown and center has a slight jiggle to it, 25 to 35 minutes. Let cool in pan on a wire rack for 2 hours. Cover with plastic wrap and refrigerate for at least 6 hours before decorating or serving.

4. *Decoration:* Ice top of pie with Classic Whipped Cream Topping or pipe rosettes around top of pie, if desired.

Blueberry Cheese Pie

SERVES 5 TO 6

Luscious blueberries make this cheese pie an excellent summer dessert. Whenever I'm in Cincinnati, Ohio, in blueberry season I make sure to pick some up at the Findlay Market.

Tip

Try to use fresh blueberries, as frozen will turn your batter a dark blue.

Variation

Garnish each slice with fresh mint leaves for a lovely aroma and color contrast.

- Preheat oven to 325°F (160°C)
- 9-inch (23 cm) pie plate, ungreased

Crust

1¼ cups	graham cracker crumbs	300 mL
3 tbsp	unsalted butter, melted	45 mL

Filling

2	packages (each 8 oz/250 g) cream cheese, softened	2
4 oz	mascarpone cheese	125 g
¾ cup	granulated sugar	175 mL
1	egg	1
1	egg yolk	1
½ cup	fresh blueberries	125 mL
2 tsp	vanilla extract	10 mL
1 tsp	almond extract	5 mL

Decoration

	Classic Whipped Cream Topping (see recipe, page 262)	
¼ cup	fresh blueberries	50 mL

1. *Crust:* In a bowl, combine graham cracker crumbs and butter. Press into bottom and sides of pie plate and freeze.

2. *Filling:* In a mixer bowl fitted with paddle attachment, beat cream cheese, mascarpone cheese and sugar on medium-high speed until very smooth, for 3 minutes. Add whole egg and egg yolk, one at a time, beating after each addition. Fold in blueberries, vanilla and almond extract by hand.

3. Pour over frozen crust, smoothing out to sides of pie plate. Bake in preheated oven until top is light brown and center has a slight jiggle to it, 25 to 35 minutes. Let cool in pan on a wire rack for 2 hours. Cover with plastic wrap and refrigerate for at least 6 hours before decorating or serving.

4. *Decoration:* Ice top of pie with Classic Whipped Cream Topping or pipe rosettes around top of pie, if desired. Top with blueberries.

Raspberry Cheese Pie

SERVES 5 TO 6

Ruby red raspberries make this a perfect Christmas or Valentine's gift for a friend or to take to a party.

Tips

If the cottage cheese has a wet look to it, drain it through a fine-mesh sieve. Too much moisture will change the texture of the cheesecake.

If small-curd cottage cheese is not available, purée cottage cheese in a food processor before adding to the cream cheese.

Use full-fat yogurt for baking. Reduced-fat versions will change the texture of the pie.

Variation

Spiral raspberry preserves on top for extra visual drama and sweetness.

- Preheat oven to 325°F (160°C)
- 9-inch (23 cm) pie plate, ungreased

Crust

1¼ cups	butter cookie crumbs	300 mL
3 tbsp	unsalted butter, melted	45 mL

Filling

1	package (8 oz/250 g) cream cheese, softened	1
1 cup	small-curd cottage cheese, drained (see tips, at left)	250 mL
1 cup	raspberry-flavored yogurt	250 mL
¾ cup	granulated sugar	175 mL
2	eggs	2
1 cup	raspberries, cut into small pieces if large	250 mL
2 tsp	vanilla extract	10 mL

Decoration

Classic Whipped Cream Topping (see recipe, page 262)

1. *Crust:* In a bowl, combine cookie crumbs and butter. Press into bottom and sides of pie plate and freeze.

2. *Filling:* In a mixer bowl fitted with paddle attachment, beat cream cheese, cottage cheese, yogurt and sugar on medium-high speed until very smooth, for 3 minutes. Add eggs, one at a time, beating after each addition. Fold in raspberries and vanilla by hand.

3. Pour over frozen crust, smoothing out to sides of pie plate. Bake in preheated oven until top is light brown and center has a slight jiggle to it, 25 to 35 minutes. Let cool in pan on a wire rack for 2 hours. Cover with plastic wrap and refrigerate for at least 6 hours before decorating or serving.

4. *Decoration:* Ice top of pie with Classic Whipped Cream Topping or pipe rosettes around top of pie, if desired.

Banana Cream Cheese Pie

SERVES 5 TO 6

Sweet cream surrounds fresh bananas in this deluxe pie.

Tip

For optimal flavor, use very ripe bananas.

Variation

Add 2 tbsp (25 mL) dark rum with the vanilla to make a Banana Rum Pie.

- Preheat oven to 325°F (160°C)
- 9-inch (23 cm) pie plate, ungreased

Crust

1¼ cups	butter cookie crumbs	300 mL
3 tbsp	unsalted butter, melted	45 mL

Filling

2	packages (each 8 oz/250 g) cream cheese, softened	2
¼ cup	sour cream	50 mL
¾ cup	granulated sugar	175 mL
2	eggs	2
¾ cup	mashed ripe bananas (about 2 medium)	175 mL
1 tsp	ground cinnamon	5 mL
2 tsp	vanilla extract	10 mL

Decoration

Classic Whipped Cream Topping
(see recipe, page 262)

1. *Crust:* In a bowl, combine cookie crumbs and butter. Press into bottom and sides of pie plate and freeze.

2. *Filling:* In a mixer bowl fitted with paddle attachment, beat cream cheese, sour cream and sugar on medium-high speed until very smooth, for 3 minutes. Add eggs, one at a time, beating after each addition. Fold in bananas, cinnamon and vanilla by hand.

3. Pour over frozen crust, smoothing out to sides of pie plate. Bake in preheated oven until top is light brown and center has a slight jiggle to it, 25 to 35 minutes. Let cool in pan on a wire rack for 2 hours. Cover with plastic wrap and refrigerate for at least 6 hours before decorating or serving.

4. *Decoration:* Ice top of cake with Classic Whipped Cream Topping or pipe rosettes around top of cake, if desired.

Banana Macadamia Cheese Pie

SERVES 5 TO 6

Bananas and rich macadamia nuts flavor this cheese pie.

Tips

Toasting brings out the natural oils and flavor of nuts. Place nuts in a single layer on a baking sheet and bake at 350°F (180°C) until fragrant, 10 to 12 minutes.

Look for dried banana chips in the health food section of your supermarket. If you use fresh bananas for decorating, they will turn black before you can serve the dessert.

Variation

Pecans or hazelnuts are a less expensive substitute for macadamia nuts.

- Preheat oven to 325°F (160°C)
- 9-inch (23 cm) pie plate, ungreased

Crust

1¼ cups	graham cracker crumbs	300 mL
3 tbsp	unsalted butter, melted	45 mL

Filling

2	packages (each 8 oz/250 g) cream cheese, softened	2
½ cup	packed light brown sugar	125 mL
2	eggs	2
¾ cup	mashed ripe bananas (about 2 medium)	175 mL
¼ cup	macadamia nuts, toasted (see tip, at left) and ground	50 mL
2 tbsp	all-purpose flour	25 mL
1 tsp	ground cinnamon	5 mL
½ tsp	freshly grated nutmeg	2 mL
½ tsp	vanilla extract	2 mL

Decoration

	Classic Whipped Cream Topping (see recipe, page 262)	
5 to 6	dried banana chips	5 to 6

1. *Crust:* In a bowl, combine graham cracker crumbs and butter. Press into bottom and sides of pie plate and freeze.
2. *Filling:* In a mixer bowl fitted with paddle attachment, beat cream cheese and brown sugar on medium-high speed until very smooth, for 3 minutes. Add eggs, one at a time, beating after each addition. Fold in bananas, macadamia nuts, flour, cinnamon, nutmeg and vanilla by hand.
3. Pour over frozen crust, smoothing out to sides of pie plate. Bake in preheated oven until top is light brown and center has a slight jiggle to it, 25 to 35 minutes. Let cool in pan on a wire rack for 2 hours. Cover with plastic wrap and refrigerate for at least 6 hours before decorating or serving.
4. *Decoration:* Ice top of pie with Classic Whipped Cream Topping or pipe rosettes around top of pie, if desired. Top with banana chips.

Lemon Cheese Pie

SERVES 5 TO 6

Expect a pleasing pucker in your mouth from the lemon curd in this tart and tangy pie.

Tips

You can prepare the Fresh Lemon Curd up to 2 days ahead.

To quickly prepare cookie crumbs, place whole cookies in a food processor fitted with a metal blade and pulse a few times. You can add the butter to the food processor and pulse until blended. When mixed with the butter, the crumbs should feel like wet sand.

- Preheat oven to 325°F (160°C)
- 9-inch (23 cm) pie plate, ungreased

Crust
1¼ cups	butter cookie crumbs	300 mL
3 tbsp	unsalted butter, melted	45 mL

Filling
2	packages (each 8 oz/250 g) cream cheese, softened	2
¾ cup	granulated sugar	175 mL
2	eggs	2
¾ cup	Fresh Lemon Curd (see recipe, page 265)	175 mL
2 tsp	vanilla extract	10 mL

Decoration
	Classic Whipped Cream Topping (see recipe, page 262)	
¼ cup	Fresh Lemon Curd	50 mL

1. *Crust:* In a bowl, combine cookie crumbs and butter. Press into bottom and sides of pie plate and freeze.
2. *Filling:* In a mixer bowl fitted with paddle attachment, beat cream cheese and sugar on medium-high speed until very smooth, for 3 minutes. Add eggs, one at a time, beating after each addition. Stir in lemon curd and vanilla.
3. Pour over frozen crust, smoothing out to sides of pie plate. Bake in preheated oven until top is light brown and center has a slight jiggle to it, 25 to 35 minutes. Let cool in pan on a wire rack for 2 hours. Cover with plastic wrap and refrigerate for at least 6 hours before decorating or serving.
4. *Decoration:* Pipe rosettes around top of pie with Classic Whipped Cream Topping. Fill center with Lemon Curd.

Citrus Cheese Pie

I am lucky to live in a citrus-growing region of California. Driving home in spring, I roll down my windows to smell the rich, fragrant aroma of citrus fruits, which inspired me to create this pie.

Tip

Zest the fruit the day before you intend to make this pie and juice it the day of baking. You will get more juice from your fruit.

Variation

Fold ¼ cup (50 mL) crushed fresh raspberries into the filling for a Citrus Raspberry Cheese Pie.

- Preheat the oven to 325°F (160°C)
- 9-inch (23 cm) pie plate, ungreased

Crust

1¼ cups	lemon cookie crumbs	300 mL
3 tbsp	unsalted butter, melted	45 mL

Filling

2	packages (each 8 oz/250 g) cream cheese, softened	2
¾ cup	granulated sugar	175 mL
2	eggs	2
2 tbsp	grated lemon zest	25 mL
2 tbsp	grated orange zest	25 mL
1 tbsp	freshly squeezed lemon juice	15 mL
1 tbsp	freshly squeezed orange juice	15 mL
1 tsp	vanilla extract	5 mL

Decoration

Classic Whipped Cream Topping
(see recipe, page 262)

1. *Crust:* In a bowl, combine cookie crumbs and butter. Press into bottom and sides of pie plate and freeze.

2. *Filling:* In a mixer bowl fitted with paddle attachment, beat cream cheese and sugar on medium-high speed until very smooth, for 3 minutes. Add eggs, one at a time, beating after each addition. Stir in lemon zest, orange zest, lemon juice, orange juice and vanilla.

3. Pour over frozen crust, smoothing out to sides of pie plate. Bake in preheated oven until top is light brown and center has a slight jiggle to it, 25 to 35 minutes. Let cool in pan on a wire rack for 2 hours. Cover with plastic wrap and refrigerate for at least 6 hours before decorating or serving.

4. *Decoration:* Ice top of pie with Classic Whipped Cream Topping or pipe rosettes around top of pie, if desired.

Pecan Cheese Pie

SERVES 5 TO 6

Although you can buy them anywhere, when traveling through Texas, Louisiana or Georgia I always stock up on the local pecans.

Tip

Buy pecans in bulk when they're in season and freeze to have handy whenever you need them. Not only will you save money, but the nuts will be fresher than those in the small convenience packages in the baking aisle of the grocery store.

Variation

Add 2 tbsp (25 mL) brandy with the vanilla.

- Preheat oven to 325°F (160°C)
- 9-inch (23 cm) pie plate, ungreased

Crust

1¼ cups	chocolate sandwich cookie crumbs	300 mL
3 tbsp	unsalted butter, melted	45 mL

Filling

2	packages (each 8 oz/250 g) cream cheese, softened	2
½ cup	granulated sugar	125 mL
2	eggs	2
½ cup	pecans, toasted (see tip, page 216) and chopped	125 mL
2 tsp	vanilla extract	10 mL

1. *Crust:* In a bowl, combine cookie crumbs and butter. Press into bottom and sides of pie plate and freeze.
2. *Filling:* In a mixer bowl fitted with paddle attachment, beat cream cheese and sugar on medium-high speed until very smooth, for 3 minutes. Add eggs, one at a time, beating after each addition. Fold in pecans and vanilla by hand.
3. Pour over frozen crust, smoothing out to sides of pie plate. Bake in preheated oven until top is light brown and center has a slight jiggle to it, 25 to 35 minutes. Let cool in pan on a wire rack for 2 hours. Cover with plastic wrap and refrigerate for at least 6 hours before serving.

Turtle Cheese Pie

One of my favorite confections, pecans sitting on a mound of caramel and covered with chocolate, inspired this sweet pie.

Tip

When cutting caramels, dip the knife blade in hot water to keep them from sticking to the blade.

Variations

Try milk chocolate instead of bittersweet for a lighter color.

Sprinkle chopped toasted pecans over top just before serving.

- Preheat oven to 325°F (160°C)
- 9-inch (23 cm) pie plate, ungreased

Crust

1¼ cups	graham cracker crumbs	300 mL
3 tbsp	unsalted butter, melted	45 mL

Filling

2	packages (each 8 oz/250 g) cream cheese, softened	2
½ cup	granulated sugar	125 mL
2	eggs	2
3 oz	bittersweet chocolate chunks	90 g
3 oz	soft caramels, quartered	90 g
¼ cup	pecans, toasted (see tip, page 216) and chopped	50 mL
½ tsp	vanilla extract	2 mL

Decoration

3 oz	bittersweet chocolate	90 g

1. *Crust:* In a bowl, combine graham cracker crumbs and butter. Press into bottom and sides of pie plate and freeze.
2. *Filling:* In a mixer bowl fitted with paddle attachment, beat cream cheese and sugar on medium-high speed until very smooth, for 3 minutes. Add eggs, one at a time, beating after each addition. Fold in chocolate chunks, caramels, pecans and vanilla by hand.
3. Pour over frozen crust, smoothing out to sides of pie plate. Bake in preheated oven until top is light brown and center has a slight jiggle to it, 25 to 35 minutes.
4. *Decoration:* While pie is still hot, grate chocolate on top. Let cool in pan on a wire rack for 2 hours. Cover with plastic wrap and refrigerate for at least 6 hours before serving.

Savory Cheesecakes

Mini Blue Cheesecakes

*I still haven't found a
blue cheese I don't like.
Use your favorite in
this recipe.*

Tips

Toasting brings out the
natural oils and flavor
of nuts. Place nuts in a
single layer on a baking
sheet and bake at 350°F
(180°C) until fragrant,
10 to 12 minutes.

Purchase a wedge of
blue cheese and crumble
it with a fork. The cheese
will be better quality than
the pre-crumbled type
and will yield a much
better result.

Variation

Add 2 tbsp (25 mL) port
or red wine to the filling
with the blue cheese to
enhance the depth and
complexity of the flavors.

- Preheat oven to 325°F (160°C)
- 24-cup mini muffin tin, lined with paper muffin cups

Crust

¾ cup	stone-ground wheat cracker crumbs	175 mL
¼ cup	pecans, toasted (see tip, at left) and ground	50 mL
¼ cup	unsalted butter, melted	50 mL

Filling

1	package (8 oz/250 g) cream cheese, softened	1
2 tsp	granulated sugar	10 mL
2	eggs	2
8 oz	blue cheese, crumbled	250 g
¼ cup	chopped green onions (about 4)	50 mL
2 tsp	dried onion flakes	10 mL
½ tsp	salt	2 mL
½ tsp	freshly ground black pepper	2 mL

1. *Crust:* In a bowl, combine cracker crumbs, pecans and butter. Press 2 tsp (10 mL) into bottom of each muffin cup and freeze.

2. *Filling:* In a mixer bowl fitted with paddle attachment, beat cream cheese and sugar on medium-high speed until very smooth, about 3 minutes. Add eggs, one at a time, beating after each addition. Fold in blue cheese, green onions, onion flakes, salt and pepper by hand.

3. Fill each cup about three-quarters full. Bake in preheated oven until cheesecakes puff up a bit, 18 to 22 minutes. Let cool on a wire rack for 10 minutes before removing from tin.

Three-Cheese Torte

SERVES 10 TO 12

I am a big fan of cheese — the more in a cheesecake, the better.

Tips

For the crust, use whatever crackers you enjoy with cheese.

Sprinkle extra cracker crumbs on top for added crunch or if the cheesecake is a little too brown on top.

Variation

A Swiss cheese, shredded, is a good substitute for the blue cheese, as its flavor blends with the other seasonings.

- Preheat oven to 325°F (160°C)
- 6-inch (23 cm) cheesecake pan, ungreased, or springform pan with 3-inch (7.5 cm) sides, greased

Crust

¾ cup	cracker crumbs (see tip, at left)	175 mL
2 tbsp	butter, melted	25 mL

Filling

1	package (8 oz/250 g) cream cheese, softened	1
2	eggs	2
1 tsp	freshly squeezed lemon juice	5 mL
¼ tsp	salt	1 mL
1 tsp	chopped fresh dill	5 mL
1 tsp	dried onion flakes	5 mL
8 oz	blue cheese, crumbled	250 g
½ cup	freshly grated Parmesan cheese	125 mL

1. *Crust:* In a bowl, combine cracker crumbs and butter. Press into bottom of cheesecake pan and freeze.

2. *Filling:* In a mixer bowl fitted with paddle attachment, beat cream cheese on medium-high speed until very smooth, for 3 minutes. Add eggs, one at a time, beating after each addition. Stir in lemon juice, salt, dill and onion flakes. Fold in blue cheese and Parmesan by hand.

3. Pour over frozen crust, smoothing out to sides of pan. Bake in preheated oven until top is light brown and center has a slight jiggle to it, 30 to 40 minutes. Let cool in pan on a wire rack for 2 hours. Cover with plastic wrap and refrigerate for at least 6 hours before serving.

Spicy Savory Cheesecake

SERVES 10 TO 12

This unbaked cheesecake goes a long way. I like to serve it with celery sticks.

Tips

This cheesecake can be refrigerated in the pan for up to 2 weeks before serving.

Parsley must be very dry to chop finely.

Variation

Use a 6-inch (15 cm) cheesecake pan if you want thick slices.

- 9-inch (23 cm) cheesecake pan or springform pan with 3-inch (7.5 cm) sides, lined with parchment paper

Filling

1	package (8 oz/250 g) cream cheese, softened	1
4 cups	shredded pepper Jack cheese	1 L
1 cup	unsalted butter, softened	250 mL
2	jalapeño peppers, seeded and diced	2
1	shallot, minced	1
¼ tsp	freshly ground white pepper	1 mL
¼ tsp	hot pepper sauce	1 mL
1 cup	pecans, toasted (see tip, page 222) and chopped	250 mL
½ cup	chopped green onions (about 8)	125 mL
¼ cup	chopped fresh parsley	50 mL

Decoration

¼ cup	pecans, toasted and chopped	125 mL

1. *Filling:* In a food processor fitted with a metal blade, in two batches, if necessary, pulse cream cheese, pepper Jack cheese, butter, jalapeños, shallot, white pepper and hot pepper sauce until smooth. Transfer to a bowl and fold in pecans, green onions and parsley by hand.
2. Pour into prepared pan, smoothing out to sides of pan. Cover with plastic wrap and press gently to compact. Refrigerate for at least 6 hours before decorating or serving.
3. *Decoration:* To unmold, place a large plate over top of cake and invert. Take sides of pan off, then the bottom. Peel parchment paper off cake. Pack sides with chopped pecans.

Pear Nutmeg Cheese Pie (page 212)
Overleaf: Blueberry Cheese Pie (page 213)

Savory Herb Cheesecake

SERVES 4 TO 6

Fresh herbs bring out the best flavor in this savory cheesecake.

Tips

For the crust, use whatever crackers you enjoy with cheese.

Serve warm or cold with crackers. (See reheating instructions for Chipotle Chile Cheesecake, page 239.)

Variation

Zest the lemon before juicing and add the zest with the fresh herbs for a wonderful aroma and extra bite of lemon.

- Preheat oven to 325°F (160°C)
- 6-inch (15 cm) cheesecake pan or springform pan with 3-inch (7.5 cm) sides, lined with parchment paper

Crust

¾ cup	cracker crumbs (see tip, at left)	175 mL
2 tbsp	unsalted butter, melted	25 mL

Filling

2	packages (each 8 oz/250 g) cream cheese, softened	2
2	eggs	2
1 tbsp	chopped fresh tarragon	15 mL
1½ tsp	chopped fresh thyme	7 mL
1 tsp	chopped fresh dill	5 mL
1 tsp	dried onion flakes	5 mL
¼ tsp	salt	1 mL
1 tsp	freshly squeezed lemon juice	5 mL
½ cup	freshly grated Parmesan cheese	125 mL

1. *Crust:* In a bowl, combine cracker crumbs and butter. Press into bottom of cheesecake pan and freeze.

2. *Filling:* In a mixer bowl fitted with paddle attachment, beat cream cheese on medium-high speed until very smooth, for 3 minutes. Add eggs, one at a time, beating after each addition. Stir in tarragon, thyme, dill, onion flakes, salt and lemon juice. Fold in Parmesan by hand.

3. Pour over frozen crust, smoothing out to sides of pan. Bake in preheated oven until top is light brown and center has a slight jiggle to it, 35 to 45 minutes. Let cool in pan on a wire rack for 2 hours. Cover with plastic wrap and refrigerate for at least 6 hours before serving.

Overleaf: Turtle Cheese Pie (page 220)
Savory Herb Cheesecake (this page)

Herbed Gorgonzola Cheesecake

SERVES 18 TO 20

When watching a football game or hosting any other large gathering, you need a savory cheesecake that can feed a crowd.

Tips

For the crust, use whatever crackers you enjoy with cheese.

Serve warm or cold with crackers or party toasts. (See reheating instructions for Chipotle Chile Cheesecake, page 239.)

Variation

If substituting dried herbs, use half of what the recipe calls for.

- Preheat oven to 350°F (180°C)
- 9-inch (23 cm) cheesecake pan or springform pan with 3-inch (7.5 cm) sides, lined with parchment paper

Crust

2 cups	cracker crumbs (see tip, at left)	500 mL
¼ cup	unsalted butter, melted	50 mL

Filling

4	packages (each 8 oz/250 g) cream cheese, softened	4
3	eggs	3
2 tbsp	chopped fresh tarragon	25 mL
1 tsp	chopped fresh dill	5 mL
1 tsp	dried onion flakes	5 mL
¼ tsp	salt	1 mL
1 tbsp	freshly squeezed lemon juice	15 mL
8 oz	Gorgonzola cheese, crumbled	250 g

1. *Crust:* In a bowl, combine cracker crumbs and butter. Press into bottom of prepared pan and freeze.

2. *Filling:* In a mixer bowl fitted with paddle attachment, beat cream cheese on medium-high speed until very smooth, for 3 minutes. Add eggs, one at a time, beating after each addition. Stir in tarragon, dill, onion flakes, salt and lemon juice. Fold in Gorgonzola by hand.

3. Pour over frozen crust, smoothing out to sides of pan. Bake in preheated oven until top is light brown and center has a slight jiggle to it, 50 to 65 minutes. Let cool in pan on a wire rack for 2 hours. Cover with plastic wrap and refrigerate for at least 6 hours before serving.

Swiss Alps Cheesecake

SERVES 10 TO 12

Swiss cheese has a great bite to it and is such a good cooking cheese — liberate it from sandwiches!

Tips

For the crust, use your favorite salted or unsalted crackers.

Serve warm or cold with crackers. (See reheating instructions for Chipotle Chile Cheesecake, page 239.)

Variation

Try Gruyère or Emmentaler cheese for extra-rich flavor. These cheeses inspired the generic Swiss-style cheese.

- Preheat oven to 325°F (160°C)
- 6-inch (23 cm) cheesecake pan, ungreased, or springform pan with 3-inch (7.5 cm) sides, greased

Crust

¾ cup	cracker crumbs (see tip, at left)	175 mL
2 tbsp	unsalted butter, melted	25 mL

Filling

1	package (8 oz/250 g) cream cheese, softened	1
1	egg	1
1	clove garlic, minced	1
1 tsp	chopped fresh dill	5 mL
1 tsp	dried onion flakes	5 mL
¼ tsp	salt	1 mL
1 tsp	freshly squeezed lemon juice	5 mL
1 cup	shredded Swiss cheese	250 mL

1. *Crust:* In a bowl, combine cracker crumbs and butter. Press into bottom of cheesecake pan and freeze.

2. *Filling:* In a mixer bowl fitted with paddle attachment, beat cream cheese on medium-high speed until very smooth, for 3 minutes. Add egg, mixing until blended. Stir in garlic, dill, onion flakes, salt and lemon juice. Fold in Swiss cheese by hand.

3. Pour over frozen crust, smoothing out to sides of pan. Bake in preheated oven until top is light brown and center has a slight jiggle to it, 30 to 40 minutes. Let cool in pan on a wire rack for 2 hours. Cover with plastic wrap and refrigerate for at least 6 hours before serving.

Blue Cheese Pistachio Cheesecake

SERVES 10 TO 12

This cheesecake is adapted from a recipe that Arlene Ward from Adventures in Cooking in Wayne, New Jersey, created for her annual cooking school party.

Tips

This cheesecake can be refrigerated in the pan for up to 2 weeks before serving.

The blue cheese that is not creamed will crumble more uniformly if it is cold. The portion to be creamed should be at room temperature.

Parsley must be very dry to chop finely.

Variation

Use a 6-inch (15 cm) cheesecake pan if you want thick slices.

- 9-inch (23 cm) cheesecake pan or springform pan with 3-inch (7.5 cm) sides, lined with parchment paper

Filling

1 cup	unsalted butter, softened	250 mL
1	package (8 oz/250 g) cream cheese, softened	1
1 lb	blue cheese or Gorgonzola, crumbled, divided	500 g
1	shallot, minced (about ¼ cup/50 mL)	1
¼ cup	Madeira wine	50 mL
¼ tsp	freshly ground white pepper	1 mL
1 cup	pistachios, toasted (see tip, page 222) and chopped, divided	250 mL
½ cup	chopped green onions (about 8), divided	125 mL
¼ cup	chopped fresh parsley, divided	50 mL

Decoration

1 cup	pistachios, toasted and chopped	250 mL

1. *Filling:* In a food processor fitted with a metal blade, in two batches, if necessary, pulse butter, cream cheese, half the blue cheese, the shallot, Madeira and pepper until smooth. Set aside.

2. In prepared pan, sprinkle half the remaining blue cheese and half each of the pistachios, green onions and parsley. Top with half the butter mixture, then layer with the remaining blue cheese, pistachios, green onions and parsley. Finish with the remaining butter mixture. Cover with plastic wrap and press gently to compact the layers. Refrigerate for at least 6 hours before decorating or serving.

3. *Decoration:* To unmold, place a large plate over top of cake and invert. Take sides of pan off, then the bottom. Peel parchment paper off cake. Pack sides with chopped pistachios.

Goat Cheese and Walnut Cheesecake

SERVES 10 TO 12

Award-winning cheeses are produced in Indiana, with organic and artisanal styles available in farmers' markets and specialty stores.

Tips

Choose a soft goat cheese that will blend easily with the cream cheese.

To serve warm, wrap in foil and bake at 300°F (150°C) for 20 minutes or until warm.

Variation

Substitute pecans for walnuts and rosemary for the chives.

- Preheat oven to 325°F (160°C)
- 6-inch (15 cm) cheesecake pan, ungreased, or springform pan with 3-inch (7.5 cm) sides, greased

Crust

½ cup	stone-ground wheat cracker crumbs	125 mL
¼ cup	walnuts, toasted (see tip, page 222) and ground	50 mL
2 tbsp	unsalted butter, melted	25 mL

Filling

10 oz	goat cheese, softened	300 g
1	package (8 oz/250 g) cream cheese, softened	1
2 tsp	granulated sugar	10 mL
2	eggs	2
½ cup	walnuts, toasted and ground	125 mL
1 tbsp	chopped fresh chives	15 mL
2 tsp	finely diced red bell pepper	10 mL
½ tsp	salt	2 mL
½ tsp	freshly ground black pepper	2 mL

Decoration

¼ cup	walnuts, toasted and ground	50 mL
1 tsp	chopped fresh chives	5 mL

1. **Crust:** In a bowl, combine cracker crumbs, walnuts and butter. Press into bottom of cheesecake pan and freeze.

2. **Filling:** In a mixer bowl fitted with paddle attachment, beat goat cheese, cream cheese and sugar on medium-high speed until very smooth, for 3 minutes. Add eggs, one at a time, beating after each addition. Fold in walnuts, chives, red pepper, salt and pepper by hand.

3. Pour over frozen crust, smoothing out to sides of pan. Bake in preheated oven until top is light brown and center has a slight jiggle to it, 30 to 40 minutes. Let cool in pan on a wire rack for 2 hours. Cover with plastic wrap and refrigerate for at least 6 hours before decorating or serving.

4. **Decoration:** Sprinkle walnuts and chives over top of cake.

Olive Pesto Cheesecake

SERVES 10 TO 12

Paired with a simple salad, this cheesecake is perfect for dining al fresco.

Tip

If the pesto has separated, stir it before adding to the batter.

Variation

Top the cheesecake with additional chopped olives and pine nuts.

- Preheat oven to 325°F (160°C)
- 6-inch (15 cm) cheesecake pan, ungreased, or springform pan with 3-inch (7.5 cm) sides, greased

Crust

¾ cup	stone-ground wheat cracker crumbs	175 mL
2 tbsp	unsalted butter, melted	25 mL

Filling

2	packages (each 8 oz/250 g) cream cheese, softened	2
2 tsp	granulated sugar	10 mL
2	eggs	2
2	cloves garlic, minced	2
1 cup	prepared basil pesto	250 mL
½ cup	pine nuts	125 mL
¼ cup	chopped pitted green olives	50 mL
1 tsp	freshly squeezed lemon juice	5 mL

1. *Crust:* In a bowl, combine cracker crumbs and butter. Press into bottom of cheesecake pan and freeze.

2. *Filling:* In a mixer bowl fitted with paddle attachment, beat cream cheese and sugar on medium-high speed until very smooth, for 3 minutes. Add eggs, one at a time, beating after each addition. Fold in garlic, pesto, pine nuts, olives and lemon juice by hand.

3. Pour over frozen crust, smoothing out to sides of pan. Bake in preheated oven until top is light brown and center has a slight jiggle to it, 30 to 40 minutes. Let cool in pan on a wire rack for 2 hours. Cover with plastic wrap and refrigerate for at least 6 hours before serving.

Pesto Sun-Dried Tomato Cheesecake

SERVES 10 TO 12

This is a great appetizer when the main course is pasta. Serve as a spread with crackers.

Tips

Serve slightly warmed, if desired, to make more spreadable. (See reheating instructions for Chipotle Chile Cheesecake, page 239.)

To serve as an appetizer, place a thin slice on a lettuce leaf.

Variation

Substitute coarsely chopped pine nuts for the Parmesan.

- Preheat oven to 350°F (180°C)
- 9-inch (23 cm) cheesecake pan or springform pan with 3-inch (7.5 cm) sides, lined with parchment paper

1 cup	tightly packed fresh basil leaves	250 mL
3 to 4	sprigs Italian (flat-leaf) parsley	3 to 4
2	cloves garlic, coarsely chopped	2
¼ cup	olive oil	50 mL
½ cup	freshly grated Parmesan cheese	125 mL
¼ tsp	salt	1 mL
¼ tsp	freshly ground black pepper	1 mL
2	packages (each 8 oz/250 g) cream cheese, softened	2
2	eggs	2
¼ cup	all-purpose flour	50 mL
½ cup	chopped drained oil-packed sun-dried tomatoes (about 10 halves)	125 mL

1. In a food processor fitted with a metal blade, pulse basil, parsley, garlic and olive oil until finely chopped. Stir in Parmesan, salt and pepper. Set aside.

2. In a mixer bowl fitted with paddle attachment, beat cream cheese on medium-high speed until very smooth, for 3 minutes. Add eggs, one at a time, beating after each addition. Fold in flour, sun-dried tomatoes and basil mixture by hand.

3. Pour into prepared pan, smoothing out to sides of pan. Bake in preheated oven until top is light brown and center has a slight jiggle to it, 20 to 25 minutes. Let cool in pan on a wire rack for 2 hours. Cover with plastic wrap and refrigerate for at least 6 hours before serving.

Roasted Garlic Onion Cheesecake

SERVES 10 TO 12

When you bake this cheesecake, your neighbors will be calling for an invitation — the heavenly aroma can't be contained.

Tip

To roast garlic: Preheat oven to 400°F (200°F). Cut about ¼ inch (0.5 cm) off the top of each bulb and drizzle with 1 tsp (5 mL) olive oil. Wrap in foil and roast for 30 to 35 minutes or until golden brown and very soft. Let cool, turn upside down and press cloves out of bulb.

Variation

Substituting shallots for the onion takes this dish to another level.

- Preheat oven to 325°F (160°C)
- 6-inch (15 cm) cheesecake pan, ungreased, or springform pan with 3-inch (7.5 cm) sides, greased

Crust

¾ cup	stone-ground wheat cracker crumbs	175 mL
2 tbsp	unsalted butter, melted	25 mL

Filling

2	packages (each 8 oz/250 g) cream cheese, softened	2
2 tsp	granulated sugar	10 mL
2	eggs	2
2	whole bulbs garlic, roasted (see tip, at left)	2
1½ cups	freshly grated Parmesan cheese	375 mL
½ cup	diced onion	125 mL
1 tsp	hot pepper sauce	5 mL

1. *Crust:* In a bowl, combine cracker crumbs and butter. Press into bottom of cheesecake pan and freeze.

2. *Filling:* In a mixer bowl fitted with paddle attachment, beat cream cheese and sugar on medium-high speed until very smooth, for 3 minutes. Add eggs, one at a time, beating after each addition. Fold in cloves of roasted garlic, Parmesan, onion and hot pepper sauce by hand.

3. Pour over frozen crust, smoothing out to sides of pan. Bake in preheated oven until top is light brown and center has a slight jiggle to it, 30 to 40 minutes. Let cool in pan on a wire rack for 2 hours. Cover with plastic wrap and refrigerate for at least 6 hours before serving.

Triple-Pepper Cheesecake

SERVES 10 TO 12

This savory cheesecake has a nice kick. It demonstrates how the taste of a fresh jalapeño, when smoked, transforms into chipotle.

Tips

Serve with toast points or bagel chips.

Use gloves while cutting the jalapeño pepper, as the oils will linger on your hands and, if you wipe your eyes, they will burn.

- Preheat oven to 325°F (160°C)
- 6-inch (15 cm) cheesecake pan, ungreased, or springform pan with 3-inch (7.5 cm) sides, greased

Crust

¾ cup	bagel chip crumbs	175 mL
2 tbsp	unsalted butter, melted	25 mL

Filling

1	package (8 oz/250 g) cream cheese, softened	1
2 tsp	granulated sugar	10 mL
2	eggs	2
2	cloves garlic, minced	2
1	jalapeño pepper, seeded and diced	1
1	chipotle chile pepper in adobo, drained and chopped	1
2 cups	shredded pepper Jack cheese	500 mL
½ tsp	salt	2 mL
½ tsp	freshly ground black pepper	2 mL

1. *Crust:* In a bowl, combine bagel chip crumbs and butter. Press into bottom of cheesecake pan and freeze.

2. *Filling:* In a mixer bowl fitted with paddle attachment, beat cream cheese and sugar on medium-high speed until very smooth, for 3 minutes. Add eggs, one at a time, beating after each addition. Fold in garlic, jalapeño, chipotle, Jack cheese, salt and pepper by hand.

3. Pour over frozen crust, smoothing out to sides of pan. Bake in preheated oven until top is light brown and center has a slight jiggle to it, 30 to 40 minutes. Let cool in pan on a wire rack for 2 hours. Cover with plastic wrap and refrigerate for at least 6 hours before serving.

Artichoke Cheesecake

SERVES 10 TO 12

My home state of California is the world's largest grower of artichokes. I know lots of ways to enjoy the bounty, and this savory cheesecake is one of my favorites.

Tip

You can use artichoke hearts that are packed in oil or even the frozen variety. Drain well and dry on paper towels before using.

Variation

Add texture, taste and visual appeal with ½ cup (125 mL) diced roasted red bell pepper, folded in with the artichoke hearts.

- Preheat oven to 325°F (160°C)
- 6-inch (15 cm) cheesecake pan, ungreased, or springform pan with 3-inch (7.5 cm) sides, greased

Crust

¾ cup	stone-ground wheat cracker crumbs	175 mL
2 tbsp	unsalted butter, melted	25 mL

Filling

2	packages (each 8 oz/250 g) cream cheese, softened	2
2 tsp	granulated sugar	10 mL
2	eggs	2
1 cup	shredded Swiss cheese	250 mL
1 cup	artichoke hearts, drained and coarsely chopped (see tip, at left)	250 mL
1 tsp	freshly squeezed lemon juice	5 mL
½ tsp	hot pepper flakes	2 mL

1. *Crust:* In a bowl, combine cracker crumbs and butter. Press into bottom of cheesecake pan and freeze.

2. *Filling:* In a mixer bowl fitted with paddle attachment, beat cream cheese and sugar on medium-high speed until very smooth, for 3 minutes. Add eggs, one at a time, beating after each addition. Fold in Swiss cheese, artichoke hearts, lemon juice and hot pepper flakes by hand.

3. Pour over frozen crust, smoothing out to sides of pan. Bake in preheated oven until top is light brown and center has a slight jiggle to it, 30 to 40 minutes. Let cool in pan on a wire rack for 2 hours. Cover with plastic wrap and refrigerate for at least 6 hours before serving.

Salsa Cheesecake

SERVES 10 TO 12

This appetizer becomes dinner when served with a green salad.

Tip

It's important that the tomato is well drained or it will change the texture drastically.

Variation

You can use 1¾ cups (425 mL) prepared salsa in place of the tomato, cilantro and onion, but drain it well.

- Preheat oven to 325°F (160°C)
- 6-inch (15 cm) cheesecake pan, ungreased, or springform pan with 3-inch (7.5 cm) sides, greased

Crust

¾ cup	tortilla chip crumbs	175 mL
2 tbsp	unsalted butter, melted	25 mL

Filling

2	packages (each 8 oz/250 g) cream cheese, softened	2
2 tsp	granulated sugar	10 mL
2	eggs	2
2	cloves garlic, minced	2
1	large Roma (plum) tomato, seeded, diced and drained (about ¾ cup/175 mL)	1
½ cup	packed fresh cilantro, chopped	125 mL
½ cup	diced onion	125 mL
½ tsp	salt	2 mL
½ tsp	freshly ground black pepper	2 mL

1. *Crust:* In a bowl, combine tortilla chip crumbs and butter. Press into bottom of cheesecake pan and freeze.

2. *Filling:* In a mixer bowl fitted with paddle attachment, beat cream cheese and sugar on medium-high speed until very smooth, for 3 minutes. Add eggs, one at a time, beating after each addition. Fold in garlic, tomato, cilantro, onion, salt and pepper by hand.

3. Pour over frozen crust, smoothing out to sides of pan. Bake in preheated oven until top is light brown and center has a slight jiggle to it, 30 to 40 minutes. Let cool in pan on a wire rack for 2 hours. Cover with plastic wrap and refrigerate for at least 6 hours before serving.

Santa Fe Cheesecake

Santa Fe is a remarkable area of New Mexico. I love the hearty foods of the region and the care with which they prepare them.

Tip

Use gloves while cutting the jalapeño pepper, as the oils will linger on your hands and, if you wipe your eyes, they will burn.

Variation

Continue your chile pepper education by substituting a roasted and peeled poblano pepper for the jalapeño — completely different, but just as good.

- Preheat oven to 325°F (160°C)
- 6-inch (15 cm) cheesecake pan, ungreased, or springform pan with 3-inch (7.5 cm) sides, greased

Crust

¾ cup	tortilla chip crumbs	175 mL
2 tbsp	unsalted butter, melted	25 mL

Filling

1	package (8 oz/250 g) cream cheese, softened	1
2 tsp	granulated sugar	10 mL
2	eggs	2
2	cloves garlic, minced	2
1	jalapeño pepper, seeded and diced	1
2 cups	shredded pepper Jack cheese	500 mL
¼ cup	packed fresh cilantro, chopped	50 mL
½ tsp	salt	2 mL
½ tsp	freshly ground black pepper	2 mL

1. *Crust:* In a bowl, combine tortilla chip crumbs and butter. Press into bottom of cheesecake pan and freeze.

2. *Filling:* In a mixer bowl fitted with paddle attachment, beat cream cheese and sugar on medium-high speed until very smooth, for 3 minutes. Add eggs, one at a time, beating after each addition. Fold in garlic, jalapeño, Jack cheese, cilantro, salt and pepper by hand.

3. Pour over frozen crust, smoothing out to sides of pan. Bake in preheated oven until top is light brown and center has a slight jiggle to it, 30 to 40 minutes. Let cool in pan on a wire rack for 2 hours. Cover with plastic wrap and refrigerate for at least 6 hours before serving.

Taco Cheesecake

SERVES 10 TO 12

When you can't make up your mind what to serve, tacos are one of the most popular options in North America, and this cheesecake is a unique presentation.

Tip

For best flavor, reheat before serving. To serve warm, wrap in foil and bake at 300°F (150°C) for 20 minutes or until warm.

- Preheat oven to 325°F (160°C)
- 6-inch (15 cm) cheesecake pan, ungreased, or springform pan with 3-inch (7.5 cm) sides, greased

Crust

¾ cup	tortilla chip crumbs	175 mL
2 tbsp	unsalted butter, melted	25 mL

Filling

2	packages (each 8 oz/250 g) cream cheese, softened	2
2 tsp	granulated sugar	10 mL
2	eggs	2
2	cloves garlic, minced	2
1	large Roma (plum) tomato, seeded, diced and drained (about ¾ cup/175 mL)	1
1½ cups	shredded Cheddar cheese	375 mL
½ cup	packed fresh cilantro, chopped	125 mL
½ cup	diced onion	125 mL
2 tsp	taco seasoning	10 mL
1 tsp	hot pepper sauce	5 mL

Decoration

2 cups	shredded lettuce	500 mL

1. *Crust:* In a bowl, combine tortilla chip crumbs and butter. Press into bottom of cheesecake pan and freeze.

2. *Filling:* In a mixer bowl fitted with paddle attachment, beat cream cheese and sugar on medium-high speed until very smooth, for 3 minutes. Add eggs, one at a time, beating after each addition. Fold in garlic, tomato, Cheddar cheese, cilantro, onion, taco seasoning and hot pepper sauce by hand.

3. Pour over frozen crust, smoothing out to sides of pan. Bake in preheated oven until top is light brown and center has a slight jiggle to it, 30 to 40 minutes. Let cool in pan on a wire rack for 2 hours. Cover with plastic wrap and refrigerate for at least 6 hours before decorating or serving.

4. *Decoration:* Place cheesecake on a serving plate with lettuce around the sides.

Cheddar Chili Cheesecake

This south-of-the-border treat is easy to make and is always a hit at parties.

Tip

To turn this into a party spread, skip the crust and bake the cheesecake right in the pan. Serve on a platter surrounded with stone-ground crackers.

Variation

You can add ½ cup (125 mL) cooked ground beef, turkey or chicken with the beans. Be sure to cool it to room temperature before adding to the filling.

- Preheat oven to 325°F (160°C)
- 6-inch (15 cm) cheesecake pan, ungreased, or springform pan with 3-inch (7.5 cm) sides, greased

Crust

¾ cup	stone-ground wheat cracker crumbs	175 mL
2 tbsp	unsalted butter, melted	25 mL

Filling

2	packages (each 8 oz/250 g) cream cheese, softened	2
2 tsp	granulated sugar	10 mL
2	eggs	2
1	large Roma (plum) tomato, seeded, diced and drained (about ¾ cup/175 mL)	1
1 cup	prepared refried beans	250 mL
¾ cup	shredded Cheddar cheese	175 mL
½ cup	chopped onion	125 mL
2 tsp	freshly squeezed lime juice	10 mL
3	drops hot pepper sauce	3

1. *Crust:* In a bowl, combine cracker crumbs and butter. Press into bottom of cheesecake pan and freeze.

2. *Filling:* In a mixer bowl fitted with paddle attachment, beat cream cheese and sugar on medium-high speed until very smooth, for 3 minutes. Add eggs, one at a time, beating after each addition. Fold in tomato, refried beans, Cheddar cheese, onion, lime juice and hot pepper sauce by hand.

3. Pour over frozen crust, smoothing out to sides of pan. Bake in preheated oven until top is light brown and center has a slight jiggle to it, 30 to 40 minutes. Let cool in pan on a wire rack for 2 hours. Cover with plastic wrap and refrigerate for at least 6 hours before serving.

Chipotle Chile Cheesecake

SERVES 12 TO 14

Southwest flavors are vibrant in this savory cheesecake. A little goes a long way.

Tips

Serve with stone-ground wheat crackers and/or fresh vegetables.

Canned chipotle chiles — smoked jalapeños with a great smoky flavor — can be found in the international food section of most large supermarkets. The adobo sauce used in some brands can be spicy. Use reserved sauce to punch up chili or tomato-based spaghetti sauce.

- Preheat oven to 325°F (160°C)
- 6-inch (15 cm) cheesecake pan or springform pan with 3-inch (7.5 cm) sides, lined with parchment paper

Crust

¾ cup	stone-ground wheat cracker crumbs	175 mL
2 tbsp	unsalted butter, melted	25 mL

Filling

2	packages (each 8 oz/250 g) cream cheese, softened	2
2 tsp	granulated sugar	10 mL
1	egg	1
2	cloves garlic, minced	2
2	chipotle chile peppers in adobo, drained and chopped	2
1	large Roma (plum) tomato, seeded, diced and drained (about ¾ cup/175 mL)	1
¼ cup	diced onion	50 mL

1. *Crust:* In a bowl, combine cracker crumbs and butter. Press into bottom of cheesecake pan and freeze.

2. *Filling:* In a mixer bowl fitted with paddle attachment, beat cream cheese and sugar on medium-high speed until very smooth, for 3 minutes. Add egg, mixing until blended. Fold in garlic, chipotles, tomato and onion by hand.

3. Pour over frozen crust, smoothing out to sides of pan. Bake in preheated oven until top is light brown and center has a slight jiggle to it, 35 to 45 minutes. Let cool in pan on a wire rack for 2 hours. Cover with plastic wrap and refrigerate for at least 6 hours before serving.

4. To serve as a warm appetizer, wrap the cheesecake in foil and place in a preheated 350°F (180°C) oven for 10 minutes to heat through. Do not microwave; it will toughen the cheesecake.

Smoked Salmon Cheesecake

If you travel to Seattle, don't miss the fishmongers at the Pike Market. Try Northwest-style smoked salmon. The smoke from alder or cedar wood really perfumes the cheeses.

Tip

Hot-smoked salmon is preferable to cold-smoked, as it has a firmer texture, but cold-smoked will also work.

Variation

Use pepper Jack cheese in place of the smoked Gouda.

- Preheat oven to 325°F (160°C)
- 6-inch (15 cm) cheesecake pan, ungreased, or springform pan with 3-inch (7.5 cm) sides, greased

Crust

¾ cup	stone-ground wheat cracker crumbs	175 mL
2 tbsp	unsalted butter, melted	25 mL

Filling

2	packages (each 8 oz/250 g) cream cheese, softened	2
2 tsp	granulated sugar	10 mL
2	eggs	2
4 oz	smoked salmon, flaked	125 g
2	cloves garlic, minced	2
½ cup	shredded smoked Gouda cheese	125 mL
¼ cup	chopped onion	50 mL
1 tsp	freshly squeezed lemon juice	5 mL
½ tsp	drained chopped capers	2 mL

1. *Crust:* In a bowl, combine cracker crumbs and butter. Press into bottom of cheesecake pan and freeze.

2. *Filling:* In a mixer bowl fitted with paddle attachment, beat cream cheese and sugar on medium-high speed until very smooth, for 3 minutes. Add eggs, one at a time, beating after each addition. Fold in salmon, garlic, Gouda, onion, lemon juice and capers by hand.

3. Pour over frozen crust, smoothing out to sides of pan. Bake in preheated oven until top is light brown and center has a slight jiggle to it, 30 to 40 minutes. Let cool in pan on a wire rack for 2 hours. Cover with plastic wrap and refrigerate for at least 6 hours before serving.

Creamy Crab Seafood Cheesecake

SERVES 12 TO 14

Make extra copies of this recipe before the party starts — everyone is going to want one after they've tasted this rich cake.

Tips

Serve with crackers and/or fresh vegetables.

Pick over the crabmeat to be sure it is free of shells.

Variation

Cooked lobster or scallop pieces work well in place of the crabmeat.

- Preheat oven to 325°F (160°C)
- 6-inch (15 cm) cheesecake pan or springform pan with 3-inch (7.5 cm) sides, lined with parchment paper

2	packages (each 8 oz/250 g) cream cheese, softened	2
8 oz	mascarpone cheese	250 g
3	eggs	3
¾ cup	all-purpose flour	175 mL
4 oz	cooked crabmeat pieces	125 g
4 oz	cooked shrimp, diced	125 g
2	cloves garlic, minced	2
¼ cup	diced onion	50 mL
¼ cup	diced green onions (about 4)	50 mL
½ tsp	salt	2 mL
¼ tsp	freshly ground white pepper	1 mL

1. In a mixer bowl fitted with paddle attachment, beat cream cheese and mascarpone cheese on medium-high speed until very smooth, for 3 minutes. Add eggs, one at a time, beating after each addition. Stir in flour. Fold in crabmeat, shrimp, garlic, onion, green onions, salt and pepper by hand.

2. Pour into prepared pan, smoothing out to sides of pan. Bake in preheated oven until top is light brown and center has a slight jiggle to it, 45 to 55 minutes. Let cool in pan on a wire rack for 2 hours. Cover with plastic wrap and refrigerate for at least 6 hours before serving.

Maine Lobster Cheesecake

SERVES 12 TO 14

Two of my good friends, Sean and Marc of Maine, took me to a lobster dinner. With the leftovers, I made this cheesecake for their party the next day.

Tips

Serve with hearty crackers.

People who love it spicy will enjoy additional hot pepper sauce. Try 1 tbsp (15 mL) hot pepper sauce.

Variation

Cooked crabmeat is a delicious substitute for lobster, and is perhaps easier to come by.

- Preheat oven to 325°F (160°C)
- 6-inch (15 cm) cheesecake pan or springform pan with 3-inch (7.5 cm) sides, lined with parchment paper

2	packages (each 8 oz/250 g) cream cheese, softened	2
1 cup	sour cream	250 mL
3	eggs	3
¾ cup	all-purpose flour	175 mL
8 oz	cooked lobster pieces	250 g
2	cloves garlic, minced	2
¼ cup	diced onion	50 mL
¼ cup	chopped green onions (about 4)	50 mL
½ tsp	salt	2 mL
¼ tsp	freshly ground white pepper	1 mL
3	drops hot pepper sauce	3

1. In a mixer bowl fitted with paddle attachment, beat cream cheese and sour cream on medium-high speed until very smooth, for 3 minutes. Add eggs, one at a time, beating after each addition. Stir in flour. Fold in lobster, garlic, onion, green onions, salt, pepper and hot pepper sauce by hand.

2. Pour into prepared pan, smoothing out to sides of pan. Bake in preheated oven until top is light brown and center has a slight jiggle to it, 45 to 55 minutes. Let cool in pan on a wire rack for 2 hours. Cover with plastic wrap and refrigerate for at least 6 hours before serving.

Holiday and Celebration
Cheesecakes

Raspberry Rose Cheesecake

SERVES 8 TO 10

Light pink in color, this cheesecake is perfect for Valentine's Day or a holiday party where color counts on the buffet table.

Tip

Rose water can be purchased at health food stores or spice vendors.

Variation

Candied petals from organic roses would be sensational scattered on top. They are easy to make: Brush both sides of the petal with beaten egg white and sprinkle both sides with granulated sugar. Dry overnight on a rack before using.

- Preheat oven to 350°F (180°C)
- 9-inch (23 cm) cheesecake pan, ungreased, or springform pan with 3-inch (7.5 cm) sides, greased

Crust

1¼ cups	butter cookie crumbs	300 mL
¼ cup	unsalted butter, melted	50 mL

Filling

2	packages (each 8 oz/250 g) cream cheese, softened	2
¾ cup	granulated sugar	175 mL
2	eggs	2
½ cup	raspberries, quartered if large	125 mL
1 tsp	rose water	5 mL

Decoration

	Classic Whipped Cream Topping (see recipe, page 262)	
½ cup	raspberries	125 mL

1. *Crust:* In a bowl, combine cookie crumbs and butter. Press into bottom of cheesecake pan and freeze.

2. *Filling:* In a mixer bowl fitted with paddle attachment, beat cream cheese and sugar on medium-high speed until very smooth, for 3 minutes. Add eggs, one at a time, beating after each addition. Fold in raspberries and rose water by hand.

3. Pour over frozen crust, smoothing out to sides of pan. Bake in preheated oven until top is light brown and center has a slight jiggle to it, 35 to 45 minutes. Let cool in pan on a wire rack for 2 hours. Cover with plastic wrap and refrigerate for at least 6 hours before decorating or serving.

4. *Decoration:* Pipe 12 rosettes around top of cake with Classic Whipped Cream Topping. Fill center with raspberries.

Shamrock Mint Cheesecake

SERVES 18 TO 20

When I was a child, my proud Irish father would paint shamrocks on everything. I still pay homage to our lucky icons. Serve this on St. Patrick's Day for good luck, whether you're Irish or not.

Tip

When making cookie crumbs, you do not have to scrape the cream filling out of the cookies; just place them whole into the food processor and pulse.

- Preheat oven to 350°F (180°C)
- 10-inch (25 cm) cheesecake pan, ungreased, or springform pan with 3-inch (7.5 cm) sides, greased

Crust

2½ cups	chocolate sandwich cookie crumbs	625 mL
⅓ cup	unsalted butter, melted	75 mL

Filling

5	packages (each 8 oz/250 g) cream cheese, softened	5
2 cups	granulated sugar	500 mL
5	eggs	5
1 tsp	vanilla extract	5 mL
2 tsp	mint extract	10 mL
1 tsp	liquid green food coloring	5 mL

1. *Crust:* In a bowl, combine cookie crumbs and butter. Press into bottom of cheesecake pan and freeze.

2. *Filling:* In a mixer bowl fitted with paddle attachment, beat cream cheese and sugar on medium-high speed until very smooth, for 3 minutes. Add eggs, one at a time, beating after each addition. Mix in vanilla.

3. Transfer 1½ cups (375 mL) of the batter to a small bowl and stir in mint extract and green food coloring.

4. Pour vanilla batter over frozen crust, smoothing out to sides of pan. Viewing the cheesecake as a clock, pool the green batter on top of white layer, about 2 inches (5 cm) from sides of pan, at 9, 11, 1 and 3 o'clock. With a wooden skewer, draw the green pools toward the center, making green heart shapes, creating a shamrock.

5. Bake in preheated oven until top is light brown and center has a slight jiggle to it, 55 to 65 minutes. Let cool in pan on a wire rack for 2 hours. Cover with plastic wrap and refrigerate for at least 6 hours before serving.

Passover Honey Cheesecake

SERVES 18 TO 20

I love the slight taste of honey in this Passover cheesecake.

Tips

Grind almonds and matzo meal together in a food processor to keep the nuts from turning to butter.

Save the egg whites in the refrigerator for up to 2 days or in the freezer for up to 6 months. Use for meringue or when a recipe calls for egg whites.

Variation

Substitute pecans for almonds for a more complex nut flavor.

- Preheat oven to 350°F (180°C)
- 10-inch (25 cm) cheesecake pan, ungreased, or springform pan with 3-inch (7.5 cm) sides, greased

Crust

2 cups	almonds, toasted (see tip, page 249) and ground	500 mL
¼ cup	matzo meal	50 mL
2 tbsp	unsalted butter, melted	25 mL

Filling

4	packages (each 8 oz/250 g) cream cheese, softened	4
2 cups	sour cream	500 mL
⅔ cup	liquid honey	150 mL
6	egg yolks	6
1 tbsp	vanilla extract	15 mL
½ cup	almonds, toasted and chopped	125 mL

1. *Crust:* In a bowl, combine ground almonds, matzo meal and butter. Press into bottom of cheesecake pan and freeze.

2. *Filling:* In a mixer bowl fitted with paddle attachment, beat cream cheese, sour cream and honey on medium-high speed until very smooth, for 3 minutes. Add egg yolks, one at a time, beating after each addition. Mix in vanilla.

3. Pour over frozen crust, smoothing out to sides of pan. Sprinkle chopped almonds on top of batter. Bake in preheated oven until top is light brown and center has a slight jiggle to it, 60 to 75 minutes. Let cool in pan on a wire rack for 2 hours. Cover with plastic wrap and refrigerate for at least 6 hours before serving.

Easter Cheesecake

SERVES 18 TO 20

*Easter always reminds
me of white chocolate
and toasted coconut.
This cheesecake will be
a hit at Easter brunch
or any spring party.*

Tips

To melt white chocolate,
bring water to a boil in
the bottom of a double
boiler and turn the heat
off. Place chopped white
chocolate in the top
portion of the double
boiler and stir until
melted. The steam is
hot enough to melt white
chocolate. Do not use
the microwave to melt
white chocolate, as it has
a lower melting point
than other chocolates. If
you don't have a double
boiler, a saucepan with a
metal bowl loosely fitted
on top will also work.
After the chocolate has
melted, remove it from
the bottom boiler and
let cool until tepid.

Make sure the chocolate
has cooled slightly
before adding it to the
filling or the cake will
have chocolate chunks.

Variation

Pecans may be more
economical than
macadamia nuts.

- Preheat oven to 350°F (180°C)
- 10-inch (25 cm) cheesecake pan, ungreased, or springform pan with 3-inch (7.5 cm) sides, greased

Crust

2 cups	butter cookie crumbs	500 mL
½ cup	macadamia nuts, toasted (see tip, page 249) and ground	125 mL
¼ cup	unsalted butter, melted	50 mL

Filling

6	packages (each 8 oz/250 g) cream cheese, softened	6
2 cups	granulated sugar	500 mL
5	eggs	5
1	egg yolk	1
8 oz	white chocolate, melted (see tip, at left) and cooled	250 g
1½ cups	flaked sweetened coconut, toasted (see tip, page 135)	375 mL
2 tsp	vanilla extract	10 mL

Decoration

	Classic Whipped Cream Topping (see recipe, page 262)	
½ cup	flaked sweetened coconut, toasted	125 mL

1. *Crust:* In a bowl, combine cookie crumbs, macadamia nuts and butter. Press into bottom of cheesecake pan and freeze.

2. *Filling:* In a mixer bowl fitted with paddle attachment, beat cream cheese and sugar on medium-high speed until very smooth, for 3 minutes. Add whole eggs and egg yolk, one at a time, beating after each addition. With the mixer running, pour in melted chocolate in a steady stream. Fold in coconut and vanilla by hand.

3. Pour over frozen crust, smoothing out to sides of pan. Bake in preheated oven until top is light brown and center has a slight jiggle to it, 60 to 75 minutes. Let cool in pan on a wire rack for 2 hours. Cover with plastic wrap and refrigerate for at least 6 hours before decorating or serving.

4. *Decoration:* Ice top of cake with Classic Whipped Cream Topping or pipe a ribbon around border, if desired. Sprinkle with coconut.

Fourth of July Cheesecake

SERVES 18 TO 20

Here's an all-American cheesecake you will be proud to serve at a picnic or summer gathering.

Tip

You can make the cheesecake weeks ahead and freeze it (see Storing and Freezing, page 22). Decorate the day of the event.

Variation

Substitute fresh cherries for the strawberries to keep the patriotic theme. Using only one type of berry is delicious, but not as colorful.

- Preheat oven to 350°F (180°C)
- 10-inch (25 cm) cheesecake pan, ungreased, or springform pan with 3-inch (7.5 cm) sides, greased

Crust

2 cups	butter cookie crumbs	500 mL
⅓ cup	unsalted butter, melted	75 mL

Filling

6	packages (each 8 oz/250 g) cream cheese, softened	6
2¼ cups	granulated sugar	550 mL
6	eggs	6
1 cup	strawberries, quartered	250 mL
½ cup	raspberries	125 mL
½ cup	blueberries	125 mL
1 tbsp	vanilla extract	15 mL

Decoration

	Classic Whipped Cream Topping (see recipe, page 262)	
1 cup	strawberries, hulled	250 mL
½ cup	raspberries	125 mL
½ cup	blueberries	125 mL

1. *Crust:* In a bowl, combine cookie crumbs and butter. Press into bottom of cheesecake pan and freeze.
2. *Filling:* In a mixer bowl fitted with paddle attachment, beat cream cheese and sugar on medium-high speed until very smooth, for 3 minutes. Add eggs, one at a time, beating after each addition. Fold in strawberries, raspberries, blueberries and vanilla by hand.
3. Pour over frozen crust, smoothing out to sides of pan. Bake in preheated oven until top is light brown and center has a slight jiggle to it, 60 to 75 minutes. Let cool in pan on a wire rack for 2 hours. Cover with plastic wrap and refrigerate for at least 6 hours before decorating or serving.
4. *Decoration:* Ice top of cake with Classic Whipped Cream Topping. Place perfectly shaped strawberries around outside edge of cake, followed by a row of raspberries. Fill center with blueberries.

Autumn Festival Cheesecake

SERVES 18 TO 20

Full of warm harvest flavors, this cheesecake is great served on a cool autumn night or on Halloween.

Tips

Toasting brings out the natural oils and flavor of nuts. Place nuts in a single layer on a baking sheet and bake at 350°F (180°C) until fragrant, 10 to 12 minutes.

If the raisins are hard, you can plump them up in a little hot water. Cover them for 10 minutes, then drain and use.

- Preheat oven to 350°F (180°C)
- 10-inch (25 cm) cheesecake pan, ungreased, or springform pan with 3-inch (7.5 cm) sides, greased

Crust

1½ cups	graham cracker crumbs	375 mL
½ cup	pecans, toasted (see tip, at left) and ground	125 mL
⅓ cup	unsalted butter, melted	75 mL

Filling

6	packages (each 8 oz/250 g) cream cheese, softened	6
2¼ cups	granulated sugar	550 mL
6	eggs	6
1	baking apple (such as Granny Smith or Pippin), peeled and finely chopped	1
½ cup	golden raisins	125 mL
2 tbsp	grated orange zest	25 mL
1 tsp	freshly grated nutmeg	5 mL
1 tsp	ground cinnamon	5 mL
½ tsp	ground cloves	2 mL
½ tsp	ground allspice	2 mL
2 tsp	vanilla extract	10 mL

Decoration

	Classic Whipped Cream Topping (see recipe, page 262)	
¼ tsp	grated orange zest	1 mL
1 tsp	ground cinnamon	5 mL
½ tsp	freshly grated nutmeg	2 mL

1. *Crust:* In a bowl, combine graham cracker crumbs, pecans and butter. Press into pan and freeze.

2. *Filling:* In a mixer bowl fitted with paddle attachment, beat cream cheese and sugar on medium-high speed until very smooth, for 3 minutes. Add eggs, one at a time, beating after each addition. Fold in chopped apple, raisins, orange zest, nutmeg, cinnamon, cloves, allspice and vanilla by hand.

3. Pour over frozen crust, smoothing out to sides of pan. Bake in preheated oven until top is light brown and center has a slight jiggle to it, 60 to 75 minutes. Let cool in pan on a wire rack for 2 hours. Cover with plastic wrap and refrigerate for at least 6 hours before decorating or serving.

4. *Decoration:* Ice top of cake with Classic Whipped Cream Topping. Sprinkle with orange zest, cinnamon and nutmeg.

Maple Pumpkin Cheesecake

SERVES 18 TO 20

Two fall flavors that go well together are maple and pumpkin.

Tip

If maple syrup is not available, you can substitute ¼ tsp (1 mL) maple extract.

Variation

Fold 1 cup (250 mL) chopped hazelnuts into the filling for a crunchy texture.

- Preheat oven to 350°F (180°C)
- 10-inch (25 cm) cheesecake pan, ungreased, or springform pan with 3-inch (7.5 cm) sides, greased

Crust

2½ cups	graham cracker crumbs	625 mL
1 tsp	ground ginger	5 mL
⅓ cup	unsalted butter, melted	75 mL

Filling

5	packages (each 8 oz/250 g) cream cheese, softened	5
1 cup	sour cream	250 mL
2¼ cups	granulated sugar	550 mL
6	eggs	6
1 cup	pumpkin purée (not pie filling)	250 mL
½ cup	all-purpose flour	125 mL
½ cup	pure maple syrup	125 mL
1 tbsp	ground cinnamon	15 mL
½ tsp	freshly grated nutmeg	2 mL
¼ tsp	ground allspice	1 mL
3 tbsp	freshly squeezed lemon juice	45 mL
1 tbsp	vanilla extract	15 mL

Decoration

	Classic Whipped Cream Topping (see recipe, page 262)

1. *Crust:* In a bowl, combine graham cracker crumbs, ginger and butter. Press into bottom of cheesecake pan and freeze.

2. *Filling:* In a mixer bowl fitted with paddle attachment, beat cream cheese, sour cream and sugar on medium-high speed until very smooth, for 3 minutes. Add eggs, one at a time, beating after each addition. Fold in pumpkin, flour, maple syrup, cinnamon, nutmeg, allspice, lemon juice and vanilla by hand.

3. Pour over frozen crust, smoothing out to sides of pan. Bake in preheated oven until top is light brown and center has a slight jiggle to it, 60 to 75 minutes. Let cool in pan on a wire rack for 2 hours. Cover with plastic wrap and refrigerate for at least 6 hours before decorating or serving.

4. *Decoration:* Ice top of cake with Classic Whipped Cream Topping or pipe a ribbon around border, if desired.

Pumpkin Praline Cheesecake

SERVES 18 TO 20

You will be delighted by the nutty taste of pecans mixed with rich pumpkin.

Tip

Look for pure pumpkin when purchasing canned. Stay clear of pumpkin pie filling and those with squash added.

Variation

Hazelnuts work well instead of pecans in this recipe.

- Preheat oven to 350°F (180°C)
- 10-inch (25 cm) cheesecake pan, ungreased, or springform pan with 3-inch (7.5 cm) sides, greased

Crust

2½ cups	gingersnap cookie crumbs	625 mL
⅓ cup	unsalted butter, melted	75 mL

Filling

5	packages (each 8 oz/250 g) cream cheese, softened	5
1 cup	sour cream	250 mL
2¼ cups	granulated sugar	550 mL
6	eggs	6
1 cup	pecans, toasted (see tip, page 249) and chopped	250 mL
1 cup	pumpkin purée (not pie filling)	250 mL
½ cup	all-purpose flour	125 mL
1 tbsp	vanilla extract	15 mL
2 tsp	ground cinnamon	10 mL
½ tsp	freshly grated nutmeg	2 mL
¼ tsp	ground allspice	1 mL
¼ tsp	ground cloves	1 mL

Decoration

	Classic Whipped Cream Topping (see recipe, page 262)	
18 to 20	pecan halves	18 to 20
1 tsp	ground cinnamon	5 mL

1. *Crust:* In a bowl, combine cookie crumbs and butter. Press into bottom of cheesecake pan and freeze.

2. *Filling:* In a mixer bowl fitted with paddle attachment, beat cream cheese, sour cream and sugar on medium-high speed until very smooth, for 3 minutes. Add eggs, one at a time, beating after each addition. Fold in pecans, pumpkin, flour, vanilla, cinnamon, nutmeg, allspice and cloves by hand.

3. Pour over frozen crust, smoothing out to sides of pan. Bake in preheated oven until top is light brown and center has a slight jiggle to it, 65 to 75 minutes. Let cool in pan on a wire rack for 2 hours. Cover with plastic wrap and refrigerate for at least 6 hours before decorating or serving.

4. *Decoration:* Ice top of cake with Classic Whipped Cream Topping or pipe a ribbon around border, if desired. Arrange pecan halves on top and sprinkle with cinnamon.

Sweet Potato Cheesecake

SERVES 18 TO 20

Who doesn't like sweet potato pie? Now try my version of this classic as a cheesecake!

Tips

Peel a medium sweet potato, wrap in foil and bake in a 400°F (200°C) oven for 60 minutes or until soft. Mash about half of it for this recipe. Add a little butter and brown sugar to the remainder for a snack.

Use drained canned sweet potatoes if fresh are unavailable.

- Preheat oven to 350°F (180°C)
- 10-inch (25 cm) cheesecake pan, ungreased, or springform pan with 3-inch (7.5 cm) sides, greased

Crust

2 cups	pecans, toasted (see tip, page 249) and ground	500 mL
¼ cup	all-purpose flour	50 mL
2 tbsp	unsalted butter, melted	25 mL

Filling

5	packages (each 8 oz/250 g) cream cheese, softened	5
1 cup	sour cream	250 mL
2 cups	packed light brown sugar	500 mL
6	egg yolks	6
1 tbsp	vanilla extract	15 mL
1½ tsp	freshly grated nutmeg	7 mL
6	egg whites	6
⅔ cup	mashed cooked sweet potato (see tip, at left)	150 mL

Decoration

	Classic Whipped Cream Topping (see recipe, page 262)	
1 tsp	freshly grated nutmeg	5 mL

1. *Crust:* In a bowl, combine pecans, flour and butter. Press into bottom of cheesecake pan and freeze.

2. *Filling:* In a mixer bowl fitted with paddle attachment, beat cream cheese, sour cream and brown sugar on medium-high speed until very smooth, for 3 minutes. Add egg yolks, one at a time, beating after each addition. Stir in vanilla and nutmeg.

3. In a clean mixer bowl fitted with whip attachment, whip egg whites on medium-high speed until soft peaks form. Fold in sweet potato. Fold into batter by hand.

4. Pour over frozen crust, smoothing out to sides of pan. Bake in preheated oven until top is light brown and center has a slight jiggle to it, 60 to 75 minutes. Let cool in pan on a wire rack for 2 hours. Cover with plastic wrap and refrigerate for at least 6 hours before decorating or serving.

5. *Decoration:* Ice top of cake with Classic Whipped Cream Topping or pipe rosettes around top of cake, if desired. Sprinkle with nutmeg.

Christmas Cheesecake

SERVES 18 TO 20

Give in to the Christmas spirit of red and green everything by garnishing this cheesecake with raspberry preserves and a ring of sliced kiwi.

Tips

Kiwis should be firm, like tomatoes, with a little give when you hold one in the palm of your hand.

Preserves are best to use here, rather than jelly or jam. They adhere to the cheesecake better because they are thicker and less runny.

Variation

Substitute strawberry preserves for the raspberry preserves.

- Preheat oven to 350°F (180°C)
- 10-inch (25 cm) cheesecake pan, ungreased, or springform pan with 3-inch (7.5 cm) sides, greased

Crust

2 cups	graham cracker crumbs	500 mL
¼ cup	pecans, toasted (see tip, page 249) and ground	50 mL
⅓ cup	unsalted butter, melted	75 mL

Filling

5	packages (each 8 oz/250 g) cream cheese, softened	5
1 cup	sour cream	250 mL
2¼ cups	granulated sugar	550 mL
6	eggs	6
⅓ cup	all-purpose flour	75 mL
1 tbsp	grated orange zest	15 mL
1 tbsp	grated lemon zest	15 mL
1 tsp	freshly squeezed lemon juice	5 mL
2 tsp	vanilla extract	10 mL

Decoration

	Classic Whipped Cream Topping (see recipe, page 262)	
⅔ cup	raspberry preserves	150 mL
2	kiwifruits, peeled and thinly sliced	2

1. *Crust:* In a bowl, combine graham cracker crumbs, pecans and butter. Press into bottom of cheesecake pan and freeze.

2. *Filling:* In a mixer bowl fitted with paddle attachment, beat cream cheese, sour cream and sugar on medium-high speed until very smooth, for 3 minutes. Add eggs, one at a time, beating after each addition. Stir in flour, orange zest, lemon zest, lemon juice and vanilla.

3. Pour over frozen crust, smoothing out to sides of pan. Bake in preheated oven until top is light brown and center has a slight jiggle to it, 60 to 75 minutes. Let cool in pan on a wire rack for 2 hours. Cover with plastic wrap and refrigerate for at least 6 hours before decorating or serving.

4. *Decoration:* Pipe a ribbon of Classic Whipped Cream Topping around border of cake. Spread raspberry preserves in the center and out toward the whipped cream. Lay kiwi slices in spirals close to the whipped cream.

Eggnog Nutmeg Rum Cheesecake

SERVES 18 TO 20

I wait patiently every year for the holiday season to start so I can make this cheesecake with fresh eggnog, which gives it a special flavor.

Tips

If the cottage cheese has a wet look to it, drain it through a fine-mesh sieve. Too much moisture will change the texture of the cheesecake.

If small-curd cottage cheese is not available, purée cottage cheese in a food processor before adding to the cream cheese.

Keep canned eggnog in the pantry so you can make this recipe out of season when you can't wait for cartons of fresh eggnog to be available.

- Preheat oven to 350°F (180°C)
- 10-inch (25 cm) cheesecake pan, ungreased, or springform pan with 3-inch (7.5 cm) sides, greased

Crust

2 cups	graham cracker crumbs	500 mL
1 tsp	freshly grated nutmeg	5 mL
1/3 cup	unsalted butter, melted	75 mL

Filling

4	packages (each 8 oz/250 g) cream cheese, softened	4
2 cups	small-curd cottage cheese, drained (see tips, at left)	500 mL
2 1/4 cups	granulated sugar	550 mL
6	eggs	6
1 cup	prepared eggnog	250 mL
1/2 cup	light rum	125 mL
1 tbsp	vanilla extract	15 mL
1 tsp	freshly grated nutmeg	5 mL

Topping

1 cup	sour cream	250 mL
1/2 cup	granulated sugar	125 mL
1 tsp	freshly grated nutmeg	5 mL
1 tsp	vanilla extract	5 mL

Decoration

	Classic Whipped Cream Topping (see recipe, page 262)	
1 tsp	freshly grated nutmeg	5 mL

1. *Crust:* In a bowl, combine graham cracker crumbs, nutmeg and butter. Press into bottom of cheesecake pan and freeze.
2. *Filling:* In a mixer bowl fitted with paddle attachment, beat cream cheese, cottage cheese and sugar on medium-high speed until very smooth, for 3 minutes. Add eggs, one at a time, beating after each addition. Mix in eggnog, rum, vanilla and nutmeg.

Variation

Substitute ground cinnamon for the nutmeg, or use in addition to the nutmeg for extra sparkle.

3. Pour over frozen crust, smoothing out to sides of pan. Bake in preheated oven until top is light brown and center has a slight jiggle to it, 60 to 75 minutes. Let cool on the counter for 10 minutes (do not turn the oven off). The cake will sink slightly.

4. *Topping:* In a small bowl, combine sour cream, sugar, nutmeg and vanilla. Pour into center of cooled cake and spread out to edges. Bake for 5 minutes more. Let cool in pan on a wire rack for 2 hours. Cover with plastic wrap and refrigerate for at least 6 hours before decorating or serving.

5. *Decoration:* Ice top of cake with Classic Whipped Cream Topping or pipe rosettes around top of cake, if desired. Sprinkle with nutmeg.

Cranberry Orange Cheesecake

SERVES 18 TO 20

This cheesecake is a staple on many of my students' holiday tables. The tartness of the cranberries and the sweet creamy filling make every bite explode in your mouth.

Tip

Use frozen cranberries right from the freezer, without thawing, to prevent the color from bleeding.

Variation

Spread top of cooled cake with Spiked Cranberry Sauce (page 273).

• Preheat oven to 350°F (180°C)
• 10-inch (25 cm) cheesecake pan, ungreased, or springform pan with 3-inch (7.5 cm) sides, greased

Crust

1½ cups	butter cookie crumbs	375 mL
½ cup	pecans, toasted (see tip, page 249) and ground	125 mL
⅓ cup	unsalted butter, melted	75 mL

Filling

6	packages (each 8 oz/250 g) cream cheese, softened	6
2¼ cups	granulated sugar	550 mL
6	eggs	6
2 tbsp	grated orange zest	25 mL
2 tsp	freshly grated nutmeg	10 mL
2 tsp	vanilla extract	10 mL
1½ cups	fresh cranberries, slightly crushed, or frozen cranberries	375 mL

Topping

1 cup	sour cream	250 mL
½ cup	granulated sugar	125 mL
1 tsp	vanilla extract	5 mL
¼ tsp	grated orange zest	1 mL

1. *Crust:* In a bowl, combine cookie crumbs, pecans and butter. Press into bottom of cheesecake pan and freeze.

2. *Filling:* In a mixer bowl fitted with paddle attachment, beat cream cheese and sugar on medium-high speed until very smooth, for 3 minutes. Add eggs, one at a time, beating after each addition. Stir in orange zest, nutmeg and vanilla. Fold in cranberries by hand.

3. Pour over frozen crust, smoothing out to sides of pan. Bake in preheated oven until top is light brown and center has a slight jiggle to it, 60 to 75 minutes. Let cool on the counter for 10 minutes (do not turn the oven off). The cake will sink slightly.

4. *Topping:* In a small bowl, combine sour cream, sugar, vanilla and orange zest. Pour into center of cooled cake and spread out to edges. Bake for 5 minutes more. Let cool in pan on a wire rack for 2 hours. Cover with plastic wrap and refrigerate for at least 6 hours before serving.

Taco Cheesecake (page 237)

Peppermint Chocolate Cheesecake

SERVES 18 TO 20

During the Christmas holidays, I love to serve hot chocolate with a peppermint stick. The combination of chocolate and mint works well in this cheesecake, too.

Tips

If candy canes are difficult to find, I use the round red and white wrapped mints.

To crush candy canes, place them in a sealable plastic bag and pound with a meat pounder until crushed to desired coarseness.

Variation

Use white chocolate chunks instead of semisweet.

Overleaf: Maple Pumpkin Cheesecake (page 250) and Cranberry Orange Cheesecake (page 256)

Peppermint Chocolate Cheesecake (this page)

- Preheat oven to 350°F (180°C)
- 10-inch (25 cm) cheesecake pan, ungreased, or springform pan with 3-inch (7.5 cm) sides, greased

Crust

2 cups	chocolate sandwich cookie crumbs	500 mL
1/3 cup	unsalted butter, melted	75 mL

Filling

6	packages (each 8 oz/250 g) cream cheese, softened	6
1 cup	sour cream	250 mL
2 cups	granulated sugar	500 mL
6	eggs	6
6 oz	semisweet chocolate, melted (see page 63) and cooled	175 g
2/3 cup	all-purpose flour, divided	150 mL
2 tsp	vanilla extract	10 mL
1/2 tsp	peppermint extract	2 mL
12 oz	semisweet chocolate chunks	375 g
1 cup	crushed candy canes (see tips, at left)	250 mL

Decoration

	Classic Whipped Cream Topping (see recipe, page 262)	
1/4 cup	crushed candy canes	50 mL

1. *Crust:* In a bowl, combine cookie crumbs and butter. Press into bottom of cheesecake pan and freeze.

2. *Filling:* In a mixer bowl fitted with paddle attachment, beat cream cheese, sour cream and sugar on medium-high speed until very smooth, for 3 minutes. Add eggs, one at a time, beating after each addition. With the mixer running, pour in melted chocolate in a steady stream. Stir in 1/2 cup (125 mL) of the flour, vanilla and peppermint extract. In a small bowl, coat chocolate chunks and candy canes with the remaining flour. Fold into batter by hand.

3. Pour over frozen crust, smoothing out to sides of pan. Bake in preheated oven until top is light brown and center has a slight jiggle to it, 60 to 75 minutes. Let cool in pan on a wire rack for 2 hours. Cover with plastic wrap and refrigerate for at least 6 hours before decorating or serving.

4. *Decoration:* Ice top of cake with Classic Whipped Cream Topping or pipe a ribbon around border, if desired. Top with crushed candy canes.

Three-Tier Wedding Cheesecake

SERVES 70 TO 80

*Anyone who can bake
a cheesecake can easily
make a fabulous wedding
cheesecake. Bake the
cakes up to 3 weeks in
advance, freeze and
thaw before decorating.*

Tips

If you do not have a
6-quart (6 L) mixer,
you can make this in
two equal batches in a
smaller stand mixer or
using a hand mixer.

Do not substitute
flavored whipped cream
for the Cream Cheese
Whipped Cream. My
recipe will hold the
form of piped borders
and decorations much
longer.

- Preheat oven to 325°F (160°C)
- 10-inch (25 cm) cheesecake pan, ungreased, or springform pan with 3-inch (7.5 cm) sides, greased
- 9-inch (23 cm) cheesecake pan, ungreased, or springform pan with 3-inch (7.5 cm) sides, greased
- 8-inch (20 cm) cheesecake pan, ungreased, or springform pan with 3-inch (7.5 cm) sides, greased
- Piping bag

Crust

4½ cups	graham cracker crumbs	1.125 L
¾ cup	unsalted butter, melted	175 mL

Filling

8	packages (each 8 oz/250 g) cream cheese, softened	8
2½ cups	granulated sugar	625 mL
8	eggs	8
¼ cup	freshly squeezed lemon juice	50 mL
1 tbsp	vanilla extract	15 mL

Topping

2 cups	sour cream	500 mL
1 cup	granulated sugar	250 mL
1½ tbsp	freshly squeezed lemon juice	22 mL
2½ tsp	vanilla extract	12 mL

Decoration

	Cream Cheese Whipped Cream (see recipe, page 262)	
12 cups	strawberries, hulled	3 L

1. *Crust:* In a bowl, combine graham cracker crumbs and butter. Press 2 cups (500 mL) into 10-inch (25 cm) pan, press 1½ cups (375 mL) into 9-inch (23 cm) pan and press 1 cup (250 mL) into 8-inch (20 cm) pan. Place pans in freezer.

2. *Filling:* In a mixer bowl fitted with paddle attachment, in two batches, if necessary, beat cream cheese and sugar on medium-high speed until very smooth, 5 to 6 minutes. Add eggs, one at a time, beating after each addition. Mix in lemon juice and vanilla.

Variation

Use an array of fresh berries, such as raspberries, blueberries and blackberries, for decoration. You can also use fresh flowers, such as roses, but make sure they have not been sprayed with pesticides.

3. Pour half the batter over 10-inch (25 cm) frozen crust, smoothing out to sides of pan. Pour about three-quarters of the remaining batter over 9-inch (23 cm) crust, smoothing out to sides of pan. Pour remaining batter over 8-inch (20 cm) crust, smoothing out to sides of pan. Check to make sure depth of batter is about the same in each pan. Bake in preheated oven until tops are light brown and centers have a slight jiggle to them. (All three may not fit on one center rack, so bake in two batches, if necessary.) The large cheesecake will take 75 to 80 minutes to bake; the medium will take 45 to 55 minutes; and the small will take 35 to 40 minutes. Let cool on the counter for 10 minutes (do not turn the oven off). The cakes will sink slightly.

4. *Topping:* In a bowl, combine sour cream, sugar, lemon juice and vanilla. Divide mixture in same proportions as batter, pour into center of each of the cooled cakes and spread out to edges. Bake for 5 minutes more. Let cool in pans on wire racks for 2 hours. Cover with plastic wrap and refrigerate for at least 8 hours or freeze for up to 3 weeks before decorating (see Storing and Freezing, page 22).

5. *Decoration:* Using a star tip, pipe Cream Cheese Whipped Cream in a ribbon around the border of each cake. Top each cake with strawberries, cut side down. Do not attempt to stack cakes one on top of the other. Instead, place cakes on a three-tiered pedestal cake plate or on three different plates at different heights.

Birthday Chocolate Cheesecake

SERVES 18 TO 20

Here's a happy birthday recipe to satisfy all the chocolate lovers in your family.

Tip
Make chocolate shavings by moving a spatula in an up-and-down motion along the side of a large bar of chocolate (or use a potato peeler on a cold bar of chocolate).

Variation
For a chocolate chocolate-chip cheesecake, fold 1 cup (250 mL) semisweet chocolate chips, dusted with 1 tbsp (15 mL) all-purpose flour, into the filling.

- Preheat oven to 350°F (180°C)
- 10-inch (25 cm) cheesecake pan, ungreased, or springform pan with 3-inch (7.5 cm) sides, greased

Crust

2½ cups	chocolate sandwich cookie crumbs	625 mL
⅓ cup	unsalted butter, melted	75 mL

Filling

6	packages (each 8 oz/250 g) cream cheese, softened	6
1 cup	sour cream	250 mL
2 cups	granulated sugar	500 mL
6	eggs	6
½ cup	unsweetened Dutch-process cocoa powder, sifted	125 mL
2 tbsp	all-purpose flour	25 mL
2 tsp	vanilla extract	10 mL

Decoration

	Classic Whipped Cream Topping (see recipe, page 262)	
3 oz	semisweet chocolate, shaved (see tip, at left)	90 g

1. *Crust:* In a bowl, combine cookie crumbs and butter. Press into bottom of cheesecake pan and freeze.
2. *Filling:* In a mixer bowl fitted with paddle attachment, beat cream cheese, sour cream and sugar on medium-high speed until very smooth, for 3 minutes. Add eggs, one at a time, beating after each addition. Stir in cocoa, flour and vanilla.
3. Pour over frozen crust, smoothing out to sides of pan. Bake in preheated oven until top is light brown and center has a slight jiggle to it, 75 to 85 minutes. Let cool in pan on a wire rack for 2 hours. Cover with plastic wrap and refrigerate for at least 6 hours before decorating or serving.
4. *Decoration:* Ice top of cake with Classic Whipped Cream Topping or pipe rosettes around top of cake, if desired. Top with chocolate shavings.

Toppings and Sauces

Classic Whipped Cream Topping

MAKES ABOUT 1 CUP (250 ML)

A whipped cream topping never goes out of style. You can use this classic on almost any cheesecake in this book.

Tip

For perfect results, see Whipping Technique (page 20).

Variation

Stir in 3 oz (90 g) semisweet chocolate, melted, to create a chocolate version.

½ cup	whipping (35%) cream	125 mL
2 tbsp	granulated sugar	25 mL

1. In a well-chilled mixer bowl fitted with whip attachment, whip cream on medium-high speed until soft peaks form. With the mixer running, sprinkle with sugar and whip until firm peaks form.
2. Pipe a ribbon or rosettes around the border of the cheesecake or ice the entire top.

Cream Cheese Whipped Cream

MAKES ABOUT 2½ CUPS (625 ML)

Adding cream cheese to the whipping cream adds texture and increases the fat percentage, enabling this topping to stay out on a cheesecake longer without refrigeration.

3 oz	cream cheese, softened	90 g
1 tbsp	milk	15 mL
2 cups	whipping (35%) cream	500 mL
¾ cup	confectioner's (icing) sugar	175 mL

1. In a mixer bowl fitted with whip attachment, whip cream cheese and milk on low speed until smooth, about 3 minutes. Pour in whipping cream and confectioner's sugar. Whip on high speed, scraping bowl occasionally, until stiff peaks form.

Truffle Fudge Topping

**MAKES ABOUT
2½ CUPS (625 ML)**

*When you just need a
little more chocolate in
your cheesecake, top
it with a layer of this
fudge topping. I use any
leftovers on ice cream.*

Tips

You can reheat this
topping in the double
boiler and use it as a
poured glaze.

The chocolate can be
a bit warm when you
incorporate it into the
butter. This will cause
the butter to melt,
creating a different
texture.

- 2-quart (2 L) double boiler

12 oz	milk chocolate, chopped	375 g
6 oz	semisweet or bittersweet chocolate, chopped	175 g
1 cup plus 2 tbsp	unsalted butter, softened	275 mL

1. In top of double boiler over simmering (not boiling) water, melt milk and semisweet chocolates, stirring until smooth. Let cool until no longer warm to the touch.

2. In a mixer bowl fitted with whip attachment, beat butter and melted chocolate on medium speed until uniform in color, about 3 minutes. Place bowl in the refrigerator for 10 minutes to firm the frosting. Return to the mixer and beat until fluffy, about 2 minutes.

3. Spread a thin layer over the top of the cheesecake. Place the remainder in a pastry bag fitted with a star tip and decorate with a shell border around the top edge and around the bottom, where the cake meets the plate.

Pineapple Topping

**MAKES ABOUT
1½ CUPS (375 ML)**

*This topping is
delicious on Banana
Split Cheesecake (page
104) or any other cake
with a tropical flair.*

Tip

If you only have
chunks of pineapple,
you can process them
until crushed, about
20 seconds.

Variation

Add 1 tbsp (15 mL)
rum with the pineapple
to make a pineapple
rum sauce.

¼ cup	cold water	50 mL
3 tbsp	cornstarch	45 mL
1	can (20 oz/567 mL) crushed pineapple in heavy syrup, drained and syrup reserved	1

1. In a small bowl, combine cold water and cornstarch. Set aside.
2. In a heavy saucepan, combine reserved syrup and enough water to equal 1 cup (250 mL). Heat over medium heat until bubbling, about 3 minutes. Whisk in cornstarch mixture until thickened, about 2 minutes. Remove from heat and stir in crushed pineapple. Let cool completely. Store in an airtight container in the refrigerator for up to 1 week.

Fresh Lemon Curd

**MAKES ABOUT
2 CUPS (500 ML)**

*This is the most useful
fruit item in any pastry
kitchen.*

Variation

You can use Meyer
lemon or tangerine
juice, if you like.

10	egg yolks	10
¾ cup	granulated sugar	175 mL
¾ cup	freshly squeezed lemon juice	175 mL
½ cup	unsalted butter, softened, cut into pieces	125 mL

1. In a large heatproof glass or nonreactive metal bowl, whisk egg yolks for 2 minutes. Gradually whisk in sugar. Whisk in lemon juice. Place on top of a saucepan of simmering water, over medium heat, making sure the bowl does not touch the water. Cook, whisking constantly, until mixture is thick enough to coat the back of a spoon, about 7 minutes.

2. Remove bowl from saucepan and whisk in butter, a few pieces at a time. Transfer to a cool bowl and place plastic wrap directly on the surface of the curd. Let cool completely at room temperature. Cover and refrigerate until chilled, about 2 hours, or for up to 2 days.

Port Wine Berry Compote

MAKES ABOUT 3 CUPS (750 ML)

Such an easy compote, and so tasty too! Serve on top of Tri-Berry Cheesecake (page 102) for added berry punch.

Tip

To make superfine sugar, place the amount called for in a food processor and process for 2 minutes.

1½ lbs	berries, such as strawberries, raspberries, blackberries and/or blueberries	750 g
½ cup	superfine sugar (see tip, at left)	125 mL
¼ cup	aged port	50 mL

1. Place berries in a large bowl. Add sugar and port; toss to coat. Let stand for at least 30 minutes before using, or store in an airtight container in the refrigerator for up to 4 days (as long as the berries are fresh).

Island Fruit Compote

MAKES ABOUT 3 CUPS (750 ML)

This compote is a great topping for any of the lemon cheesecakes. If you have any left over, you can use it on chicken breasts.

Tip

To tell if a mango or papaya is fresh, hold it in the palm of your hand and gently squeeze. It is ready to use if it feels soft, like a tomato.

1 cup	diced pineapple	250 mL
½ cup	diced mango (about 1 medium)	125 mL
½ cup	diced papaya (about 1 medium)	125 mL
½ cup	flaked sweetened coconut	125 mL
1 cup	rum	250 mL

1. In a bowl, combine pineapple, mango, papaya and coconut. Add rum and toss to coat. Cover and refrigerate for at least 1 hour before using, or store in an airtight container in the refrigerator for up to 1 week (as long as the fruit is fresh).

Orange Mist Glaze

**MAKES ABOUT
1½ CUPS (375 ML)**

*After placing fresh
berries on top of a
cheesecake, you can
mist this glaze over
them for a wet look.*

Tip

I like to use a spray mister
for this glaze. It will coat
more evenly than if you
use a pastry brush.

1 cup	granulated sugar	250 mL
¼ cup	water	50 mL
¼ cup	orange-flavored liqueur or rum	50 mL

1. In a saucepan, bring sugar and water to a rapid boil over medium heat. Boil until sugar is dissolved, 5 to 8 minutes. Remove from heat and stir in liqueur. Transfer to a spray mister bottle and use immediately, or store in an airtight container in the refrigerator for up to 2 weeks.

Coffee-Flavored Syrup

**MAKES ABOUT
1 CUP (250 ML)**

*This sauce is fast and easy
to make, but your guests
will think you worked
all day on it. Drizzle on
top of Chocolate Espresso
Swirl Cheesecake
(page 72).*

Tip

Make sure to heat the
sugar and water to a full
boil and cook until sugar
is dissolved; otherwise,
the sugar may crystallize.

Variation

For a nutty taste,
substitute almond-
flavored liqueur for the
coffee-flavored liqueur.

½ cup	granulated sugar	125 mL
¼ cup	water	50 mL
¼ cup	coffee-flavored liqueur	50 mL

1. In a saucepan, bring sugar and water to a rapid boil over medium heat. Boil until sugar is dissolved, 5 to 8 minutes. Remove from heat and stir in liqueur. Use warm or let cool. Store in an airtight container in the refrigerator for up to 2 weeks.

Espresso Cream Sauce

MAKES ABOUT 1½ CUPS (375 ML)

Pool this cream sauce on a plate before placing a slice of cheesecake on top. Use it with any chocolate- or coffee-flavored cheesecake.

Variation

Substitute orange- or almond-flavored liqueur for the coffee-flavored liqueur.

1 cup	whipping (35%) cream	250 mL
¼ cup	granulated sugar	50 mL
¼ cup	brewed espresso	50 mL
2 tbsp	coffee-flavored liqueur	25 mL

1. In a saucepan, heat cream, sugar and espresso over medium heat until bubbles form around the sides and sugar is dissolved, about 3 minutes. Remove from heat and stir in liqueur. Use warm or cold. Store in an airtight container in the refrigerator for up to 2 weeks. To reheat, warm in the microwave for 1 minute on Medium (50%).

Cherry Almond Sauce

MAKES ABOUT 2 CUPS (500 ML)

This sauce tastes great with Brownie Cheese Pie (page 210).

Tip

If using frozen cherries, try to purchase ones that have been individually quick-frozen and are not packed in juice. If the cherries are packed in juice, drain before using.

Variation

To create a creamy sauce, fold ¼ cup (50 mL) warm whipping (35%) cream into the cooked cherries.

1 tbsp	cornstarch	15 mL
2 tsp	cold water	10 mL
12 oz	fresh cherries, pitted and drained, or frozen cherries, thawed	375 g
¾ cup	granulated sugar	175 mL
½ tsp	almond extract	2 mL

1. In a small bowl, combine cornstarch and cold water. Set aside.
2. In a heavy saucepan, bring cherries and sugar to a boil over medium heat. Add cornstarch mixture, reduce heat to low and whisk until mixture starts to thicken, 2 to 4 minutes. Heat for an additional 2 minutes. (If the cherries do not break up while cooking, use a potato masher to slightly smash the fruit.) Remove from heat and whisk in almond extract. Let cool completely. Store in an airtight container in the refrigerator for up to 1 week.

White Chocolate Macadamia Midnight Sauce

MAKES ABOUT 2 CUPS (500 ML)

I named this sauce when I was working late one night. It was close to midnight, and there was a full moon. You can use this sauce on top of a pound cake, as well.

Tips

When purchasing white chocolate, look at the ingredients and purchase one made with cocoa butter. Avoid those made with palm kernel, cottonseed or tropical oils, which will give the sauce a coconut flavor.

Do not use the microwave to melt white chocolate. It has a lower melting point than other chocolates and burns easily.

Variation

Substitute hazelnuts or cashews for the macadamia nuts.

• 2-quart (2 L) double boiler

12 oz	white chocolate, chopped	375 g
1 cup	whipping (35%) cream	250 mL
½ cup	macadamia nuts, toasted (see tip, page 249) and chopped	125 mL

1. In top of double boiler, over hot (not boiling) water, melt chocolate and cream, stirring until well blended. (The steam will melt the white chocolate without the burner being on.) Let cool until lukewarm. Stir in macadamia nuts. Use warm or cold.

Fresh Blackberry Sauce

**MAKES ABOUT
2 CUPS (500 ML)**

*Plump blackberries,
fresh from the produce
stand, make this a rich,
decadent sauce. I use
leftovers on pancakes
for brunch.*

Tip

Use a strawberry huller
to remove the insides
of the blackberries. The
hulls sometimes create
a bitter taste.

1 tbsp	cornstarch	15 mL
2 tsp	cold water	10 mL
1 lb	blackberries, hulled (see tip, at left)	500 g
1/3 cup	granulated sugar	75 mL
1/4 tsp	almond or rum extract	1 mL

1. In a small bowl, combine cornstarch and cold water. Set aside.
2. In a heavy saucepan, bring blackberries and sugar to a boil over medium heat. Add cornstarch mixture, reduce heat to low and whisk until mixture starts to thicken, 2 to 4 minutes. Heat for an additional 2 minutes. Remove from heat and whisk in almond extract. Let cool completely. Store in an airtight container in the refrigerator for up to 1 week.

Fresh Raspberry Sauce

**MAKES ABOUT
2 CUPS (500 ML)**

*Raspberry sauce is
a staple in all pastry
kitchens, including mine.
Fold into whipped cream
for a mousse, use as a
topping for ice cream
or drizzle over warm
chocolate brownies.*

Tip
You can use frozen
berries that have been
individually quick-
frozen and are not
packed in sugar syrup.
Make sure to thaw the
berries before using.

Variation
Omit the liqueur for
a thicker sauce.

2 tbsp	cornstarch	25 mL
1/4 cup	cold water	50 mL
2 1/2 cups	raspberries	375 mL
1/2 cup	granulated sugar	125 mL
2 tsp	freshly squeezed lemon juice	10 mL
1/4 cup	raspberry-flavored liqueur	50 mL

1. In a small bowl, combine cornstarch and cold water.
   Set aside.

2. In a heavy saucepan, bring raspberries and sugar to a
   boil over medium heat.

3. Press raspberry mixture through a fine-mesh strainer
   to remove the seeds. (You can leave the seeds in, if you
   prefer.) Return to heat and bring to a boil. Add cornstarch
   mixture, reduce heat to low and whisk until mixture is
   thickened, ruby red in color and no longer cloudy, about
   2 minutes. Remove from heat and whisk in liqueur. Let
   cool completely. Store in an airtight container in the
   refrigerator for up to 1 week.

Fresh Strawberry Sauce

**MAKES ABOUT
3 CUPS (750 ML)**

My dinner party guests always linger in my kitchen, watching me prepare stuff. This flavorful sauce is a great choice to make in front of your guests.

Tips

You can ignite the liqueur with a match after you have heated it.

If using large berries, cut them into smaller pieces before cooking so they will cook faster.

¼ cup	unsalted butter	50 mL
½ cup	packed brown sugar	125 mL
4 cups	strawberries, halved	1 L
¼ cup	orange-flavored liqueur	50 mL

1. In a large skillet, melt butter over high heat. Add sugar and cook, stirring, until dissolved, 3 to 5 minutes. Add berries and cook, stirring, until mixture is a brick red color, 5 to 8 minutes. Remove from heat and whisk in liqueur. Serve warm or let cool. Store in an airtight container in the refrigerator for up to 1 week.

Spiked Cranberry Sauce

**MAKES ABOUT
2 CUPS (500 ML)**

*I first served this
sauce alongside my
Thanksgiving turkey,
and then tried it on
top of Blood Orange
Cheesecake (page 120).
I knew I had a winner.*

Tip

Fresh orange juice
makes a substantial
difference in the flavor.

Variation

Blood oranges, when
in season, are flavorful
in this topping.

1 cup	granulated sugar	250 mL
½ cup	water	125 mL
12 oz	fresh cranberries (about 3 cups/750 mL)	375 g
1 tbsp	grated orange zest	15 mL
¼ cup	freshly squeezed orange juice	50 mL
¼ cup	orange-flavored liqueur	50 mL

1. In a heavy saucepan, bring sugar and water to a boil over medium heat. Add cranberries, orange zest and orange juice; return to a boil. Reduce heat and boil gently until cranberries thicken and break open, about 10 minutes. Remove from heat and stir in liqueur. Use warm or let cool.

Marshmallow Sauce

**MAKES ABOUT
2 CUPS (500 ML)**

*Drench a piece of dark
chocolate cheesecake
with this white sauce —
pure decadence.*

Tip

You can prepare this
sauce up to 2 days
ahead and store it in an
airtight container in the
refrigerator. However, it
will thicken as it cools,
so reheat over a double
boiler to the desired
consistency before using.

Variation

Add 1 tsp (5 mL)
peppermint extract for
a mint marshmallow
sauce.

3 cups	miniature marshmallows	750 mL
1 cup	whipping (35%) cream	250 mL
1 tsp	vanilla extract	5 mL

1. In a heavy saucepan, heat marshmallows and cream
   over medium heat, stirring constantly, until fully melted,
   about 4 minutes. Remove from heat and stir in vanilla.
   Serve warm.

Maple Pecan Sauce

*Large pecan halves
in a rich sauce will
transform any simple
cheesecake (or ice cream)
into an elegant dessert.*

Tip

Use real maple syrup
for full flavor.

Variation

Substitute any variety
of nut.

1 cup	pure maple syrup	250 mL
½ cup	whipping (35%) cream	125 mL
1 cup	pecan halves, toasted (see tip, page 249)	250 mL
1 tsp	vanilla extract	5 mL

1. In a heavy saucepan, heat maple syrup and cream over medium heat until bubbling, about 4 minutes. Remove from heat and stir in pecans and vanilla. Serve warm.

Sources

Equipment and Services

Calico Cake Shop
7321 Orangethorpe Avenue
Buena Park, California 90621
714-521-2761
www.calicocakeshop.com
Sells cake and decorating supplies.

George Geary, CCP
www.georgegeary.com
Author's website, full of recipes, tips, culinary tour information and information on classes. Magic Line baking pans also sold here.

Golda's Kitchen
866-465-3299
905-816-9995
www.goldaskitchen.com
Online shopping site. Offers a large range of baking, cooking and measuring equipment; specialty cake decorating, chocolate and confectionery supplies; and a wide assortment of kitchen tools, knives and appliances. Ships worldwide.

KitchenArt
1550 Win Hentschel Boulevard
West Lafayette, Indiana 47906
765-497-3878
www.k-art.com
Privately owned kitchen store and cooking school outside of Purdue University. Full catalog of equipment. Ships to U.S. only.

Parrish's Cake Decorating Supplies
225 W. 146th Street
Gardena, California 90248
800-436-8443 (U.S. only)
310-324-2253
www.parrishsmagicline.com
Offers Magic Line baking pans, offset spatulas and cake decorating supplies. Website under construction at time of printing.

Ingredients

Charles H. Baldwin and Sons
1 Center Street, P.O. Box 372
West Stockbridge, Massachusetts 01266
413-232-7785
www.baldwinextracts.com
Manufactures Baldwin's flavoring extracts — pure extracts from anise to peppermint to vanilla. Also sells baking supplies, flavoring oils and spices.

C.S. Steen's Syrup Mill
800-725-1654
www.steensyrup.com
Manufacturers of Steen's 100% Pure Cane Syrup.

Nielsen-Massey Vanillas
1550 Shields Drive
Waukegan, Illinois 60085-8307
800-525-7873
847-578-1550
www.nielsenmassey.com
Fine producers of vanilla and oil products. Organic products also available.

Penzeys Spices
800-741-7787
www.penzeys.com
Over 30 stores across the U.S. Check online for stores and recipes.

The Spice House
312-274-0378
www.thespicehouse.com
One of the best spice companies. Owner Patty Erd's folks started Penzeys Spices, so spice is in her blood. Four stores in Illinois and Wisconsin. Ships to Canada.

Acknowledgments

INSPIRATION FOR THIS BOOK came from so many friends and family members. My father has always guided me in the right direction. My mom is my biggest fan and the world's premier expert on the best cheesecake. Monica and Pattie, you are the best sisters. Thank you, Neil, for putting up with all my travels and a dirty kitchen, and for tasting never-ending cheesecakes. Jonathan and Teri, you are both always there for me.

Thanks also to all my testers and taste-testers: Chris, Ted, Don, Eilena, Sean, Joel and Ross. To Sean and Chris at Sephno Systems for keeping my computer systems top-notch, even in the middle of the night. To Val, Jo, Kathy and Jill at the Los Angeles County Fair, where I received my first blue ribbon for cheesecakes back in 1980.

To Lisa Ekus-Saffer, a real friend and a great agent. To Bob Dees at Robert Rose for believing in me yet another time — here's to many more projects. To Karen Tripson for all the checking and editing. To Carol Sherman for guiding me the first time and Sue Sumeraj for editing this latest book. To Jennifer MacKenzie for testing, editing and double-checking until all the recipes were perfect. To Colin Erricson for the beautiful photography and Daniella Zanchetta for the perfect graphic design.

Thanks especially to the thousands of students I have taught over the years. I enjoyed teaching you to make perfect cheesecakes.

Library and Archives Canada Cataloguing in Publication

Geary, George
The cheesecake bible : includes 200 recipes / George Geary.

Includes index.
ISBN-13: 978-0-7788-0192-4.--ISBN-10: 0-7788-0192-6

1. Cheesecake (Cookery). I. Title.

TX773.G422 2008   641.8'653   C2008-902422-2

Index